ALL PALS

TOGETHER

ALL PALS
TOGETHER
The Story of Children's Cinema

TERRY STAPLES

EDINBURGH UNIVERSITY PRESS

© Terry Staples, 1997

Edinburgh University Press
22 George Square, Edinburgh

Typeset in Sabon by Pioneer Associates, Perthshire
Printed and bound in Great Britain

A CIP record for this book is available
from the British Library

ISBN 0 7486 0718 8

The right of Terry Staples to be identified as author of
this work has been asserted in accordance with the
Copyright, Designs and Patent Act (1988).

This book is dedicated to my parents,
Fred and Doris Staples, for letting me go
(or do I mean sending me?)

Contents

Autobiographical Note

By Vernon Scannell (born 1920)

Beeston the place, near Nottingham:
We lived there for three years or so.
Each Saturday at two o'clock
We queued up for the matinee,
All the kids for streets around
With snotty noses, giant caps,
Cut down coats and heavy boots,
The natural enemies of cops
And schoolteachers. Profane and hoarse
We scrambled, yelled and fought until
The Picture Palace opened up
And we, like Hamelin children, forced
Our bony way into the hall.
That much is easy to recall;
Also the reek of chewing gum,
Gob-stoppers and licorice,
But of the flickering myths themselves
Not much remains. The hero was
A milky wide-brimmed hat, a shape
Astride the arched white stallion:
The villain's horse and hat were black.
Disbelief did not exist
And laundered virtue always won
With quicker gun and harder fist,
And all of us applauded it.

Yet I remember moments when
In solitude I'd find myself
Brooding on the sooty man,
The bristling villain, who could move
Imagination in a way
The well-shaved hero never could,
And even warm the nervous heart
With something oddly close to love.

1. Wall of Dominion Cinema, Walthamstow,
where children used to queue up, coins in
hand, on Saturday mornings

Acknowledgements

TEXT CREDITS

The poem 'Autobiographical Note' is from *New and Collected Poems 1950–1993* by Vernon Scannell, published by Robson Books (1993); the Wickham Common material referred to in Chapter 10 is copyright to the Trustees of the Mass-Observation Archive at the University of Sussex, and is reproduced by permission of Curtis Brown Group Ltd, London; the extract from 'Chicks at the Flicks' is reproduced by permission of Michael Cudlipp; the extracts from Hansard are parliamentary copyright.

PICTURE CREDITS

Acknowledgements are due to:

- ❏ The Vestry House Museum, London E17, for picture 1
- ❏ BFI Stills, Posters and Designs for 2, 6, 10, 11, 15, 16, 17, 18, 31 and 33
- ❏ The Scottish Film Archive for 3, 5 and 32
- ❏ The Cinema Theatre Association for 4, 9, 28 and 29
- ❏ The Special Materials Unit of the British Film Institute Library for 7 and 21
- ❏ Derek Parsons for 8
- ❏ Odeon Cinemas for 12, 20 and 37
- ❏ Con Docherty for 13
- ❏ Boyd Catling for 14
- ❏ Allen Eyles for 19
- ❏ Allan Scott for 22, 23 and 30
- ❏ Mary Evans Picture Library for 24 and 25
- ❏ Maurice Ambler for 26
- ❏ The Carnegie United Kingdom Trust for 27a, 27b and 27c

- ❏ Ned Williams for 34 and some of the badges
- ❏ The Scottish Film Archive for 35
- ❏ Arthur Frost for 36
- ❏ ABC Cinemas Ltd for 38
- ❏ The Children's Film and Television Foundation Ltd for 39
- ❏ Stephen Herbert for most of the badges
- ❏ Chris Willis for providing ONCC magazine no. 1, July 1947, on which is based the design on the front cover of this book

Research assistance was provided by Leon Brown and Heather Osborn. Helpful critical comments on the text as it progressed were offered by Cary Bazalgette and David Buckingham, while initial impetus and sustaining enthusiasm for the project over many years came from correspondence with Jeffrey Richards.

CONTRIBUTORS

Without the co-operation, research facilities, written memoirs and taped interviews so generously given by so many, this book would have had neither the inspiration necessary to get it started, nor the encouragement which eventually saw it finished. Whether or not they are directly quoted in the text, these people and organisations made the book possible. I wish to place on record my gratitude to all of them.

Organisations

ABC Cinemas Ltd; Barbican Cinema, London; British Film Institute Library; The Chapter, Cardiff; Children's Film and Television Foundation Ltd; Cinema and Television Veterans; Cinema City, Norwich; Cinema Exhibitors' Association; Cinema Theatre Association; CineMagic, Belfast; City and Islington College, London; Cornerhouse, Manchester; Filmhouse, Edinburgh; Glasgow Film Theatre; Midland Arts Centre, Birmingham; National Association for the Teaching of English; National Film and Television Archive; National Film Theatre, London; Odeon Cinemas; Scottish Film Archive; Tyneside Cinema, Newcastle; UCI (UK); Welsh Film Archive.

Individuals

Alexander Briggs Allan	G. F. Arnold	Ed Bazalgette
Boise Allan	Robin Baillie	Angela Bell
Maurice Ambler	Roy Bainton	Halla Beloff
Morce Ambler	John Barnes	Roger Bennett
Elaine Anderson	Maureen Barnes	Chris Beresford
Edith Archibald	Zelda Barron	Eric Beresford
Alison Arnold	Nicholas Baumfield	Christopher John Bishop

Jeff Boston
Stephen Bourne
Olwyn Bowditch
Ron Brewer
Sid Brooks
Dot Bryant
Elizabeth Burdis
Margaret Callander
Kingsley Canham
Boyd Catling
Annie Chandler
John Coates
David Cole
Vic Cope
Jeff Cottis
Patrick Cottrell
David Crabtree
Gordon Crandles
Keith Crane
Ian Davidson
John Davies
Maire Messenger Davies
Robert Davies
Yvonne Davies
Andy Dent
Con Docherty
Bertha Downes
Don Easton
Barry Ecuyer
Paul Edmunds
Marjorie Edwards
Grace Ewen
Robert Ewan
Natasha Fairbairn
Harry Fairbairn
Dick Fiddy
Elaine Forman
Bob Fowler
Arthur Frost
Mrs D. Frost
Andy Garner
Clive Garner

Henry Geddes
Glenda Gee
John Gibson
Mel Gibson
Denis Gifford
V. T. Gilchrist
Peter Good
Bernard Goodsall
Murray Gordon
Richard Gray
Keith Green
Linda Greenwood
Douglas Hague
Barry Haigh
Stuart Hall
K. R. Hammond
Gillian Hartnoll
Alun Harvey
Peter Harvey
Molly Helley
Stephen Herbert
Doreen Higgins
Veronica Hitchcock
Colin Honey
Maureen How
Keith Howes
Roy Hubble
Colin Hunter
Pat Hursey
Christine James
Brett Jarrold
Clyde Jeavons
Mrs M. Jones
Rene Keats
John Keenan
Wendy Kitchingman
Steve Kloppe
Patricia Latham
Andrew Linham
Sonia Livingstone
Pam Logan
Steve Longworth

David Lusted
James Lyon
Steve McAusland
Matt McCarthy
D. N. MacCormick
Jaki McDougall
Bert McGuffie
Alex Macintosh
Paul Maddison
Roger Marley
Peter Meachen
Joe Mendoza
Alfred Montgomery
Jim Moore
Tony Moss
Alison Munro
Mabel Nichols
Walter Nichols
Denis Norden
Sheila O'Connell
Terence O'Connell
Mike O'Hara
Steve Oldman
Eva O'Rourke
Derek Parsons
Mrs R. Patt
Mary Pearce
Edna Pearson
Hilda Pearson
Jeremy Perkins
Thelma Perkins
Vivienne Phillips
John Platford
Edward Plunkett
John Pocock
William Porter
Joyce Pringle
David Puttnam
Tony Ray
Jackie Reeve
Robert Rider
William Riefe

Ian Rintoul
Norman Robins
Gil Robottom
Mrs U. M. Rogers
Ron Rogers
Esther Samuels
Allan Scott
Allan Selkirk
Ken Sephton
Sue Sewell
Aubrey Singer
June Skinner
Jane Slade
Tony Sloman
Ralph Smart
Elizabeth Smillie

Ken Smith
Donald Soper
Fred Staples
John Staples
Norma Stedman
Peggy Steven
Mrs Stevenson
James Stirling
John Sturdy
Cleo Sylvestre
Veronica Taylor
Melanie Tebb
Constance Townsend
Royce Trafford
Paula Visocchi
Ena Warminger

Pat Waterman
Peter Watson
Grahame Wear
David Webb
Steve Wheal
Ned Williams
Peggy Williamson
Chris Willis
Harry Willis
Fred Windsor
Shiona Wood
Chris Woodcock
Giles Woodforde
Doreen Woolley
Bill Wren

and everyone whose contribution was sent anonymously

Preface

In the late forties, at the age of nine, for a short while I became a Panda. I didn't mean to, but the Spider Lady lured me in. Instead of going as usual on Saturday mornings to the Luxor to be an ABC Minor and see Shirley Temple, Roy Rogers or Old Mother Riley, I went for a few weeks to an independent cinema where the serial *Superman* was freshly arrived. Within minutes, it held me with its glittering eye and compelled my attention. In the story, Superman's chief adversary – the glamorous Spider Lady – uses a web made of bare, inter-linked electric cables to murder anyone who hinders her. Near the beginning of one particular episode an incompetent minion is hypnotised into walking backwards into the web. Sparking and sizzling, it envelops and kills him. That did not trouble me much, as he had never been seen before, but fifteen minutes later it is Lois Lane, attractive and sympathetic heroine, who is in the Spider Lady's power. As the episode ends, she is only inches away from the strands of the electrocuting web. How could Superman possibly get there in time? Even though I was fairly sure that he would, an image of Lois Lane writhing in the web burned itself into my brain. For a week I lived alternate scenarios – one exhilarating, one terrifying. In the first I did Superman's job for him, and rescued Lois Lane with ease. In the other I myself, powerless, was being steadily backed into the Spider Lady's deadly mesh.

I did not know at the time that a government committee was then investigating the effects of cinema attendance on children, with special reference to Saturday cinema clubs. They particularly wanted to know whether serials such as *Superman* were poisoning my daydreams. I found that out only in the early eighties when, programming films for children, I too had to grapple with the question of 'suitability'. My own Saturday morning childhood experiences kept coming to mind, and in my quest for an understanding of past thinking on the subject I frequently came across references to 'the matinee movement', and to a specialist production organisation called the Children's Film Foundation.

Wishing to know more about Minors, movers and makers I was drawn deeper into researching and studying this neglected area of British culture.

In my task I was spurred on by the discovery that there is a national Saturday Pictures memory bank. Over the course of more than eighty years, thousands of clubs and matinees and special shows and separate performances entertained or baffled or stimulated or bored or frightened many millions of children. While researching this book I received a taped or written account of children's matinees from someone, somewhere, virtually every day. The salient characteristics of such memoirs were captured concisely in the short celebratory film that was shown throughout the country in the run-up to Cinema 100's British Cinema Day, 2 June 1996. Reminiscing about early cinema experiences, John Major affectionately recalled Roy Rogers, while Arthur Smith sang the first line of the ABC Minors' song before commenting: 'During the love bits, you'd go "Eugghhh! – he's kissing her!"'. Then Bob Hoskins joined in: 'There were sweet wrappers and all that, flying around. We had Hopalong Cassidy, the Cisco Kid, Flash Gordon – it was great!'

Everyone who was there, it seems, remembers the confectionery, the mucking about, the stars, the week-by-week suspense, bits of the songs, and the collective rejection of the soppy stuff. Such elements were central to audience experience, and I have sought to make sure that they are given ample expression.

There is, however, more to be said in any attempt to tell the whole story. Recent media debates have characterised the present decade as one in which children's culture finally assumed a real significance on the public agenda. This proposition blindly ignores the fact that such a focus has been attained many times before. As I trawled the political controversies and public inquiries sparked by children and cinema from 1910 onwards, a sense of repetition was inescapable. Just as television and computer games are blamed and feared in the nineties, so in the past public anxiety and political expediency seized upon children's cinema diet as a source of society's ills. The only significant differences between then and now is that previously there were more people willing to engage in practical, subsidised argument with those whose attitudes were purely censorious.

Above all, what the attempt to understand children's cinema shows clearly, because it happened on such a wide scale and so much of it was public and collective, is that children's media culture cannot be usefully defined in terms of what adults present to them. It is, rather, what children bring to it and make of it. There can be a world of difference between what children are given, and what they take. That difference is what, in essence, this book is all about.

TERRY STAPLES
London, February 1997

1 *The Happy Hunting Ground*

So long as something moved the subject did not matter. To see waves dashing over rocks in a most natural way, to see a train arriving and people walking about as if alive, was admitted to be very wonderful, but what was the good of it all? All it seemed to be good for was to provide a 'turn' at Music Hall, or a subject for a booth show, or an entertainment for children.

(James Wilkinson, Victorian film-maker, 1926)

Two boys may visit a picture house together and see a drama which will inspire one to petty larceny and land him in a penitentiary, while the other may thereby be induced to become a Boy Scout and qualify for the Victoria Cross.

(*The Bioscope*, 14 November 1916)

To be able to make the poor pinched-faced, half-clad, and half-nourished boys and girls in the crowded slums in cities forget their pain and misery and their sad lot is a great thing, and the pictures do it.

(Witness giving evidence to the National Council for Public Morality inquiry into the influence of cinema, 1917)

Four major themes dominate the story of children and cinema: exploitation, corruption, edification and diversion. Since the invention of the medium, people have variously tried to make money out of children, to protect them from moral and physical harm, to inject uplift into their experience or to entertain them on their own terms. Where this involved adults it is well documented. The children's own perception and use of cinema's possibilities is not so easily available, but I believe it to be just as important. Reconstructing the front row view largely from individual memories, I set out in this book to tell both halves of the story.

It is often suggested that children's cinema began in 1900 in Mickleover, Derbyshire. In that town, at 5.30 p.m. on Tuesday, 7 February, there was a

INFANT
SCHOOLROOM
MICKLEOVER.

One Night Only, WEDNESDAY, Feb. 7th. at 8.

Doors open at 7.30.

Great Attraction!

THE EXCELSIOR
DIORAMAS
And Great American
BIOSCOPE

The above Exhibition is a Good First-class Entertainment, and free from Vulgarity throughout.

The First Part consists of

TOUR ROUND THE WORLD!

Consisting of over

100 Scenes 100

Beautifully shown by Limelight. Splendid Effects!

Sights of London, Paris, Rome, Constantinople, Beautiful Sights of

VENICE.

A Visit to the HOLY LAND

Scenes of Joppa, or Jaffa, which is the principal Seaport of Palestine, and landing place for most Visitors to the Holy Land. Views of Jerusalem, Mount of Olives, Mosques of Omar, and the Holy Sepulchre, Bethlehem, Nazareth &c.

Cairo & the Pyramids, a Splendid journey through the Suez Canal en route to India, Malta, Genoa Gibraltar and the beautiful Island of Maderia.

A delightful journey through Hong Kong, Singapore, Pekin, Jokohama, New Zealand, Sydney Melbourne, San Francisco, the Josemite Valley and States of California

Also a visit to the Salt Lake City, and other principal places of Interest of the World.

Concluding with a Series of Moving Pictures on the great American

BIOSCOPE

War Scenes, Comic Scenes Interesting Scenes of all sorts, with all the latest and up-to-date Pictures added

Refined, High-class & Thrilling Entertainment!

Admission, Front Seats 1/- Second 6d., Back 3d.

CHILDREN'S PERFORMANCE

At 5.30.

Admission 1d. Adults 3d.

Proprietor Mr. WALTER FEARN.

separate performance for children of the Great American Bioscope (and the accompanying magic lantern show). However, this visit was not unique to Mickleover. The show would have been somewhere else a day or two before and somewhere else again a day or two later. The only reason we know about it is that the publicity poster has survived. Nonetheless, precisely because it was not a unique event, it is a useful starting point. It exemplifies the general situation of children and cinema at the dawn of the twentieth century.

The showmen's approach was straightforwardly commercial and exploitative. Once the equipment had been set up, it was bad business to let it stand idle if that could be avoided, especially as the films to be shown had been bought outright from the company that made them and not, as became the practice later, rented on a fee-per-show basis. In these circumstances, there were two main things about children that were of interest to showmen. First, they were available at a time of day when most adults were still at work. Second, they were smaller, so more of them could be compressed on to one bench, and the benches could be set closer together.

The custom of charging children half-price was not sentimental in origin: it derived solely from the presumption of their being half-size. Nor did the promotional slogan that the show was 'free from vulgarity throughout' relate to any idea that children particularly needed to be protected. It was simply an attempt to persuade the respectable citizens of Mickleover that anything disreputable that they might have heard about animated pictures – for certain films had been criticised on the ground that they were vulgar – did not apply to the Bioscope show.

Exactly what vulgarity-free films the penny-paying children saw that afternoon is not known. It is, however, possible to suggest what the Bioscope might have shown that day, for the only films compatible with that equipment were those sold by the Warwick Trading Company. Among the fifty-second silent scenes that could have flickered briefly on the Mickleover screen were music hall items such as *Tiller's Six Diamonds* (synopsised by Denis Gifford as 'Six dancing girls in three skipping scenes'); comedies such as *Four to One* ('Scene painters get drunk and paint policeman'); dramas such as *An Affair of Honour* ('Duellist kills opponent and is arrested'); and character sketches such as *A Jolly Old Couple* ('Man smokes pipe and drinks beer, while woman plays with cat and sews'). There is no record of what the children made of this first experience of moving pictures.

Five years later, in Hull, children saw films in an auditorium which at other times was a roller-skating rink or a dance hall. For one penny, each child was given a stick of Hull rock, and saw about ten five-minute films. The highlight of that year's viewing must have been Cecil Hepworth's *Rescued by Rover*, the first film to present a dog as its protagonist. While the parents helplessly wring their hands over the stealing of their baby daughter from a pram in the park,

Rover tracks her down and eventually manages to get the father to follow him to the thief's hovel. The baby is rescued; the family reunited; Rover is the dog of the day. This film was so successful that it sold over four hundred copies. For children, it offered a hero they could identify with, in a quest they could understand. Many must themselves have frequently had to look after a younger sibling – sometimes at a picture show. Rover was the forerunner of Rin Tin Tin and Lassie, and the sight of him leaping out of the window in search of the stolen baby is, as I have witnessed, after more than ninety years, still capable of rousing children to enthusiastic support.

From Hull again come glimpses of the fun the children had, as well as the management's attitude to them, in this memoir written about shows for children given around 1909:

> It was a real joy to queue up on winter Saturdays outside the circus building in Anlaby Road soon after mid-day, and be admitted to the gallery at about 1.00 p.m. with 2,000 other yelling youngsters. Admission was still 1d., and again included the stick of Hull rock. We were packed into the building by two very energetic young men wearing blazers and straw hats and carrying large walking sticks, which they didn't hesitate to use on the young bodies who wouldn't be packed in too close on the plain, backless, wooden benches. While we were waiting, chocolate slabs and nougat bars were available for sale at one penny each from youths of around fifteen who had bought them wholesale in boxes at about half-a-crown per gross. At about 2.50 p.m. the operator used to climb up a steep iron ladder at the back of the gallery to the box, and the ushers began putting up the shutters over the windows and turning down the gas jets. Imagine the noise from 2000 yelling youngsters in pitch darkness. I dread to think what would have happened in case of fire or panic. At 3.00 p.m. a white spot on the sheet heralded the opening of the show. Hollywood was unknown then; the films we saw were mainly French and Italian. There were also British films, from Hepworth and others. The show lasted about one-and-a-half hours, including a twenty-minute interval for the sale of more chocolate and nougat. (Quest, 1953)

In fact, what could happen if anything caused panic must have been well known to the management, for a recent incident had brought such shows to the attention even of King Edward. It occurred in Barnsley in 1908. In its basic set-up this event was typical of hundreds that had taken place all over Britain. Only in its climax, recorded in detail by the press, was it unique.

A cinematograph show was to be presented in the Harvey Institute at three o'clock on Saturday, 11 January, by a travelling outfit called The World's

Animated Picture Company. For its evening shows the company put on a mixture of films and variety turns, but on the Saturday afternoon there were to be films only. Such shows were not exclusively for children, but they were at pocket-money prices – especially in the gallery, which cost 1d. There were also 2d. and 3d. seats downstairs. Children had been heavily targeted during the week before the show, teachers in various schools having been persuaded to give out pieces of coloured card advertising the event. Some children had the idea that these cards were admission tickets; there were even rumours that some of the cards bore lucky numbers and that somebody would win a substantial cash prize that Saturday afternoon.

Of the company's two managers, one was primarily an acrobat and gymnast, while the other was an equilibrist and juggler. For the Saturday show the other artistes would have the jobs of supervising the audience all over the Hall. An experienced attendant had asked for a job for that Saturday afternoon, but was turned down on the ground that they had all the staff they needed. In fact, to supervise around 1,500 children, fewer staff were to be deployed than would have been normal for an adult function. Seventy-five minutes before the show was due to start, more than 100 children were already waiting outside the Hall. Nobody from the company was there, so builders from a neighbouring yard attempted to get them to line up. Many were so young that they were carried by an older sibling. Children of that age were taken, whether or not they were capable of enjoying the show, because it was customary for babes in arms to be admitted free.

When the doors were finally opened, at 2.30 p.m., the sights of many children were fixed firmly on the gallery. Most of them had only one penny. They clamoured outside the downstairs door, where one attendant was stationed. He let them through in batches of around a dozen, not keeping a count of how many he had admitted. The children then had to go up a winding stone stairway, consisting of four flights, with rises of seven inches and treads of eleven, before reaching the gallery. There the only other attendant in this part of the building – actually one of the managers – held out a bag for them each to drop a penny into, and let them in. Soon there were four hundred there – the standard number for adults – but more continued to be admitted. This was not exceptional: there were no individual seats.

The low price of admission to the gallery meant that the children so eager to get into it were those from the poorest and largest working-class families. Down below, on the ground floor, there was no such crush, and probably not such a proportion of babes in arms. When there were about 550 children packed into the gallery the manager, prompted by the fact that children were coming back out claiming they could not see the screen, finally stopped letting more in, and told the freshly arriving children to go back down the stairs the way they had come. To placate them, he said that they would be admitted downstairs for the price they had been expecting to pay for the gallery. However, the attendant on the outside door knew nothing of this turn-around. He still had hundreds of prospective customers, and was letting in regular batches. Near the bottom of the stairway, the children climbing down collided with the children climbing up. The resultant crush and chaos was described by the Hall caretaker in the account he later gave:

> I was first made aware of the incident by the downstairs checker call-ing out: 'Tell them to come. The children are falling down the steps.' I rushed round to the bottom of the gallery steps. There, at the bottom of the longest flight, I saw a mass of terrified children struggling for life. There would be, I should say, about 200 of them altogether on the stair-case, and about thirty or forty were lying at this point in a heap. Those on top were struggling, crying piteously for help. Some at the bottom of the pile seemed to be already dead, and most of them were lying head foremost as if they had been struggling to get out when they fell from the pressure behind. I called in the help of some builders employed nearby, and we did all we could to rescue the living. When the bodies had been cleared away, I found lots of pennies lying on the stair just as they had dropped from the hands of the little ones.

Of the sixteen children who suffocated that day, four were aged eight, three were seven, two were six, five were five, and two were four. At the inquest, the jury found that the deaths were due to the company's negligence in not pro-viding sufficient staff to regulate the children on the staircase. As a result, three months later, the government inserted into its Children Bill a clause stipulating that at any kind of performance for children it was the organisers' duty to station enough adult attendants to control movement and prevent the entrance of more children than could be accommodated. This did not, however, put an end to overcrowding.

A more benevolent form of exploitation was being practised in Glasgow on the day the Barnsley sixteen died. J. J. Bennell, former manager of a travelling cinematograph show, acquired an enormous hall in the Gorbals called the Wellington Palace, and planned to settle there. Two and a half weeks before the Barnsley disaster he opened it as a home for the Permanent Exhibition of Animated Pictures, despite the warnings of critics that people would never pay to see films on a regular basis. In proving them wrong, Bennell used help from children. The name he gave to his venture applied to all screenings, but was calculated to appeal to children especially. He took the phase 'bright and beautiful' from the well-known hymn and shortened it to 'BB'. Every Saturday afternoon up to 3,000 children (in a space that would later occupy only 2,000 adults) paid one penny each to be a BB and see the BBs. The films were the same ones that adults would see in the evening, but there was nonetheless a feeling of this being their own special place and time. It came from eating together, singing together and occasionally getting in free. The children enjoyed the solidarity and the darkness, and through their pleasure spread the name of BB Pictures better than any amount of paid-for advertising could ever have done, as is illustrated by this composite version of the recollections of three ex-BBs, recorded by the Scottish Film Archive:

> The BBs were pretty well the only entertainment we ever got, and gave us lots to talk about. The Wellington was rather gloomy inside, because there were no windows on the ground floor, only great tall ones above the balcony, but going there was nonetheless a huge treat. Many of us would have been given twopence, and we'd maybe spend a half-penny of that, or just a farthing, on nuts or chews before we got there, and we'd be eating while waiting, so even the queuing was fun. We knew each other from school, and a lot of friendly teasing went on while we were queuing up. When they finally opened the doors, there was such a noise going in! We had a wee book and they used to stamp it every week, and if you attended for a whole season and got a full card you got in free on one special day, but the others had to pay as usual. We would have our photograph taken by flash that day, with Mr Bennell standing on the stage pointing the camera at us. However, we never saw the result. Mr Bennell must have used it as publicity.
>
> There were no individual seats, just plain benches with a back, but it was not uncomfortable. Once in, we used to scramble and rush to get the places near the front. While the hall was filling up, two men were going round the balcony pulling down the big dark-blue blinds, and down below another two were each carrying a cardboard box full of sticks of rock, each about the thickness of a pinkie. They went to the end of every row of seats, handing them out. We sat sucking the rock before the pictures started, and carried on for as long as possible. The screen was almost the full length of the stage, and it went right up to the ceiling. When the last blind was pulled down, a great roar went up, but before the pictures could start, Mr Bennell appeared at the front in long dark clothes. He held up his hands for silence. He had no microphone or anything like that – just the power of his personality, but it was enough. Then he started singing the song he'd written. We had to join in too. If our singing wasn't good enough, we had to sing it again. That could happen four or five times. He must have been just killing time, trying to get the noise out of our system. The song went something like this:

BB Pictures they're all right,
Always beautiful and bright.
We will sing with all our might,
Come and see them every night.

It was a very high-spirited atmosphere. There would always be some-body shouting out comments. Mr Bennell would be back on the stage at once, saying: 'There'll be no pictures until you've sung it properly!' Finally he'd say 'All right, all right', and then away he'd go, and the pic-tures would start, and we'd quieten down, sucking our rock. While the films were on, we had a piano playing tunes and making sound effects, to help the story along. Whenever the inter-titles came on the screen there'd be lots of children reading them out loud. It was all wonderful fun.

The actual films the BBs saw are hardly remembered at all. Just as with later matinee-goers, it's mainly the comedy and adventure series, and the cliff-hanging serials, that stick in the mind several decades later, not only because of the familiarity with certain faces bred by the fact of seeing them so fre-quently, but also because of the special pleasure those two forms gave. They were designed to stimulate regularity of cinema-going, and with children they certainly succeeded.

The first fictional hero to achieve recognition with children was Lieutenant Rose RN, in a series of two-reelers produced between 1910 and 1914. Their titles all began: *Lieutenant Rose and the . . . .* Among the characters and inci-dents that the lieutenant got involved with were: The Chinese Pirates, The Gunrunners, The Moorish Raiders, The Foreign Spy, The Robbers of Fingall's Creek, The Sealed Orders, The Royal Visit, The Stolen Battleship, The Stolen Bullion, The Stolen Code, The Stolen Submarine, The Trainwreckers, The Hidden Treasure and The Patent Aeroplane. The stories are very much of the type found in the contemporary *Boys' Own Paper*. Rose is not characterised in detail; he's just patriotic, loyal and willing to give all in the service of king and country. It is easy to imagine that children, perhaps mainly boys, found Rose a fairly attractive hero, one with whom they could identify, one whom they looked forward to seeing again.

For the girls there was another series, also very successful for a few years before the war. Produced by Hepworth, it featured two tomboys – Tilly and Sally. The films, however, had only Tilly's name in the title: *Tilly and the Fire Engines, Tilly the Tomboy Goes Boating*. Together, the two girls behave dis-reputably, and enjoy doing so, in a variety of incidents involving dogs, smugglers, a Mormon missionary, an election, a football match, a boarding house, a roll of linoleum and an unsympathetic uncle. Chrissie White (Sally) recalled later that during the course of the series she had fallen through a pane of glass, and had been nearly run over by motor cars, burned, knocked off a bicycle, stunned by a golf-ball, thrown from a horse and almost drowned.

The first early comedians to appear often enough to find a place in children's hearts and memories were European: Frenchmen Max Linder and André Deed were hits with the BBs and elsewhere. Elegant, silk-hatted, debonair Max, the first star to have his name in the titles of virtually all his films, played a young man innocently causing havoc. The other Frenchman, André Deed, created for an Italian company a buffoon character called Cretinetti. Known in English as Foolshead, his plotless slapstick appealed strongly to children, perhaps even more than Linder's subtler approach. One of Foolshead's particular attractions was that in his films communication is conveyed not by inter-titles but by facial and bodily expression.

Nobody objected to children seeing Lieutenant Rose or Tilly or Foolshead, but anxiety about possible corrupting effects was beginning to be felt in relation to other films in general circulation – principally some of those arriving in ever greater numbers from North America. Before 1909 such concern would not have bothered cinema managers much, but in that year the first Cinematograph Act required local authorities to make regulations about safety in cinemas. The Act was explicitly concerned with physical safety, particularly danger from fire, but some local Watch Committees sought to apply it more widely, and to ban from their area films which they considered a danger to moral safety. When the film industry challenged this interpretation, it lost its case. A High Court judgement agreed that fire risk need not be the limit of the Act's scope. This ruling had force only in England and Wales; from then on, for more than forty years, film shows for Scottish children operated within a different legal framework from those in the rest of Britain.

This confirmation of local power gave rein to individuals and pressure groups within each of the over 700 licensing areas in England and Wales, and there followed several years of what the trade referred to as 'anti-cinema agitation'. It could come in the form of pinpricks of interference, as when the Chief Constable of St Helens (*The Bioscope*, 22 September 1910) complained to the magistrates that the management of a gymnasium where children's matinees were sometimes held had advertised the fact that nuts and sweets would be given to children attending. This had resulted in children 'scrambling all over the place' to get their share, and could have been 'very dangerous', he claimed. He had heard also of a place where balloons were given to children. This too should be stopped, he argued. The bench agreed and ruled that children's entertainments within their area must henceforth desist from giving away 'objectionable things'. More frequently the agitation related to the content of films, with children being invoked as the touchstone. Walsall Council, for example, objected to local cinemas screening a film of a 1910 American boxing match in which a black man, Jack Johnson, defeated a white man, Jim Jeffries. In their opinion it 'tended to demoralise and brutalise the minds of young people especially'.

Individual managers responded to attacks by such ploys as taking out one of the films from their general programme, and replacing it, for the children's matinee, with a nature documentary. A special programme of Boy Scout films was trumpeted. Some cinemas displayed signs proclaiming that they showed only Clean and Moral Pictures, and *The Bioscope* promoted among managers a Fresh Air Fund which would take city children on outings to the countryside.

Such efforts did little to mollify local or national disapproval, and fearing that the government was likely to respond to it by imposing crippling regulations on film exhibition, the industry set up its own watchdog committee, the British Board of Film Censors (BBFC), which started work in 1913. Because so much of the criticism had related to the presumed effects of films on children, one of the BBFC's first acts was categorisation. Being put in category U meant, as it still does, that a film was regarded as being universally acceptable, totally safe for children to see. Inclusion in category A meant that the film was regarded as being more suitable for adults – defined as people of sixteen or over. A film not given a certificate at all was judged by the BBFC as not fit to be seen by anybody.

These classifications had no legal force, for it was the local authorities that held the statutory powers; and the BBFC did not even propose that children should be kept out of category A films, merely that they and their parents should be advised of their unsuitability. Initially fewer than fifty of the hundreds of local licensing authorities committed themselves to accepting the BBFC as a competent judge. A few large towns though, such as London and Birmingham, did take up the idea of treating children as a separate category. A proposal that found some municipal favour was that children should be kept out of the cinema completely except for special shows which would contain only geographical films (*Views of Ilfracombe and Clovelly*), science films (*From the Ostrich Egg to the Feather Boa*) and national interest films (*Our Troops in South Africa*).

Another perception of children as a special case derived from the danger of their being sexually molested inside cinemas, an offence for which, within the London County Council (LCC) area, two men were convicted in 1916. Further, there were some children, boys and girls equally, who had been taught to take the initiative and actively solicit strangers in cinemas, making arrangements there for a later liaison. By the end of the year, the LCC had discussed this with the London branch of the Cinematograph Exhibitors Association (CEA), and the two bodies agreed on a scheme whereby in every hall that allowed unaccompanied children there would be a special attendant – wearing a distinguishing badge – on duty the whole time the premises were open to the public, with no other duty than the care of the children.

Despite such local co-operation there was still no general endorsement given to the BBFC by licensing authorities, and the trade anticipated the government stepping in with heavy-handed legislation. The Chair of the London CEA put it like this: 'We are afraid that, if it becomes purely a Government matter, certain hard and fast acts and trying conditions will be imposed, such as that a film which a child of nine can view is the kind we shall have to show to adults.' In an attempt to avert such government intervention, the trade turned to the National Council for Public Morality (NCPM) for help in bringing clarity of thought to the overall national picture. The NCPM was a voluntary body composed of religious, scientific and educational leaders; its inspiration came from a speech made by King George V: 'The Foundations of National Glory are set in the homes of the people. They will only remain unshaken while the family life of our race and nation is strong, simple and pure.' Among the Council's more prominent members were: Russell Wakefield, the Bishop of Birmingham; Sir Robert Baden-Powell, who had saved the nation's honour at Mafeking in 1900 and founded the Boy Scout movement in 1907; and Dr Marie Stopes, soon to become controversially famous when she published her two books *Married Love* and *Wise Parenthood* in 1918. Bodies represented included the Sunday School Union, the Child Study Society, the Salvation Army, the National Union of Teachers, the Jewish Community, the Education Committee of the London County Council, the Ragged School Union, the National Free Church Council and the YMCA. Their task was 'to conduct an independent inquiry into the physical, social, moral and educational influence of the cinema, with special reference to young people'. To do this, they set up a commission consisting of twenty-two of their own members and four representatives of the film trade, among them the chief censor and the chairman of the CEA. A few of them doubled up as witnesses. The rest of the evidence came from probation officers, chief constables, film producers (including Hepworth), head teachers, exhibitors, a senior ophthalmic surgeon, the principal of the Institute of Hygiene and nine unidentified children, whose testimony provides a unique sketch of children's cinema-going in the middle of the Great War.

What they were seeing at this time was almost entirely American. Max and Foolshead had been replaced by Chaplin and Harold Lloyd. Gone too were Lieutenant Rose and Tilly, supplanted by the hold-over suspense of the twenty cliff-hanging episodes of Pearl White in *The Perils of Pauline* and *The Exploits of Elaine*. When the Commission began work, a serial called *Liberty, a Daughter of the USA* was being advertised in the trade press as 'a magnificent, sensational masterpiece – a 20-week money-maker'. There were also one-hour features, prominent among them being westerns featuring William S. Hart or Tom Mix, and stories of crime, detection and court cases. Virtually the only British presence on screens came in the form of films about the war and about vital supply services.

The concerns in the minds of the Commission, when questioning the children, were primarily to do with the character of the current films and their alleged capacity to inspire imitation. Even Chaplin was not immune to this kind of criticism: a member of the Union of Woman Workers, engaged in compiling evidence for a police report, had complained that some Chaplin shorts were 'vulgar and suggestive to evil', because of the tramp's occasional pilfering. Secondly, the Commission was interested in bodily integrity and health, particularly in relation to eye-strain, sleeplessness and sexual molestation. The latter was not confined to molestation by adults: the Commission had been told by a probation officer about an occasion when she had 'seen the boys behave in a very nasty manner towards the girls'. A third question was the one that some local authorities had raised: could cinema shows be made more worth while by having a larger scientific and documentary element? At the time of the inquiry some programmes contained ten to fifteen minutes of such material, never more; other cinemas showed none at all. One member of the Commission had in a previous session referred to 'excellent films showing the changes in the life of insects, and other scientific subjects like that', and asked why more could not be done with such items.

The schoolchildren, all from London, were questioned in groups, boys and girls separately. Despite their seeming tendency sometimes to give the assembled worthies what they wanted to hear, the combined responses of these nine provide a first-hand account of children's perception of their priorities. At the same time, the questions show the commissioners' ignorance of basic matters such as the location of the cheaper seats. For all these sessions, the Bishop was in the Chair. What follow are shortened versions of the published NCPM (1917) transcript:

> CHAIRMAN: How often do you go to the cinema?
> GIRL: I don't go very often, as it is very injurious to my eyes when I go.
> CHAIRMAN: Do you sit right in the front?
> GIRL: Well, if they put you there you have to.
> CHAIRMAN: What do you pay generally?
> GIRL: Fourpence.
> CHAIRMAN: Do you only go for entertainments which are for children?
> GIRL: Not always.
> CHAIRMAN (to second girl): Are you a great cinema-goer?
> GIRL: Yes. I go once a week.
> CHAIRMAN: What seats do you go in?

GIRL: I pay sevenpence.

CHAIRMAN: You sit right at the front?

GIRL: No, it is all according to how much you pay. If you pay a low price you go into the front. For sevenpence, I sit just about in the middle of the cinema, and I can see all right from there.

CHAIRMAN: How long do you sit in the cinema?

GIRL: Two and a half or three hours.

CHAIRMAN (to third girl): Do you go very much?

GIRL: About once every three weeks.

CHAIRMAN: Do you like seeing people breaking into rooms and taking things?

GIRL: Not very much.

CHAIRMAN: It never gives you any idea that you want to go and do it yourself?

GIRL: No.

CHAIRMAN: How about your eyes? Do you get a headache?

GIRL: No.

CHAIRMAN: Where do you sit?

GIRL: I pay fourpence and sit about two or three rows away from the front.

CHAIRMAN: Do the girls sit amongst the boys?

GIRL: Yes, all mixed up, and if the boys start whistling about the attendant turns them out.

CHAIRMAN: Do you go to the late entertainment?

GIRL: No, mother won't let me.

CHAIRMAN: What about you?

GIRL: I normally get out of the cinema about nine-thirty.

CHAIRMAN: Do you feel the influence next day?

GIRL: No, I do not feel any bad effects.

CHAIRMAN: What sort of picture do the children like best?

GIRL: When the cowboys and Indians come on they clap very loudly.

CHAIRMAN: Do you like films of flowers?

GIRL: No, not very much.

CHAIRMAN: What about films about birds' nests?

GIRL: No, they don't like those.

CHAIRMAN: Charlie Chaplin?

GIRL: Yes, they like those.

CHAIRMAN: Do you get bored when they begin to show views and landscapes?

GIRL: Sometimes some of them do. And when they show the *Topical Budget* newsreel then a lot of them go out.

STOPES: Supposing you went into a picture house and you met a fairy at the door who told you you could see any picture you liked, what kind would you like to see?

GIRL: I should like to see a picture about a circus.

GIRL: I should like a good drama, but not a love drama.

STOPES: You never got any disease at the cinema?

GIRL: No, I once got scarlet fever, but not in a cinema.

ADELAIDE COX (*Salvation Army*): Have you seen anything that frightened you?

GIRL: I saw one picture where a man was in the cell, and he was supposed to have an apparition, which breaks through the wall, and then the wall falls over.

COX: And when you went to bed, did you think about these things?

GIRL: No, I went to sleep.

MR A. P. GRAVES (LCC *Elementary Schools*): Have you seen any pictures which help you in school?

GIRL: I have seen that picture about Nero. [*Nero and Poppaea*, which had earlier been summarised by a Commissioner as 'the case of a woman trying to lure Nero'.]

MR. C. W. CROOK (*President*, NUT): Have you never had a man who wanted to pay for you at night?

GIRL: No.

SIR JOHN KIRK (*Ragged School Union*): Is the place very dark?

GIRL: Yes, very dark – but you can see over it while the performance goes on.

REVEREND GARVIE: Have the boys ever been rude to you in the cinema?

GIRLS: No, but they have pulled our hair, and taken our hats off.

Later, the Commission questioned six boys, first two together, and later four together. Three of them were eleven, the other three thirteen. Of the pair, one boy went to Saturday afternoon shows, while the other went on a weekday. In the first of these two sessions the commissioners seemed to be unaware of the importance of blackout to the quality of the image on the screen; there was a misunderstanding between questioner and witness about how a film might cause sleepiness; and an older medium than cinema was invoked as the source of anti-social ideas:

CHAIR: How often do you go to the cinema shows?

BOY: About once a week.

CHAIR: And what price seats do you go in?

BOY: Twopence.

CHAIR: And you?

BOY: I always go in the fourpenny.

CHAIR: And your parents like you to go, and give you the money to go with?

BOTH BOYS: Yes.

CHAIR: About what time in the day do you go?

BOY: On Saturday afternoon.

BOY: On Friday after school.

CHAIR: And what time do the performances begin?

BOY: About a quarter to three.

BOY: Five o'clock.

CHAIR: And it lasts about two hours?

BOYS: Yes.

CHAIR: Have you any particular fancy for any particular kind of picture?

BOY: Well, I like war pictures, and I like geography pictures, about the different kinds of things that come into England.

CHAIR: You like to see things unshipped?

BOY: Yes.

CHAIR: Do you like the films where people are stealing things, and where the clever detective discovers them?

BOY: Yes.

CHAIR: Have you ever thought it would be a fine idea to copy these people and steal these things?

BOY: Yes.

CHAIR: Seeing a bad man trying to kill a good fellow, you never want to go and kill the best boy in the school?

BOY: No.

CHAIR: Now, why do you especially like that film?

BOY: It rather makes you – like, jumpy.

CHAIR: Does that excitement last after you leave the theatre? Do you feel nervous?

BOY: I feel rather nervous when I get home and when I go upstairs in the dark.

CHAIR: Do you feel nervous next morning when you go to school?

BOY: No, I have never felt any effects in the daytime, only at night.

CHAIR: But you still like it?

BOY: Yes.

CHAIR: What else do you like besides?

BOY: Robberies are all right.

CHAIR: And you like to see how a fellow cleverly cuts things with a glass and gets into a window and over walls?

BOY: Yes, a man has to be pretty good and have a good bit of sense to do all that.

CHAIR: Have you ever met any boys who are thieves?

BOY: There are one or two ruffians who sometimes go for other people's things.

CHAIR: And have they told you that the pictures made them anxious to do that?

BOY: I do not believe the pictures do, but they read some of these penny books.

CHAIR: Do you know those pictures which show you birds growing up and flowers coming out?

BOY: Yes, I like them all right.

CHAIR: Would you like the whole entertainment to consist of that kind of film?

BOY: No.

CHAIR: Do you find that seeing these things teaches you something?

BOY: Yes.

T. P. O'CONNOR (*MP, and Chief Censor of* BBFC): Do you find that films assist you with your geography? If you saw a picture about Russia, say, would that make you study up your geography more about that country?

BOY: Yes.

RABBI PROFESSOR H. GOLLANCZ (*Jewish Community*): Have you ever had any headaches on the same evening?

BOY: No.

GOLLANCZ: Have you ever noticed any rough behaviour to some of the girls?

BOYS: No.

MR GAVAZZI KING (*CEA*): Have you ever felt sleepy because of the pictures?

BOY: Yes, when there is a dry picture and you don't care about looking at it.

GRAVES: Would you like cinema lessons to be given in your schools the same as magic lantern lessons?

BOY: Yes, that would not be bad.

MONSIGNOR BROWN: Supposing a geography film lasted for half an hour, how do you think the children would take it?

BOY: They would not like it.

BROWN: Are the children crowded in at the cinemas?

BOY: Not in all the places, but there was one place I went to where they were crowded together and there were no divisions or arms to the seats.

REVD CAREY BONNER (*Sunday School Union*): Have you seen any rough play going on?

BOY: No, there has always been decent behaviour – unless some ruffians get in.
CHAIR: Do you see these films better if the hall is lighted better?
BOY: No, the darker the place the better you can see the pictures.

The four boys giving evidence in the final children's session all came from the Bethnal Green neighbourhood of East London. The Commissioners' questioning followed the usual lines, but also elicited information about the age of babies in 1917, the overwhelming popularity of Charlie Chaplin against all opposition and the stirrings of consumer resistance.

CHAIR: What do you like best about cinema?
BOY: All about thieves, and Charlie Chaplin.
CHAIR: And you others?
BOYS: Mysteries, and then Charlie Chaplin.
BOY: Cowboys, and then Charlie Chaplin.
CHAIR: What do you mean by mysteries?
BOY: Where stolen goods are hidden away in vaults so the police can't get them.
CHAIR: When you have seen these pieces, showing thieving and people catching the thief, has it ever made you wish to go and do the same thing?
BOY: Yes.
CHAIR: Do you think the fellow who steals, then, a fine man?
BOY: No.
CHAIR: Do you like the adventure or what?
BOY: I like the adventure.
CHAIR: You have no desire, then, to steal in order to get things for yourself, but you like the dashing about and getting up drain-pipes and that sort of thing?
BOY: Yes.
CHAIR: Do you like pictures where you see flowers growing?
BOY: No.
CHAIR: What do you have to pay?
BOYS: Penny-halfpenny or twopence.
CHAIR: Do you ever have to sit on the ground?
BOYS: No, we always have a seat.
CHAIR: Have you ever seen the boys behave roughly to the girls?
BOY: Yes.
CHAIR: What do they do?
BOY: Aim orange peel at them.

CHAIR: Do they pull the girls about?

BOY: Yes, their hair.

CHAIR: And do the girls pull back again?

BOY: No, they seem to enjoy it.

CHAIR: Do your sisters go?

BOY: I take baby every night when I go; it is four and a half years old.

CHAIR: Does baby like it and laugh?

BOY: Yes. She likes Charlie Chaplin best.

CHAIR: I suppose mother is very busy on a Saturday night, and she gives you the baby to take to the pictures?

BOY: Yes.

CHAIR: Do you pay for the baby?

BOY: Yes, a penny.

CHAIR: Do you go to Sunday School?

ONE BOY: Yes

OTHER THREE: No.

CHAIR: Are you three then able to sleep long on a Sunday morning after going to the pictures the previous evening?

BOY: I do not feel tired.

GARVIE: Can you tell me the film you like best?

BOYS: *The Red Circle* – it's a serial about a woman who has a red circle on her hand and it forces her to do crime.

BROWN: If there were two picture houses together, and one was showing flowers and geography films, and the other one Chaplin films, which would you go to?

BOYS: The one showing Charlie Chaplin.

BROWN: If they put on some of the films you do not like, what would the boys do?

BOYS: They would grumble and shout 'Chuck it off!'

In the following month the Commission heard evidence from one of its own members, Dr Kimmins. As LCC chief inspector he had arranged for 6,701 children in twenty-five different schools to write an account of 'the moving picture they liked most of all those they had seen at the cinema'. They wrote for fifteen minutes, all at the same time, without preparation or preliminary discussion. The resultant statistical table correlated more or less with the oral, anecdotal evidence of the nine interviewed. The main new piece of data that emerged was that a high proportion of children never went to a cinema at all, even though in London access was no problem. This was attributed to a general adult perception that cinemas were not hygienic, and that the pictures shown there were morally questionable. Some cases of abstinence from the cinema were quoted in detail, most invoking health as their reason for not going: 'The heat gives me a headache. I also found that germs like the dark, it don't do your eyes any good, and it's not healthy to be stuck inside a hot place taking other peoples' breath, so father and mother decided I better not go.' Only rarely was cost cited as a reason for not going: the cinema was at that time the most affordable public entertainment that had ever been available.

While the Commission was still holding its sessions, more children died. Purpose-built in 1910, the Deptford Electric Palace had run matinees since it opened. Adult seating capacity was 726, but on 28 April 1917 there were 1,007 children present. Many were older siblings looking after younger ones, some of whom sat on low movable benches at the front. The cinema was well staffed, having four attendants on duty, as well as a pianist, a doorman and a projectionist. The show started at 2.00 p.m. and was due to finish at 4.00 p.m., but just before that three loud noises were heard in the auditorium, and were taken to signify either bombs or fire. In instant panic, hundreds of children got up and fought to get out of the auditorium, or to find their siblings, disregarding the attempts of the staff to assure them that there was no danger. Children started shouting 'Fire!' The piano stopped playing. All three exit doors were quickly opened. Adults in the crowded shopping street nearby, hearing the cry of 'Fire!', forced their way into the cinema against the outflowing stream. It was Barnsley all over again, though on a smaller scale. Some children, mainly the smallest, got knocked over in the crush, and suffocated. Four died that day – one aged eight, two aged seven and one aged three. There were also ten injured, ranging in age from three to thirteen.

The subsequent inquest, reported in the *Kentish Mercury* (4 May), came to the conclusion that the noise which prompted the panic had been caused not by bombs or fire but by two flints which had been found on a grating near the large electric ventilating fan at the back of the hall. The surmise, unproven, was that a child (presumed to be 'a boy') had thrown them through the apertures in the fan-casing. When revolved, they would cause sharp metallic cracks until ejected on to the grating. As a result of this incident, the LCC imposed a new licence condition on cinemas in the London area. In the belief that overcrowding exacerbated the panic, they required exhibitors henceforth to accommodate only one child in a seat or space intended for one person. (Elsewhere the one-child-one-seat argument made progress only very slowly: it was, for example, 1939 before the Watch Committee of Newcastle decided that the practice of allowing twenty-five children to share ten seats must be discontinued.)

The NCPM did not stop to consider Deptford. Six months after opening the inquiry, it published its evidence and conclusions in a 400-page report (1917) which rejected most of the allegations levelled against the film industry during the previous seven years. It was welcomed not only by the trade, but also by such organisations as the Church Army, previously one of cinema's sternest critics. The report by no means stifled criticism entirely, and individual films continued to cause concern in particular districts, but it offered a well-documented rebuttal of the idea that moving pictures were all in principle inherently and irredeemably evil. On the contrary, said the report: 'Under wise guidance, the cinema may be a powerful influence for good.' Among the proposals for wise guidance was a recognition, drawn partly from the interviews with children, that education and amusement should not be conflated:

> The educational film, with no interest other than the educational, has been given a fair trial in the picture house and has not proved to be of sufficient general interest in the ordinary programme of the cinema. A film, however beautiful, of the life history of a plant or insect sandwiched between a Charlie Chaplin film and a thrilling episode of *The Exploits of Elaine* has little chance of survival. The interest – if ever it has been aroused – is soon switched off, and a feeling of boredom results.

A related recommendation in the report was that the industry should in future turn its attention to the 'adequate filming of stories of acknowledged literary merit'. This notion that the classics of English literature could be transferred to the screen, and would thereby solve the problem of how to combine entertainment with improvement, was to come up repeatedly in discussions of children and cinema.

In the absence of such adaptations, the NCPM report came to no conclusion either way as to whether separate Saturday matinees, whether or not they included a natural history film, were any better for children than ordinary performances. It was more concerned to call for the introduction of certain health and safety measures: that children should not be allowed at any time to sit closer to the screen than a distance of one and a half times the screen's height; that the cinema must be adequately ventilated; that capable attendants must be on duty; and that no child under fourteen should be allowed to remain in a cinema after nine in the evening. Such conclusions, however, had no binding force on anyone. In particular, a recommendation that censorship should be the job of the state, not the industry, was totally rejected by the government, on the ground that the real power, quite properly, lay with individual licensing authorities.

Indeed it did. The LCC, for example, came very close to banning completely the simple, companionable pleasures recalled in this memoir:

> From about 1920, when I was eight, I used to go with my older brothers to a cinema in Strutton Ground, Westminster, on Saturday mornings.

We looked forward to this each week. It was our time. The cinema was not very big, and I never even knew its name, but it was a real neighbourhood meeting place. Everybody you knew was there, everybody from your school. Being a market-place, Strutton Ground was very busy all day Saturday, since everybody in the neighbourhood went there to shop. We all stopped there and stocked up on oranges, and peanuts in their shells. Outside the cinema there was nothing like a single queue, just lots of pushing and shoving, lots of 'I'm minding this place for my brother' – that kind of thing. We finally paid our pennies to the man on the door, whose job was to keep us in order, and went in. Even though it was a small place, there were hundreds of us there. It was absolutely packed. You all stuck together with your brothers and sisters, inside the cinema just as much as on the way there and home. The older children had been specifically given the job of looking after the younger ones.

When the films started we normally settled down a bit. We saw cowboy things and the Keystone cops and Pearl White tied to the railway. It was still noisy, because we used to shout out 'Look behind you, guv'nor!' and 'Oh, oh, he's got you', and things like that. There were inter-titles for the dialogue, and sometimes kids used to read them out loud, but that didn't matter, because the film was silent. All the while, there was a lady pounding away on the piano, making galloping noises for the cowboys. Sometimes it developed into absolute chaos, with kids shouting out and throwing peanuts. Those up in the balcony used to drop things down on to the rest of us. There were two attendants inside, one on each aisle, and their job was to keep us sitting down while the films were showing, but when there was a break between films, children could get out to go to the toilet, and then there was a lot of running around. The attendants had to chase kids and try to get them back to their places. We certainly had plenty to talk about on our way home.

What nearly stopped the conversation was a reversal of the LCC's attitude to the BBFC. For eight years the LCC had refused to recognise BBFC judgements. However, in October 1921, following a court ruling, the LCC notified the BBFC that from now on only films with a BBFC certificate would be permitted to be shown within its licensing area. That was what the BBFC wanted to hear. But the LCC went even further, and declared that all films shown in London must henceforth be shown to adults only, regardless of what certificate the BBFC had given them. This would have barred everyone under sixteen – including young men and women who may have been in a job for more than two years – from London cinemas completely, on any day of the week, and was definitely not what the BBFC wanted to hear. Such an action, if widely copied, would have rendered pointless the categorisation of films, and would have significantly reduced the film trade's profits.

From hastily arranged meetings between the LCC, the BBFC, the Home Office and the CEA emerged a compromise which was to affect children's cinema-going in England and Wales for half a century. The new rule was that under-sixteens were after all to be allowed to see U films freely, but would be kept out of A films unless they were accompanied by a parent or bona fide adult guardian. This system, which came into effect within the LCC from July 1922, was deemed within a year to be such a success that the Home Office advised all other local authorities in England and Wales to follow suit. Most, but not all, did. There was thus from 1923 a larger measure of clarity and uniformity about film categories in England and Wales than ever before. Scottish licensing authorities continued to have no powers to restrict children's admission on any ground other than physical safety, but this situation caused no great public concern till the coming of sound.

This was partly because Hollywood, virtually the only source of the films seen on British screens, had in the early twenties gone through the same debate about screen morality as had taken place in the UK. The consequent self-imposed restrictions resulted in a coming to the fore of the comedies and swashbucklers for which the decade is now largely remembered. By 1923, when the LCC had just introduced its policy of excluding unaccompanied children from A films, only 13 per cent were placed in that category; and during the rest of the decade the percentage of A certificates was never higher than twenty.

In the main, therefore, the films that children saw in the twenties at matinees were the same as everyone else saw at other times: Charlie Chaplin, Buster Keaton, Harold Lloyd, Jackie Coogan, Mary Pickford, Douglas Fairbanks, the Keystone Cops. A particular favourite was Tom Mix, now top screen cowboy. His credentials – at least, according to his publicity – were impeccable. Before getting into films he had been a real Texas Ranger, US cavalryman, and deputy marshal. More importantly for the Saturday matinee crowds, he looked impressive in his close-fitting white outfit, and he could certainly ride like a cyclone. Though in his forties, his stunts involving horses, stage-coaches, trains and ropes provoked vigorous vocal participation from matinee audiences. To cap it all, he had a horse, Tony, which could put on an unbeatable turn of speed when the need arose and which had an independent resourcefulness that saved him more than once.

The twenties also saw the re-emergence of animals as stars. Hollywood made a series of films featuring an Alsatian, Rin Tin Tin, who like Rover eighteen years before was loyal, resourceful and good at rescuing babies. In *Where the North Begins* he uses the warmth of his body to stop an injured man from freezing to death; later he skilfully gains entrance through a high window in order to come to the rescue; at the climax, when everybody else is powerless to stop the villain escaping on horseback, Rinty darts in pursuit, jumps up on to him, frees the heroine, pulls the villain off the horse and engages him in a cliff-top fight from which he falls to his death. He could also be gentle, loving, trustful and winsome. His storylines were more complex than Rover's in that his qualities are not recognised by all the humans: he comes under suspicion of sheep-killing and baby-mauling. The audience knows he is innocent, but Rinty cannot understand or explain. This situation aroused strong emotions, and Rinty became one of the major box-office attractions of the decade. Children responded with particular excitement and pleasure to the directness and simplicity of his appeal; in addition, his films have the advantage of containing few inter-titles, since he never spoke.

Despite their U certificates, for some managers there was still a problem with certain of these films as far as children were concerned: they were too long. The point of running a special show was to make a little extra money, without affecting the main audience. For some managers, the penny or tuppence that children paid bought them a maximum of two hours of screen time, from two till four. They wanted the children out then so that they could get the place disinfected before the full-price audience came in. So, if the full programme was two and a half hours long, the managers' solution was to omit the first three reels of the feature, leaving children to work out for themselves what had happened in the missing half hour.

The serials of course could not be left out, for their purpose was to bring the children back week after week. Pearl White was still everywhere, though she had given up that line of work in 1922. In addition to *The Perils of Pauline*, she appeared in ten other serials. Since each of them had an average of twenty episodes, it meant that when she retired she had made enough to fill every Saturday afternoon serial slot for four years. It is little wonder that she is remembered as the Queen of the Screen. But she had a rival, Ruth Roland, whose first serial appearance was in the psychological thriller *The Red Circle* (mentioned by one of the boys giving evidence to the NCPM). In it Roland plays a split-personality heroine with a circular stigma on one hand, which drives her to commit criminal acts until she is redeemed by love. Another ten Ruth Roland serials followed, until she too retired in 1922.

A third suspense exponent was Harry Houdini, who had won fame as an escapologist, and at the age of forty-five brought his skills to a customised story called *The Master Mystery*. In it he plays Federal Agent Quentin Locke, who tangles every week with a mastermind known as The Automaton. At the end of each episode The Automaton tries once again to think of a surefire way of getting rid of Locke. By turns Locke is strung up by his thumbs; shackled and thrown into a river; bound with barbed wire before being put into a bath of acid; secured to the bottom of a shaft to await the plunging elevator; and forced into a complex garroting device by the Madagascar Strangler. This serial is vividly remembered by some people because of the nightmares its cliff-hanging images could cause.

What became another standard ingredient of children's matinees was also established at this time – a regular, familiar, likeable cartoon character. In the twenties this was Felix the Cat. With Felix, the children had a cartoon friend created with them in mind – the first film character to have that orientation. Otto Messmer, who designed Felix in 1919, and did most of the animation all through the twenties, wanted him to influence children by exemplifying kindness. Felix is a loner, willing to roam anywhere to lend a helping hand. In one story his mission is to persuade the weather controller to send sunshine rather than rain. His altruism is made entertaining by ingenious picture gags which foreground the fact that he and his environment are drawings. When he needs a hook, he strides along looking puzzled, until the animator draws a question mark over his head. Felix reaches up, takes hold of it, turns it upside down and puts it to use within his story. There's no evidence that he ever had the moral impact that Messmer hoped for, but he was certainly well loved, and his special verse, though unsung, lives on in folk-memory:

> *Felix kept on walking*
> *Kept on walking still.*
> *With his hands behind him*
> *You will always find him.*
> *Blew him up with dynamite*
> *But him they could not kill,*
> *'Cos Felix kept on walking,*
> *Kept on walking still.*

In Govan, Glasgow, where there were two picture houses opposite each other, it was probably Felix, Tom Mix and Pearl White whichever one you went to. Managers therefore needed to devise other attractions in order to compete successfully. People there recall the benefits of this rivalry:

In those days there was no radio, no nothing, and the Saturday matinee was the highlight of the week. So you might have three or four hundred children on one side of the street, and four or five hundred on the other. Then the manager of one of them would come out with sticks of rock and he would wave them about, saying 'Sticks of rock! Into the pictures!' And the kids would rush across the street. Next week it would be the other manager's turn, and he would come out with strings of balloons. This battle would go on week after week, every Saturday afternoon. Great fun for the kids. (McBain, 1985)

A cry of 'Free pomegranates!' would probably not have had the same persuasive effect as 'Free sticks of rock!', but they were the refreshment favoured by some children. 'You had to remember to take a pin with you as well. Using the pin to spear one globule of flesh at a time, you could make a pomegranate last all through the show.' Another seasonal matinee snack, particularly popular in the North of England, was a stick of raw rhubarb, repeatedly dipped into a bag of sugar.

Commercial afternoon shows dominated the twenties, but there were occasions when an education authority, prompted perhaps by the NCPM conclusion that moving images could be a force for good, wanted its schoolchildren to see a particular instructional or patriotic film. Such a film could not be shown in schools because they lacked the technical equipment; and could not be shown on a Saturday afternoon because it was not American. The solution was to require all the children from several schools within one area to attend a particular cinema on a Saturday morning. Having to give up their time like this caused resentment, even resistance, among children, as this memoir relates:

> When I was at senior school in Kingston in the twenties we were drafted in to the Elite Cinema one Saturday to see a show which was probably organised in conjunction with the Empire Marketing Board. We were somewhat upset at having our morning taken away, and this feeling was compounded when it turned out that the reason for our being there was so that we could be shown a film about rice-growing. After the screening someone made a long speech, and I think we were supposed to write a competitive essay about what we had seen. By this time we were getting restless, and after someone else, probably the Mayor, had had his say, we were supposed to applaud. I never knew which school started it, but the applause gradually developed into a slow handclap. Very angrily, the officials left the stage; and, a bit earlier than planned, the National Anthem was played on the organ. We got a good wigging for our bad manners, but I don't think any of us ever did write that essay on rice-growing.

In one way this decade came to an end twenty-one months early when in March 1928 Sidney Bernstein instituted, within his Granada chain of cinemas, the first British attempt at turning matinees into a social service rather than a money-making enterprise (see Chapter 3). Alternatively, the decade may be perceived as ending on schedule, on the very last day of 1929, when there occurred the worst and last catastrophe to befall children in a cinema. On the afternoon of 31 December 1929 approximately one in seven of the capacity audience at the Glen, Paisley, suffered or died in a panic caused, according to the official report (Crozier, 1930), partly by overcrowding and understaffing.

Though licensed as a cinema since 1910 the Glen had never acquired individual tip-up seats. Instead, it still had wooden benches, with backs but no divisions, which could seat 612 adults, or an unspecified larger number of children. On this particular afternoon, 'there cannot have been less than 700 children and there may have been many more'. It seems that the management did not run a proper ticketing system, but just took money off children as they came in. Once inside, the 700 or more children, some of them as young as four or less, were supervised by one single male attendant. There was also a young woman selling chocolates. In the balcony there was no supervision at all, because for children's matinees it was meant to be closed. However, some children had managed to get up there, as was shown by the peanut shells, orange peel and chocolate wrappers found there two days later, and by the testimony of survivors.

3. Frame still from Paisley Children's Happy Hunting Ground, *a promotional film for the Alex Cinema, Paisley, shot on the afternoon of Saturday, 31 August 1929. Captions urge parents to 'note the happy smiling contented faces, and be sure to send yours to share in the good fare offered'* (Scottish Film Archive)

One of the films to be shown that afternoon was a silent two-reel western, packed with non-stop action and gunfire, called *Dude Desperado*. It featured hard-riding, two-fisted Fred Gilman. Soon after the first reel finished, dense clouds of irritant brown fumes began to penetrate the auditorium. Someone shouted 'Fire!' Within seconds there was panic. Children rushed for a double exit which was down some steps, behind the screen, away from the source of the smoke. They got the doors open, and were able to go through, a few at a time, but then found their escape blocked by a gate. As had happened at Barnsley and Deptford, a heap of bodies piled up. It went right the way to the top of the steps. The fire brigade and police arrived quickly and extricated the fallen from the pile. After bodies had been rushed to hospitals by car, tram and bus, it was found that seventy children were dead, and thirty-five had been injured. One of the survivors of that day, eleven at the time, remembers it like this in a Scottish Film Archive recording:

> I was settled in my seat, right at the back, under the balcony. Soon after the film started, children started running towards the screen, and I got caught up in the rush. I ran down and went behind the screen. I wanted to get out of the door but I saw all these bodies piled up. Children were screaming and running all over the place, so I turned around and ran back inside. Everyone was scrambling around. Petrified, I went into a toilet, took my shoe off, and smashed a window with it. A policeman who was up a ladder grabbed me and took me down to safety.

Another member of that audience, four years older, ascribes his survival to being above it all:

> I sneaked into the balcony to get a better seat. We weren't supposed to, but we always managed to get up there because there were no usherettes around. When the panic started, I got out as quickly as I could, through the front. I saw them filling the trams with children to take them to the hospital. There were sixteen children living in my street, and all of them were at the Glen that day. They all died, except me. It was a disaster that need never have happened.

The danger was indeed over even before the children started screaming and running. The cause of the smouldering film was a six-volt accumulator in the rewinding room, on which the projectionist's assistant had put the can containing the first Fred Gilman reel. The way the can was placed, across terminals, caused a short circuit which ignited the film within four seconds. However, after a delay of a few minutes, during which time the flames were contained but the smoke permeated the auditorium, the manager kicked the can through an exit door on to a patch of waste ground before the fire could escape and spread. In the Inspector's view, the panic was partly Fred Gilman's fault: 'A very exciting film was being shown, and excitement would lead to the children getting out of hand more easily, and this in itself points to the very great necessity of having an adequate number of attendants present . . . .'

The manager of the Glen was prosecuted on a charge of culpable homicide, the principal issue at stake in his trial being the question of whether or not he had been responsible for the gate being locked. He admitted that in the past he had adopted the practice of keeping it locked, because otherwise children had a habit of slipping in without paying. However, on this particular occasion, he testified – and on this point he was supported by the chocolate seller – he had definitely unlocked and pushed open the gate at 1.30 p.m. The court eventually delivered a verdict of 'Not Guilty'. Nonetheless, the Glen never again functioned as a cinema.

The deaths and injuries sustained that day brought matinees back into the national consciousness. The Prime Minister, Ramsay MacDonald, immediately sent a message of condolence to the Provost of Paisley. Three weeks later, when Parliament had reassembled, the MP for Western Renfrew, Dr Robert Forgan, asked the Home Secretary to consider the possibility of permitting at children's matinees the use of non-inflammable film only. This parliamentary concern for children's physical safety in cinemas soon broadened to include once again the danger of moral corruption. The new factor in the situation was what Hansard called American Talking Films.

2 Flagrant and Dangerous Evils

It was not a proper Children's Matinee. The last thing I saw was that a married woman and her admirer were about to go to a room to misconduct. I was compelled to go out as I had two young children with me.

(Parent in Birkenhead report, 1931)

It is a great misfortune that thousands of children should spend Saturday afternoon in cinema houses, not because it does them moral injury, but because it is clearly an inappropriate expenditure of time. Time spent playing in the streets is better spent.

(LCC Education Committee report, 1932)

When the subject of children and cinema got on to the public agenda at the outset of the thirties it was kept there not by the dangers of fire or panic or overcrowding but by the advent of sound. Children were not the only section of society thought to be at risk from this threat, but they were again the touchstone. In February 1930 Sir Alfred Knox, Conservative MP for Wycombe, asked the President of the Board of Trade 'whether, in order to protect the English language as spoken by the people of this country, he will take steps to limit the import of American talking films and to encourage the production of British films?' Less than a year later James Lovat-Fraser, Labour MP for Lichfield, called for an official inquiry because of the 'constant complaints made of the injurious effect of cinemas on children, and of their being the cause of juvenile offences'. Both these questions received a ministerial brush-off, but the Scottish dimension fared better when the Duchess of Atholl, MP for West Perth, asked the Secretary of State for Scotland whether he thought that Scottish children were receiving fair treatment 'when one remembers that for over ten years there have been regulations under the English Home Office which have protected many children and young persons from the exhibition of unsuitable films?' The reply to this was an agreement that the matter was important; it would receive 'careful consideration'.

The arrival of talkies at the end of the twenties had indeed changed drastically the character of the movies. The comedies and swashbucklers of the silent era were swept away by horror films and stories of high society, sex, crime and alcohol. What few British films existed were mainly about the Great War. In 1929 over 300 films had scenes cut out by the BBFC. Whereas for the bulk of the silent twenties the number of feature films receiving an A certificate was on average only around 20 per cent, in the mid-thirties the equivalent figure was around 50. Inevitably, therefore, since children were persistent film-goers, and an A and a U were frequently coupled in double bills, they were seeing a high proportion of A films. They got in either through being accompanied by a bona fide parent or guardian, through persuading unrelated adults to see them past the box-office, through bunking in by the fire doors, through passing themselves off as older than they were or through happening to live in Scotland or one of the 35 per cent of licensing areas in England and Wales which had not accepted the Home Office guidelines of 1923. Nor was this confined to the ordinary programming: even children's Saturday matinees sometimes included A-certificate films.

One reason given by the government for keeping out of the arguments as far as possible was that they were waiting to see the report of an investigation being conducted by the LCC Education Committee. But there were also four other committees enquiring into the influence of the cinema on children. Taken together, these five reports – from London, Birmingham, Sheffield, Birkenhead and Edinburgh – provide a unique compendium of facts and attitudes relating to children and cinema in the early thirties.

Four of them were researched by self-appointed vigilance groups. First off was Birmingham, where a Cinema Enquiry Committee was set up in May 1930, under the presidency of Sir Charles Grant Robertson, Vice-Chancellor of the city's university and author of a book on *The Rise of the English Nation*. His Committee began from the premiss that the type of film then prevalent was having a 'baneful effect' on children. With the help of local teachers the Committee got information – sometimes written, sometimes oral – from 1,439 children between the ages of eight and fourteen about frequency of attendance, reasons for going, preferred stars and types of film, eye-strain, sleep problems, what they had learnt from films and how they thought cinemas could be improved. They also sent observers to actual matinees. The Birkenhead Vigilance Committee later adopted both Birmingham's presumptions and its methodology, and conducted a similar survey.

The Birmingham figure for average attendance was once a week for each child. A small percentage never went at all, and a larger group went twice a week or more. This pattern was, broadly, replicated in three of the other inquiries. More boys went than girls; older children preferred evenings; younger ones were more likely to go on Saturday afternoon, often with siblings.

Film-preferences were similar across the five towns. Adventure, cowboys, comics, crime, mystery and war were still top of the poll, as they had been in 1917. The only new vote-catcher was the cartoon – outgoing Felix and incoming Mickey Mouse were both mentioned enthusiastically. There was also a significant vote among the girls for films of romance, a taste obscured in the overall figures because the boys hated such stuff.

However, the reports showed that what children preferred to see, and what they mainly did see, was not the same thing – at least not on Saturday afternoons. Birmingham matinees could not, by the terms of the exhibitors' licences, include any A-certificate films, but there was still much that was found objectionable. In one matinee an observer noted 150 children, brought there for a treat by the British Legion, having to sit through *The Woman who Was Forgotten*, described by the observer as 'very long drawn out and dull'. The children were 'restless and bored'. The observer's plot synopsis makes clear why: 'Pathetic story of teacher's life. Sees her young lover drowned before her eyes. Devotes herself to career. Wrongfully accused of fraud, becomes outcast, poor, penniless, finally reinstated. Slushy love-making and harrowing descriptions of her poverty and sorrow.' Other objections referred to imitable crime ('he shows the necessity for wearing gloves to prevent his fingerprints being taken') in *Too Many Crooks*; and to a film which the children were judged to have liked too much, called *Balaclava*, of which the observer wrote that: 'In addition to the fighting when the Light Brigade charges it included a duel, murder, and fighting with sword and axe. The children shouted and cheered. It is not a bad film of its kind, but far too exciting for children.'

In both Birkenhead and Sheffield it was at the time of the investigations perfectly legal to show unaccompanied children A films. Thus members of the Birkenhead Vigilance Committee found children at matinee screenings of the A-certificated *Uneasy Virtue*, and *Soldiers and Women*. The latter was judged to be not entirely bad: 'Hero showed restraint and thoughtfulness. However, film suggests that if married life proves unhappy, the way out is divorce and that there is no harm in finding consolation in the company of a friend of the opposite sex.' Even the lone cinema which put on special programmes for the matinee, rather than simply repeat its ordinary show, was judged to have got it wrong. Both its films were U-certificated silents. One, *Bright Eyes*, was evaluated as: 'Fast hotel life, much drinking, sex appeal'. The second contained an element that the audience could respond to – other children – but which the observer would nonetheless have preferred them not to see. Called *Second Husband First*, it was put down as: 'A most unhealthy film, inciting to do really naughty things. Mischievous pranks of two boys to prevent their widowed mother marrying again. Children hugely delighted.'

Only two Birkenhead matinees offered programmes which won the complete approval of the observers. *The Second Honeymoon* was 'sufficiently clean and healthy in moral tone for children to see, and they followed it with laughter'; while its companion, *Men on Call*, was 'educational, showing an engine driver at his work and coastguards rescuing life, which the children followed with interest'. The other approved programme started with an episode of the silent serial *The Lone Ranger*; then went on to *The Freshman's Goat* ('quite clean, fair amount of rough and tumble, some quite funny situations, very well received'); and finished with the melodrama *Laughing at Death*, in which virtue triumphed.

In Sheffield the investigators started with more of an open mind. They too found, and deplored, A-certificate films being shown at four of the twenty-one matinees. *The Redeeming Sin*, *The Girl From China*, *Girl of the Port* and *The Bellamy Trial* were found to be 'positively harmful', portraying as they did night-club life, the Chinese underworld, sailors and dancing girls, and the cross-examination of trial witnesses in an unsavoury court case. At these screenings the children were observed to be so restless that the film's dialogue became inaudible. In three other cinemas, however, the Sheffield investigators found matinees of which they could wholly approve. Two were special programmes; all three consisted of silents. The special programmes both showed *Kidnapped*, which won this approbation:

> An American romantic drama which provided a feast of excitement. Swimming, acrobatics, motor racing, a fight in a balloon in mid-air, riding and chasing and a final rescue. A strongly characterised hero and villain were, respectively, warmly cheered and disapprovingly hissed by the children, who appeared to enjoy the show immensely. A healthy thriller.

Another silent winner was *Helter Skelter*, which showed again how strongly children can relate to animals:

> An exciting rough and tumble film showing the adventures of a small boy and his dog . . . The supposed death of the dog in a street accident towards the end of the film produced the deepest gloom in the audience, but this was changed to transports of wild delight when, in the last scene of all, the dog turned up with its leg in splints. A splendid entertainment for young children.

The remaining fourteen programmes were castigated by the Sheffield investigators not so much for immorality as for being boring. Some of them were rated as excellent for adults, but completely incomprehensible for children. This resulted in long stretches of chattering, rowdiness, throwing things around and general inattention. The attendants frequently had to switch on the lights and shout for order, with the film still running on the screen. Younger children left their seats and started wandering around the cinema until they were caught and returned by an attendant. The thrill of this chase could often be much more fun than anything in the film. Some older ones at the back of the cinema 'organised a game which they were playing quite oblivious of what was going on on the screen'. Remarks such as 'I don't want no more of this', 'Take it off!', 'I'm fed up' and 'I'm going home' were clearly heard. Isolated moments of action on the screen – fires, fights, stabbings, a chase, a rescue – would rouse the children to cheering or booing for a while, and then they returned to their chatting and games-playing.

The only one of these five reports to come from a statutory body – the LCC – is in many ways the most authoritative. For a start, its sample was ten times greater than any other. A total of 21,280 children between three and thirteen, from twenty-nine schools in varying parts of London, were asked about their frequency of attendance, how much they paid, their preferences, and the effects films had on them. Some of the questions were asked and answered in writing, while others were put orally, by teachers who knew the children well. The information gathered showed that in London attendance started early. Only 37 per cent of under-fives never went to a cinema at all. Despite these high figures, the overall average came out at rather less – only thirty-two cinema visits per child per year – than the once-per-week-per-child that other reports found to be the norm. This may have been because the preferred time for visiting a cinema was Saturday afternoon, and yet a smaller proportion of LCC cinemas ran Saturday matinees than was the case anywhere else. One suggested reason for this low proportion of children's matinees was that managers in tough, densely populated areas of London feared that their cinema would be damaged if a children-only audience was allowed in (especially if they were shown a film they could not understand and enjoy). In some areas, there was even an influence from the fact that the Salvation Army was at that time throwing its weight against cinema attendance of any kind.

On the question of the acceptability to adults of what the children were seeing, the LCC report differed from the others, finding the films 'at least free from what most people would regard as plainly unsuitable matter'. Unfortunately, the LCC investigation had not included observers actually visiting Saturday afternoon cinemas to see for themselves, so the report gives no evidence of children's spontaneous responses. Mainly on the basis of the children's answers to questions, most of the commonly supposed 'bad effects' of cinema are more or less dismissed. Children who saw 'morally questionable' elements in A films, at evening shows, were bored by them rather than corrupted. Behaviour imitative of film action amounted to no more than coming to school with a ruler stuck down a belt, after the manner of a gun or sword. The only Americanism that had entered children's speech to any degree was 'OK, Chief', used instead of 'Yes, Sir'.

In Edinburgh, where the last of these major investigations was conducted a year later by the Edinburgh Cinema Enquiry Committee, the situation on the ground was different, as the Duchess of Atholl had complained. The report found that the proportion of children regularly present at evening performances was about 25 per cent, regardless of whether the programme contained an A film or not. In fact, information about a particular film's category was in most cases not available till the BBFC certificate was displayed at the start of the screening.

The twenty-one schools that took part provided a total of 1,580 children, from an older age-range than that used in the other towns – between nine and eighteen. Another spin used only in Edinburgh was that the schools were classified as type A or type B according to whether they were located in the 'better

districts' of the city, or in the more densely populated areas. The basic finding that arose from making this distinction was that children from type-B schools went nearly 40 per cent more often than children from type-A schools. This difference was attributed to the social conditions of the type-B children, 'which must make a visit to the cinema all the more alluring'. Half of the cinema visits were made on a Saturday; mainly in the afternoon for the 9–12 group, mainly in the early evening for the older children. The programme of films was exactly the same in the afternoon as in the evening, but admission was cheaper in the afternoon.

The actual films being exhibited in Edinburgh were monitored for eight weeks in the first half of 1932. Of the 144 features reported on, one was a U silent, 17 were A talkies and 126 were U talkies. Even though the BBFC categories had no legal force in Edinburgh, the investigators spent much time discussing them. They agreed with the certification of the A talkies, except for one which they thought could have been a U, and three (including *Romeo in Pyjamas*) which they found objectionable even with A certificates. It was the U certificates that brought significant dissent. Forty-six of them were declared to be totally wrong. An example given was *The Second Honeymoon*, the very same film which, even in censorious Birkenhead, had been evaluated as 'sufficiently clean and healthy in moral tone for children to see'. Other U certificates objected to were those given to *Strangers May Kiss*, *What Wives Don't Want* and *Tarnished Lady*.

Uniquely, the Edinburgh survey included parents. From

4. The Saturday afternoon queue posing for a photograph outside the Rialto, Bermondsey, in south London, 1932. In that year the LCC Education Committee's report noted: 'The film habit starts early'
(Cinema Theatre Association)

5. Frame still from silent promotional film for the Playhouse Cinema, Inverness, shot on Saturday, 16 February 1935. The film the children are queuing for is Treasure Island, *starring Jackie Cooper, which has been playing there since the preceding Monday. A caption at the end of the film says: 'Oh my! Have they enjoyed Jim Hawkins' adventures on Treasure Island! Look at them!'*

(Scottish Film Archive)

them came a resounding dismissal of the notion that attendance at a cinema caused eye strain, sleeplessness or behavioural problems. Nonetheless they favoured special matinees showing travel, educational, biblical and nature films, with a leavening of comics. There was a general plea for an end to the predominance of films showing American culture. One parent, perhaps mindful of Paisley, wanted to 'stop the noise and smoking in matinees, and have less crowding in seats'.

Edinburgh teachers were at odds with the parents over behavioural effects, more than two-thirds being convinced that children who attended frequently suffered in the classroom from restlessness. There was also a majority in support of the proposition that children acquired false ideas from the pictures. Janet Gaynor's films were offered as an example of this; one teacher quoted a child as saying, as a description of Gaynor's normal film roles, that 'She frequently takes the part of a poor girl and always reaches a higher position in society.' Such an escape from poverty, commented the teacher, 'gives a decidedly false idea of life'.

A question that no other inquiry asked was: 'Do you think that there should be special films for children?' Seventy-five per cent of teachers gave an outright 'Yes' to this, which led to one of the principal recommendations of the Edinburgh report, a visionary idea that was to be dismissed as completely impossible for over a decade. The report put it like this: 'There ought to be a more serious effort on the part of the cinema industry to provide pictures for its child patrons. There should be special pictures for children as there are special books for children. The cinema awaits its R. M. Ballantyne and its Louisa May Alcott.'

No other report had this perception, but the other four all homed in on a separate factor that the Edinburgh report barely touched on – fear. In the Birmingham report around 400 children, out of 1,439, are referred to as saying that films sometimes or always kept them from sleeping or gave them night-mares. One boy had written: 'When I see war pictures I shout and kick the bedclothes and I never seem to settle down properly.' An observer at a Saturday matinee wrote that during the climax of *The Lily of Killarney* – about the attempted drowning of the heroine by a hunchback from a boat in a moonlit lake – a little girl of about ten squealed with fear, clutched her neighbour and said: 'Oh my, I shan't arf be walking in me sleep after this.' In Birkenhead an even higher proportion claimed to be affected by the remem-brance of certain characters or incidents: 'When I am in bed, I think of the picture, and it sends a cold shiver down my back. I feel frightened to go to sleep in case the person is there, and I put my head under the clothes.' Some of the films that caused such disturbance had undoubtedly been seen at a Satur-day matinee, the report stated. Even the LCC report, which in every other respect took a different line from Birmingham and Birkenhead, refers to fear as 'the one distinct evil' that children suffered as a result of attendance at the cinema.

There was of course no unanimity about the overall conclusions these reports came to. The evidence that Birmingham gathered confirmed the dis-satisfaction which had been felt at the outset. Robertson wrote that the Committee was determined to persist in its endeavour to get government action 'until the abuses and dangers – intellectual, physical and moral – partic-ularly for children and adolescents, which at present make what might be an instrument of untold good into an instrument of incalculable and irreparable harm, have been extirpated'. The Birkenhead Vigilance Committee gave its support to Birmingham, deplored the lack of worthy films that 'provoked mental effort and braced the moral fibre', and tried unsuccessfully to use its evidence to get the Birkenhead Justices to amend local licensing regulations. The Sheffield Committee, conversely, succeeded even without trying. Within a month of the visits which took place on 29 November and 6 December 1930, the cinemas in Sheffield stopped showing A films at matinees. The irony was that it was not A films as such that the Sheffield Committee was targeting.

They were actually more concerned with the dullness of children's average film experience.

The LCC report was similarly low-key. The education officer's overall impression, after studying all the evidence, was that 'there is no need for serious alarm'. The only problem was that war films, such as *Journey's End* and *The Victor of Verdun*, in their attempt to depict the violence and cruelty of war, did more harm by frightening children through their use of realistic and memorable detail than all the romances and crime films did – because most children knew the latter to be false to life. The report suggested that ways should be found to keep children out of screenings of war films; and, with the Paisley crush and panic in mind, that not just babes in arms, but all children under seven should be excluded from cinemas completely. (Within the LCC area, a modified version of this – that children under seven were kept out unless accompanied – did in fact become standard after 1933.)

The Edinburgh report had more to say than any of the others about the positive aspects of the influence of cinema on children. Around one-third of the teachers involved had noticed ways in which children's school work gained. One of them, working at a type-B school, wrote: 'In this district, the cinema provides an extension of knowledge, as so many of the pupils see little or nothing beyond the area in which they live.' On a similar tack, some teachers thought that through cinema children got 'a knowledge of books they are not likely to read'.

Even if these five reports had all come to exactly the same conclusion, they would not have stifled the debate. To many people it was self-evident that to represent immorality was necessarily also to promote it; and that those who made up the bulk of audiences – mainly the working class, especially children – were least able to resist such corruption. The differences between the reports' findings could have been used to indicate the complexity of the situation and the unsatisfactory nature of some of the methodologies employed. But for most commentators it simply meant that they could choose which report to refer to, and ignore the rest. The most prominent example of this, and the most extended of the decade's parliamentary interventions, came in a long Commons speech made in 1932 by Sir Charles Oman, Conservative MP for Oxford University. Seventy-two at the time, and a distinguished historian, Oman represented the backbone attitudes of the Church of England. Having read the Birmingham report and found its conclusions to his liking, he contrived an opportunity to speak his mind, though the Bill being debated was not about children. Rather, it proposed to give licensing authorities the power to permit ordinary commercial screenings on Sundays. Oman said:

> The main point I wish to adduce as my reason for voting against the Bill is as follows. The film industry as at present conducted is a deleterious

agency corrupting the children of England. I am not saying this from vague newspaper knowledge, but after very grave consultation with Sir Charles Grant Robertson and the Birmingham Committee, who have gone into the cases of hundreds of thousands of children. It is not the product of the views of a body of fanatical clergy. Some 285 films were shown in Birmingham last year. The Committee has held that 79 were in every respect objectionable, and of those 79 more than half were films licensed for children as well as for adults. You may guess what the films licensed for children were like by a few of their titles: *The Compulsory Husband, One Mad Kiss, His Other Wife*, and *Too Hot for Paris*. This is the sort of stuff which, under this Bill, can be shown to children in Birmingham on Sunday evenings.

The second group of films, 81 in number, of the total of 285, dealt not with exactly the same subjects as the first group but were films which the Committee resolved might not be too deleterious possibly for adults, but which were absolutely unsuitable for children for various reasons. For instance, firstly emphasis laid on drunkenness or sexuality; secondly, horrors and murder and unhealthy excitement; and thirdly, details of gambling, burglary and cardsharping. You may guess the sort of films they were from their titles: *The House of Horror, The Godless Girl, The Man Who Was Girl-Crazy* and *The Unkissed Man*. It is clear that all these subjects are absolutely things which are wicked to lay before children.

Unfortunately, the films are at present educating more than the schools. They are the greatest educative force in England. It is absolutely certain that of the films those Birmingham children went to see a great many must have been absolutely deleterious. In fact, we know that they were deleterious because we have the answers of the children to the Birmingham Committee's very interesting set of inquiries as to what was their main impression after seeing so many films. The comments by the Birmingham children may be interesting to the House. 'What have you learned [from films]?' was a question. One answer was 'Discontent', a second was 'I have learned how the idle rich live', a third was 'How to murder people'. Another was, 'How to kiss'. A further comment is still more worth preserving: 'When you have a woman without clothes on it is called a love story'. Another answer to the question 'What have you learned?' was, 'Oh, I have learned a lot about American gangsters who throw knives at people and kill them'. There is a similar answer, probably of a child who had seen a similar film, 'I think that the best way of shooting people is to shoot out of your pocket before they notice'. Again: 'I have learned how to choke wild animals'. Those are the sorts of films these children must have been seeing. I think there is something rotten in the film production of England when these things go to Birmingham. What is the use of the film censors when films are allowed with these objectionable names and features?

Oman's speech summed up a prevalent mainstream attitude of the early thirties. He magnified the Birmingham sample of 1,439 children into 'hundreds of thousands of cases'; he judged films unseen, on the basis of their titles; and he chose not to bother with the LCC report. Nonetheless, he was not an extremist, not a lone voice. The government got its Bill through Parliament despite his opposition, but his stance was one with which thousands of teachers, parents, justices and ministers of religion, and many Members of Parliament, sympathised.

Only two tangible and new regulatory actions emerged from this public and parliamentary outcry. One was a 1933 Home Office circular urging that local authorities should require all cinemas in their area to display category notices for each film being shown on any particular day, in large clear lettering in prominent positions. The other was a codification of horror as particularly dangerous. By the end of 1933 the BBFC had developed a new category – H – which was meant to operate in exactly the same way as an A, but more strongly. Such attempts to keep children out made them all the more determined to get in, and they did. Again, questions were asked in the House. The government insisted that a system based on informed parental responsibility was still the best option; and that in any case, local authorities had the power to interpret BBFC categories as they thought fit. Shortly at least four areas – Surrey, London, Essex and Liverpool – had made it a condition of licences that no child should be allowed in to an H-film screening in any circumstances; and by 1937 most other local authorities, urged to do so by the Home Office, had followed suit.

Neither of these two changes affected Scotland, where the situation remained for some a matter of urgent concern throughout the thirties. The 'careful consideration' that the Duchess of Atholl had been promised had resulted in a voluntary agreement that members of the Scottish CEA would not show A films at children's matinees. Within a year, however, a deputation from the National Council of Women and other bodies met the Prime Minister and the Secretary of State for Scotland to plead for better protection for Scottish children. The voluntary agreement was not working, they claimed. In two picture houses that ran crowded children's matinees every week in an industrial area of Glasgow, fifty out of sixty features shown had carried an A certificate. The Prime Minister was moved to concern, and spoke of 'these flagrant and very dangerous evils'. The Secretary of State promised action; but in fact another twenty years were to pass before Scottish children would be subject to the same restrictions as English and Welsh children.

Parliamentary approaches to the problem of children and cinema were essentially negative and prohibitive. There was also a more positive response, one based on special programming and the encouragement of film appreciation, one that took place far away from Westminster, in birthday parties and chapels and village halls and museums and East End missions – and even in some cinemas.

3 'Our Tomcat Swallowed a Kangaroo'

It was maintained at that time, particularly by those in the social services, that the cinema trade had no social conscience and lacked a true sense of civic duty; that we were there solely for what we could get out of the cinema, without any thought or reference to what social service could be rendered.

(Sidney Bernstein, 1937)

Some people in the film business anticipated the disquiet of the early thirties even before talkies arrived. Chief among these was Sidney Bernstein, owner of Granada cinemas, a small chain concentrated in the South of England. A prominent member of the Film Society, the first British organisation devoted to film appreciation, Bernstein believed that there should be children's cinema for the same reason that there are children's libraries. He realised, like the Edinburgh report, that the logic of his position was that just as children's libraries need special books, so children's cinemas need special films. He could, however, see no way to make that happen, so from March 1928 to July 1929 he employed Miss J. M. Harvey, secretary of the Film Society, to do the best she could with what was available in the service of the children of Willesden, Enfield, Leytonstone and Edmonton.

The Granada scheme differed in four ways from what was going on all around. First, the performances were not run for profit: a letter from Harvey to a local paper proclaimed, 'our books are open to inspection'. Second, they took place on Saturday mornings, not afternoons, even though this involved the expense of employing staff at a time when they would otherwise be off duty. Third, seeking public support, Bernstein launched the scheme at a special Savoy luncheon attended by influential journalists. He invited parents, schools and local authorities to co-operate – and some did. For the audience, it was the fourth change that was the most important: the films were not derived from the cinemas' ordinary show. Instead, they were specially selected as offering 'clean, healthy entertainment'. This included an attempt to represent British culture when possible, rather than settle for the easy option of one hundred per cent Hollywood.

For sixpence in the circle, or threepence in the stalls, Harvey's normal Granada matinees – all silent – consisted of a cartoon, a short and a feature. Foremost among the cartoons were two American series, *Koko the Clown* and *Felix*; but there was also a British series about Bonzo, a chubby, mischievous puppy. The shorts were largely animal documentaries, such as *The Wonderland of Big Game* and *Dinner Time at the Zoo*. A British series, *The Secrets of Nature*, focused on smaller creatures such as bees, moths, magpies and those found within *An Aquarium in a Wine Glass*. Harvey's real challenge was to find features which would meet her proclaimed criteria, and she ranged over the past decade in her quest. Chaplin's *The Circus*, Fairbanks' *The Thief of Baghdad* and the films of Rin Tin Tin were probably well received, but other choices – often based on stories or plays that were thought of as children's literary classics, or on the lives of national heroes – seem not to have gone down so well. There was, for example, the 1924 version of *Peter Pan*, which lasts two hours, is fairly stagey, and has thickly-strewn inter-titles. Moreover, because of its running time, the children may have had to go without their Koko that morning. Others chosen in this spirit were the British 1927 *Robinson Crusoe*, and the 1926 biopic *Nelson*.

Attendance at these matinees started well, with over 200 children left outside at the Willesden Granada on the opening day, but after that diminished from week to week, till the project was abandoned in the summer of 1929 because of the low numbers turning up. Bernstein himself said that the main reason for the failure was the lack of co-operation from the local education authority, but it seems more likely that the principal problem was the programming. Children preferred to go to an ordinary show of a newly released film, especially as it would not cost any more than a Granada morning programme, parts of which must have been perceived as old-fashioned, high-minded and long-winded.

For five years the Granadas let the idea of special programmes lie dormant, but as the implications of the arrival of sound became clear, other bodies took it up. Some thought the answer was to make the selection much more explicitly educational. In Bath a Children's Cinema Council was formed, and from 1929/30 onwards, for many years, it organised screenings, during the winter months only, of instructional short films, with a slight element of entertainment. The Belfast Museum was equally upfront about its aims: its series of nine programmes of short silents, shown every Saturday morning and afternoon in February and March 1930, was billed as 'Exhibitions of Educational Films embracing Nature Study, Industry and Life in Other Lands'. Among the films screened in that first season – each introduced by a talk with lantern slides –

were: *Studies in Animal Motion, Scenic Wonders of New Zealand, Persian Carpet Making, Skilled Insect Artisans, Busy Bees, The Story of Concrete* and *Infant Welfare in the Bird World.* Some of these had also figured in the Granada programmes. Another similarity was that parents and teachers were 'cordially invited to co-operate'. There the resemblance ended, however, for the Belfast Museum shows were free and did not allow in children under twelve unless they were accompanied by an adult. These shows were popular enough to justify a second, longer, season; it featured *The Economy of the Cow, The Story of a Glass of Water* and *Lifeboat Drill on the Acquitania.*

In a totally different environment, another approach flourished for a while. East End missions film shows for children were praised by the LCC report (1932) as providing 'healthy performances showing vigorous adventure and amusing films, as well as travel, natural history, etc.'. They were run by ministers who believed in stressing the cinema's potential for good. Lorimer Rees, for example, began work in 1930 as curate of St Mary's, Somerstown, an area regarded as being one of the worst slums in the country. He saw it as his job to offer more than just Sunday morning uplift, and in so doing encountered the babes-in-arms syndrome that had been so marked a feature of the previous two decades. Fifty years on, he recalled:

> Children were the main victims of the situation. There was no room for them to play in their homes – there was only the street. So I used to run a film show on Saturday mornings, for all the children in the area. It cost tuppence if you could walk, but was free if you were in arms. What I found was that a small child of four would come staggering along carrying another one about the same size as itself! It was a way of releasing the women of the parish to get on with other things. As far as I remember we used to show just wild westerns and Charlie Chaplins, silent, in 16 mm. I'd get up to 300 children in the Mission each Saturday. If you went outside for a moment for fresh air it was virtually impossible to go back inside because the smell of the children's clothes and bodies was absolutely unspeakable. (Rees, 1984)

A rather more technically ambitious operation, but with similar aims, took place a few miles away, in Islington Central Methodist Hall. There Donald Soper, superintendent of the Methodist Mission, remembering that the cinema had had an irresistible appeal to him as a boy, decided that 'instead of pretending that it wasn't there, one should make better use of it, and provide for youngsters a cinematic experience which was more acceptable than that offered by the commercial cinema'. Accordingly, he acquired a 35 mm. projector, roped in a projectionist, and persuaded a former cathedral organist, whom he had met as an inmate while working as a prison chaplain, to provide musical accompaniment. Speaking to me about those years, Soper expounded his aims and methods:

> My aim was to provide an entertainment which avoided the excesses of sexual presentation, and in general terms was of a good quality. What I was looking for was not an evangelical opportunity, nor films that were educational. I wanted run-of-the-market stuff which was morally acceptable to me, and at the same time entertaining for the children. With this object I went up to Wardour Street and begged for films. I realised immediately that many silent films had been shelved, films that were not going to be reshown because of the burgeoning number of sound films emerging at that time, yet which were very much worth seeing. I remember in particular a German film called *The Last Command*, which to me was a brilliant piece of cinematography. It was just lying around more or less in dust covers. They seemed to think I was a bit potty, but nevertheless they were very kind to me, and gave me very reasonable terms. The films I wanted were just cluttering up the premises, so that in one sense I was an agreeable customer.
>
> In most cases I had not seen the film before we showed it, so I had to rely on the synopses they gave me in Wardour Street. I felt I didn't need to see a film to distinguish between one which was erotic and one which was not. It was a bit of a hit-and-miss situation, but I normally got it right. There were, however, a few occasions when I made a mistake and realised, after I'd seen the beginning of a film, that it was not good enough. In those situations I shut it up, gave the children their money back, and sent them home. Apart from those few lapses, it was a fairly professionally-run operation. The projector was in a separate room, so the children did not hear the noise of the machinery. The police supported me because they felt it was a very useful way of keeping children off the streets on Saturday mornings. My own view was rather loftier – that it was a piece of social engineering.
>
> Every Saturday we used to get between 300 and 400 children, each paying twopence, mainly sitting on the floor. Some parents came occasionally, but we didn't want them, and they didn't stay, even though they were pleased to see that we were sometimes showing a film which they themselves had seen many years before, and had almost forgotten. We started every week with a hymn – 'O Jesus I Have Promised'. This was my spiritual gesture, my concession to piety. I don't know what good it did, but they sang it with great gusto. They knew they couldn't see the film till they'd sung the hymn. It was always

a feature film that we showed, except for one week when we showed four shorts. Of all the films we showed, the ones they liked best were those of Chaplin, Keaton and – especially – Fairbanks.

Among religious bodies it was not only London's East End missions which saw it as necessary to provide social and educational service, as well as worship. In Hulme, Manchester, the non-conformist Zion Congregational Church sponsored over forty different non-Sunday activities, including an orchestra, a savings bank, a Women's Social Hour, a rambling club and Zion Saturday Entertainment. The last was easily the most popular, attracting twice as many as its nearest rival, the Zion Boys' Brigade. Regularly every Saturday, in the early evening, around 1,000 children gathered at the Zion for a programme of silent films. The silent stars enjoyed there several years after the coming of sound were various: the standard serials, comedies and swashbucklers; the peril-prone Pauline; Elmo Lincoln as Tarzan; hard-riding cowboys Buck Jones, Hoot Gibson and Tom Mix; the young Mickey Rooney, then known as Mickey McGuire, after the tough bowler-hatted character he played in silents; and the children in the series *Our Gang* (now better known as *The Little Rascals*). Another obvious choice for the Zion was *Ben Hur: A Tale of the Christ*. Zion Saturday Entertainment was not, however, confined to action, comedy and religion. Almost anything, as long as it was silent, was deemed acceptable. Thus the children saw the master of horror, Lon Chaney, in the two-hour 1923 *Hunchback of Notre Dame* and in the 1926 *Phantom of the Opera*; and Matheson Lang playing the evil oriental master-criminal Fu Manchu, whose face reportedly gave nightmares to thousands of children (not just at the Zion). One image in particular caused fear: 'They used to zoom his face large on the screen. Later I would lie in bed in terror, waiting for "the flower of death" to descend on me.' But even when the actual films might not have been regarded as edifying, there was still edification in Zion Entertainment. This came from the pianist, who played classical tunes when she could, rather than improvise. One memoir relates:

> She used to play furiously when the chase was on, and gently during love scenes. When there was a cowboy and Indian chase she played a galloping tune which I now know is *The Poets and Peasants*. She played the march tune from *Aida* so often that we soon fitted our own words to it – 'Our tomcat swallowed a kangaroo'. The overture from William Tell was likewise soon hackneyed to our ears. I thus became familiar with classical music without knowing it.

In Glasgow it was schools, rather than religious bodies, which tried to steer a course between entertainment and edification: in May 1933 the Educational

Cinema Society, with the support of the Director of Education, ran matinees. *Sight and Sound* (summer 1933) reported: 'They planned a scheme to show the cinema-minded school children of Glasgow that a children's matinee, even if there were no 'screamy' pictures and only a scrap of 'comic', could be a thing of delight.' Some of the films chosen with this end in view were: *Rango*, a jungle story featuring two orang-utans, directed by Ernest Schoedsack, who two years later made *King Kong*; *Kamet Conquered*, a documentary record of a British mountain-climbing expedition; *The Egg*, an exploration from the *Secrets of Life* series; and a Disney cartoon. These all had sound, and were shown in regular cinemas – the Regal and the Coliseum – using 35 mm. prints. As well as the twopennies downstairs, there were balcony seats for sixpence. Together the two cinemas, showing the same programme, could hold 5,000 children. For both Saturdays over 10,000 children applied for tickets. Despite this success the matinees were not repeated: the organisers just could not find enough 'good educative matter of general interest'.

A similar but longer-lasting body, the Scottish Educational Film Association (SEFA), was based in Edinburgh but reached out to Glasgow as well. A committee of teachers previewed and selected the films, then sent teaching notes on them to schools taking part. Each film programme went round four cinemas – the admission price being fixed at 2d. in all of them – and was then changed. One month the feature was *Dick Turpin*; next it was *S.O.S. Iceberg*. The Hollywood *Midsummer Night's Dream*, with James Cagney as Bottom and Mickey Rooney as Puck, was regarded as a great success and a good illustration of what the SEFA were trying to do: induce children to see films which they would otherwise pass by.

Shakespeare figured in another semi-commercial attempt to square the circle. This time it was the newly emerged Associated British Cinemas ABC chain that provided the screens, while the programming drive came from British Instructional, makers of the *Secrets of Nature* series. When education manager Marjorie Locket launched the scheme in January 1932 there were only four cinemas involved – West Norwood, Barking, Manor Park and East Ham – but the children turned up in their thousands, so Golders Green, West Ealing, Winchmore Hill, Willesden, Lewisham and Croydon came in as well. As with Granada four years earlier, initial contact was made through schools, but unlike the Granadas, the ABCs charged the same price for any seat. 'For twopence', said Locket in an interview (Locket, 1932), 'we want to give the children as good as and perhaps better value than their parents can get for their one-and-sixpence at the evening show'. Explaining her observations in detail, she returned to the 1917 idea that the answer lay in literary classics:

Love interest bores children, unless it serves as an excuse for an exciting rescue, duel or fight. They give all their applause to pictures of courage and enterprise, hardship endured for the sake of achievement, a goal won under difficult and exacting conditions. As such a story grips their interest they make comments aloud such as 'Look, he's sacrificing himself for his tribe'. In the old days there were plenty of films of this type, but since the talkies came children have lost much of their interest in the cinema. They don't like to be told what is happening; they don't like to keep quiet as if they were in school; they find it a strain to look and listen at the same time. Modern comedies depend more on wisecracks than on custard pies. If this venture fails it will not be for lack of support or money; it will be for lack of pictures. We shall soon exhaust the supply of suitable silent films, and unless the talkies develop along different lines the Saturday morning shows will find themselves hard put to it to fill their screens. We have plenty of classic stories just waiting to be filmed, and it would be well worth while to look into school libraries for possible film heroes and heroines from the modern child's reading.

The programming through which she sought to embody her beliefs was different from most of what had gone before in that it mixed silent films with talkies. A typical programme consisted of a two-reel Chaplin, a *Secret of Nature*, a Felix, a talkie newsreel, and then a feature which, if it was silent, could be Buster Keaton in *Steamboat Bill* or a western if it was a talkie. There were also crossovers like *Dassan*, a British travelogue about jackass penguins in South-West Africa, which had no synchronised sound, but did have an overlaid commentary. In the same spirit Locket sought to yoke together sound and silents, English heritage and American star power, by putting on one of the first talking Shakespeare adaptations – the 1929 *Taming of the Shrew*. Starring the king and queen of the silent era – Mary Pickford and Douglas Fairbanks, this very condensed version lasts only sixty-eight minutes; even so, it has 'additional dialogue' by the director. As a result, its inclusion was hotly debated: teachers argued that it was not proper Shakespeare, and that therefore the children would be misled; the ABC managers said that because it was Shakespeare, proper or not, the children would be bored. Locket insisted that its justification was that it was entertaining. The screenings went ahead, with Locket judging them to be 'an uproarious success'. Nonetheless, overall the project failed within a few months. By Easter, despite what Locket had claimed, there was simply not enough support to make the operation financially viable. Like Bernstein, the ABC circuit might have been content to break even, but they were not prepared to suffer a loss.

At around the same time, a travelling experiment in Yorkshire dealt in much smaller numbers and even lower charges. Villages around Halifax and

Bradford were visited by a unit of enthusiasts who went to children's parties, or Sunday schools, by arrangement, and there put on a ninety-minute 16 mm. programme of short films: *Toy-Making in Germany*, *Child Life in Rumania*, *A Day Trip to Scarborough*, *Monkey Land up the Barito River* and *Animals in Algonquin Park*. There were also cartoons and short comedies, regarded by the organisers of this and other such events as regrettable but necessary. The children were charged only one penny, but since overheads were low the shows did not lose too much.

In more populous London, two very middle-class approaches were tried. At the Everyman Theatre, Hampstead, a Children's Film Society (CFS) was formed in 1934. For five shillings a member could attend the six programmes, consisting of short films only – Disney's *Silly Symphonies* (but not Mickey Mouse), early Chaplins, newsreels, documentaries – which were shown each winter. One of the purposes in showing only short films was to make it possible to have several intervals, since the programmer believed that the members could not watch for long without getting tired. She had difficulty in finding exciting dramas short enough for her purposes, but there were plenty of factual films which, in her perception, the members found sufficiently interesting. One which particularly aroused them, because it was about children, was *Wharves and Strays*. Each CFS session included a discussion led by film workers such as Mary Field, director of some of the *Secrets of Nature*.

The same year saw the birth and death, in Oxford Street, of Junior Academy. Manager Elsie Cohen had made her name by importing from the USSR, Germany and other countries films which would not otherwise have been shown in the UK. She never normally showed an English-dialogue film. However, she did not import any Russian made-for-children films. Nor did she bring back *Emil and the Detectives*, the already sub-titled German film of the celebrated children's novel, even though when she had shown it the year before it had been hailed in *The Times* as 'the first sign the cinema has given of being able to do for boys what has been done by the stage with *Peter Pan*, and by the novel with *Treasure Island*'. Instead, she stuck mainly with the same short films and cartoons that were on offer elsewhere, charging sixpence for the front rows and a shilling at the back. She did try three features as well, one of them being a western, *Trailing North*, which landed her in trouble with parents who demanded: 'How dare you show our children a revolver?' After only eleven weeks, Junior Academy was abandoned.

Both the Children's Film Society and Junior Academy depended heavily on parents, either to transport the children there, or to pay the high admission fees, or both. Some parents stayed for the performance as well. As Bernstein put it: 'This meant that both theatres had to satisfy, not the child's idea of what is entertainment, but the parent's idea of the child's idea of what is entertainment.'

The children at these two cinemas must have had very little sense of it being their own space; nonetheless, the Children's Film Society carried on for several years.

None of these approaches ever developed into a significant national effort. Some of them were remarkably successful in their own terms, but they were too localised, or too loss-making, or too sporadic, ever to add more than a token punch in what was perceived by the Yorkshire organiser (Margerison) as the battle between 'the good or harm that is being done to the moral, mental and physical well-being of the child by the cinema'.

Fortunately, Mickey Mouse was at hand.

4   *Square Shooting*

96 Oxo cubes, 230 cigarettes, several ounces of tobacco and 56 eggs sent to the local hospital. One hundredweight of oranges, one gross of bananas, two large packets of custard powder, four jig-saw puzzles, three dozen women's journals, a large number of apples, a tea chest full of silver paper, several boxes of cheese and one bunch of daffodils sent to the Manchester Institute for Old Women.

(Charitable donations made by the members of Whalley Range Odeon Mickey Mouse Club, Manchester, in a three-month period in 1938. Quoted in Ford, 1939)

In the United States of the twenties and thirties, debate about the effects of the cinema on children ran parallel to that in Britain. As early as 1913, there was a Children's Motion Picture League organising children's matinees in New York City, and the idea soon spread to other states. In 1925 the major industry body – the Motion Picture Producers' and Distributors' Association of America – joined in and sponsored matinees through a campaign endorsed by over sixty organisations, including the Boy Scouts of America, the YMCA and the National Council of Catholic Women. There was, in parallel, a National Committee for Better Films, which disseminated information and worked closely with PTAs.

When the talkies arrived, concern grew stronger, and out of it came co-operation between Disney and the Better Films Committee. Thus was born the Mickey Mouse Club, offering a new and different kind of matinee package. The key factor was that it involved collective rituals additional to movie-watching. Before seeing the standard programme of a Disney cartoon, a serial episode and a specially chosen feature, children saluted the American flag and joined in community singing. Soon these activities extended to include picnics, competitions, prizes and fund-raising on behalf of tubercular children. Members were given a taste of democracy by electing their own club officers, and had a creed which they were expected to learn and live by:

I will be a square-shooter in my home, in school, on the playgrounds, or wherever I may be. I will be truthful and honorable and strive always to make myself a better and more useful little citizen. I will respect my elders, help the aged, the helpless and children smaller than myself. In short, I will be a good American.

Mickey, though only three years old, was then at the peak of his fame. In 1928 *Steamboat Willie*, the first Mickey cartoon to use synchronised sound, had been such an overwhelming success that Disney immediately went into full-scale production. During the following year new Mickey cartoons appeared at the rate of one a month. They were still in black and white, but their sophisticated use of music put them in a totally different league from previous front-runners such as Felix. Realising that he had started an international craze, Disney licensed the use of the Mickey Mouse name and image in toys and other products, using the income thus generated to help fund his ambitious, and not so commercial, parallel animation series, *Silly Symphonies*.

Within a year, all over the world, shops were full of Mickey Mouse cups, toothbrushes, saucers, plates, tea-pots, tea-strainers, pennants, drums, tool chests, beakers, combs, biscuits, spoons, fish-knives and an enormous variety of Mickey and Minnie figurines. At least two companies – the makers of Ingersoll watches, and Lionel trains – were rescued from the threat of bankruptcy by getting the Mickey Mouse name on their product. At the same time King Features arranged with Disney for Mickey to become a printed comic strip character, five days a week. Mickey Mouse was thus a daily presence in the life of the Western world, not just an occasional nine-minute flicker. To crown all this, Disney got an Oscar nomination in 1931 for *Mickey's Orphans*, and a Special Award Oscar in the following year for his overall achievement in developing the Mouse.

To have Mickey associated with clubs for children thus offered the promise of both popularity and respectability. Cinema clubs could arrange to use the name as long as they showed a Mickey Mouse cartoon – there were fifty in existence by the end of 1932 – or other Disney short (a *Silly Symphony*, or after 1934 a Donald Duck) every week. They had to pay more for Disney products than for rivals such as Oswald the Lucky Rabbit or Popeye the Sailor, but for them it was worth it to be associated with the mouse of the moment. Mickey Mouse clubs, promoted jointly by the industry and by parent organisations, spread quickly, and this successful combination of child-appeal and parent-placation, prestige and profit, was soon noted in Britain. By 1934, the Mickey Mouse Club had come to Worthing.

There the original American creed was adopted with only a few changes. The first sentence, about being 'a square-shooter', was left out entirely, doubtless because of the American-ness of that idiom and its apparent endorsement of guns; the next sentence became the first sentence of the British version, with just the spelling of 'honorable' anglicised and the phrase 'useful little citizen' changed to 'useful young citizen'; the third sentence was taken over wholesale; the fourth, instead of 'I will be a good Briton', became 'I will be kind to animals always'.

As well as the creed, there was a Mickey Mouse club song, and this was very much home-grown. It was written by Sydney Parsons, manager of the Odeon, Worthing, in 1934. He wrote it initially just for his own Saturday morning customers. His intention was to promote the Odeon name – then still fairly new; to bring in the patriotism missing from the club creed; and to get parents to think of the Worthing Odeon as a good place for keeping children off the streets. A supporter of the Boy Scout movement, and a good company man, he put these words to a simple, original tune that many thousands of people still recall singing with great pleasure:

> *Every Saturday morning, where do we go?*
> *Getting into mischief? Oh dear, no!*
> *To the Mickey Mouse Club with our badges on,*
> *Every Saturday morning at the O - DE - ON!*
>
> *Play the game, be honest, and every day*
> *Do our best at home, at school, at play;*
> *Love of King and Country will always be our song,*
> *Loyalty is taught us at the O - DE - ON!*

The children's singing of this song was heard by an area manager, who liked it and promoted it in other Odeons, until three years later it became, with two more verses added, the official song for all Odeon Mickey Mouse clubs. (There were non-Odeon cinemas that also ran Mickey Mouse clubs.) All in all, the song lasted for nine years.

In this new Mickey Mouse era, Bernstein restarted Saturday matinees in his Granadas, launching in 1935 a children's club called Kinemates. A privilege of being a Kinemate was the right to book seats in advance, a scheme intended to reduce the crush that could build up outside a cinema long before the box office opened. The name Kinemates was short-lived, perhaps because nobody was sure how to pronounce it. It was replaced in 1937 by Granadiers clubs in Granadas, and Rangers clubs in Empire cinemas. There came to be a Disney connection, but it was Donald Duck, not Mickey Mouse. On the Granadiers' badge he was in military uniform, and for Empire children he was dressed as a Ranger. There was soon too a special Granadiers' song, which combined several elements: patriotism, in its tune (*The British Grenadiers*); swashbuck-ling, in its use of the rallying cry of the Three Musketeers; a declaration of civic probity; and promotion both of the company and of each cinema. In Grantham, for example, children sang:

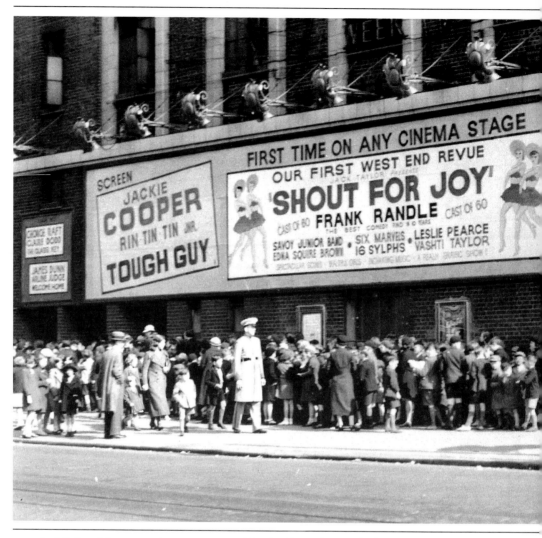

6. *Mickey Mouse matinee queue outside the Trocadero, Elephant and Castle, south London, spring 1936. The Trocadero was at that time part of the Gaumont chain, and had no connection with the Odeons* (British Film Institute)

We're one for all and all for one,
The Grantham Granadiers.
We play the game at work or fun,
The Grantham Granadiers.
And if the skies are overcast
We'll find a silver lining.
You'll know us when we shout 'I serve'
The Grantham Granadiers.

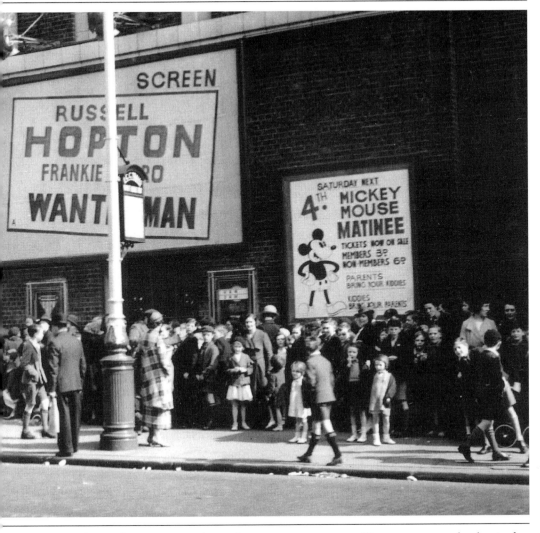

Granada were not the only group to use a military tune as the basis for their song. From around 1935 the Union circuit, the individual cinemas of which were known as Ritz cinemas, had taught its matinee members (called Union Chums) to sing these words to the tune *Blaze Away*:

> *Now come along and join our party*
> *Let's enrol you as a Chum.*
> *With all your friends so gay and hearty*
> *You can hardly wait for Saturday to come.*
> *Such fun is had at every meeting*
> *Good old Ritz can take some beating,*
> *That's why I shout 'Whoopee!*
> *I'm glad that I'm a Union Chum!'*

Blaze Away remained in use till the end of the matinee movement, but is now associated primarily with ABC Minors rather than Chums, because ABC took over Union in 1937, discarded the Chums club words and fitted new ones. This new song had to stress the identity of the parent company, as its cinemas did not share a common name. The result was a set of words which first came into use in 1937, and carried on for more than forty years. Because of the singability of the tune, the fact that the lyrics never changed and the size of the ABC circuit, it is certainly one of the two best-remembered Saturday morning songs. There must be millions who, like me, cannot hear the tune *Blaze Away* without thinking of the ABC Minors; and from their song I have taken the title for this book.

> *We are the boys and girls well known as*
> *Minors of the ABC,*
> *And every Saturday all line up*
> *To see the films we like and shout aloud with glee.*
> *We like to laugh and have our sing-song*
> *Just a happy crowd are we – e*
> *We're all pals together*
> *We're Minors of the ABC!*

The Odeon had nothing like such a confident start or such staying power. Having a creed, as well as a song, exposed them to more public comment, since the words were written on membership cards that parents could see. Around 1936 it was decided that they were no longer to be called Mickey Mouse clubs, and the creed was no longer to be a near-copy of the American original. Instead, there was to be an Odeon Children's Circle; the membership cards were to be organised centrally; a set of rules would replace the creed; and 'matinees' would become 'meetings'. The new rules contained an implicit reference to the Paisley disaster of 1929, the introduction of parents as people to be respected, and a defensive assertion of the Britishness of the operation. The last five rules ran like this:

3. You must uphold the dignity of the Club and when in a place of public entertainment behave yourself properly, and in case of emergency carry out the directions of those in charge of the building.
4. Always respect old people and help them when you can.
5. To instil into each member a desire to be loyal and patriotic.
6. Respect your parents and love your brothers and sisters.
7. The Club is British, same as the Odeon, and we are all united under the one flag – 'The Union Jack'.

POPEYE THE SAILOR CLUB

ORGANISER:
M. PACY

TELEPHONE:
MUSEUM 3307-8

HEADQUARTERS:
91, GT. TITCHFIELD ST.,
LONDON, W.1

By permission of Paramount Film Service, Ltd., also French C. Betts, Ltd., Literary and Editorial Agents for King Features Syndicate Inc.

By arrangement with King Features Syndicate Inc. and Segar.

Dear Sir,

In response to many inquiries, it has been decided to form a POPEYE THE SAILOR CLUB, and as we are convinced that all alert and progressive Cinema Managers will want to share in the publicity which such a scheme offers, especially when it is appreciated that the cost will be nothing, we have taken the liberty of sending you this letter.

The Club has been organised in such a way as to offer a very wide and attractive field of publicity to all Cinemas showing Popeye films.

Briefly, the scheme is as follows: Upon receiving an application from you, we will forward a free slide announcing the formation of the Club in your Cinema which will encourage the younger members of your audiences to apply for the special Application Forms which will be sent to you with the slide.

When the applicants send the signed Application Form to us, together with a small registration fee, we shall forward, direct to their homes a POPEYE THE SAILOR CLUB Badge, Certificate of Membership with the name of your Cinema on it, and Secret Rules Book.

All you have to do to obtain this attractive publicity is to apply to us for the free slide and state how many Application Forms you will require.

Yours faithfully,

M. Pacy

(ORGANISER)

7. *Circular letter written to cinema managers around 1937, seeking to promote Popeye as a rival to Mickey Mouse*

Another major chain of cinemas, the Gaumonts, were also developing centralised Saturday cinema clubs in these years, and from them came the other club song which, with some changes, lasted for several decades and still remains strong in the memories of millions. This one did not take over an existing tune, but was specially written by the resident organist at the Camden

Town Gaumont, Con Docherty, in January 1937, a few weeks after the Gaumonts had started running matinees. Talking to me about that era, Con Docherty recalled:

> At that time the number one singing star in the country was Gracie Fields, and the children greatly enjoyed singing the songs that she had popularised. In the month that I was pondering the problem, her big hit was *Sing as We Go*, so I stole the first four notes of that, and fitted to them the words 'We come a-long'. Then I gradually worked out the rest of the tune and words. I was trying to curry favour with the Gaumont company, and deliberately chose words that I thought would appeal to the management and to the children's parents. I finally settled on these:
>
> > *We come along, on Saturday morning*
> > *Greeting everybody with a smile;*
> > *We come along, on Saturday morning*
> > *We know it's well worth while.*
> > *Our parents know that when we're here*
> > *We're in the best of care;*
> > *We all agree the shows we see*
> > *Are the best of anywhere.*
> > *We come along, on Saturday morning*
> > *Greeting everybody with a smile, smile, SMILE,*
> > *Greeting everybody with a smile.*

I then went to see the manager of the Camden Town Gaumont, and got his agreement to put that song on a slide so that the words could be projected on to the screen. The following Saturday I said: 'Come on boys and girls, I've got a special song for you.' First an assistant manager and I sang it while I played the tune on the organ. Then I said: 'Well, do you think you can sing it?' Their response was enthusiastic, so we put the words on the screen, and I played the tune a couple of times. Within five minutes they could sing it, and certainly seemed to enjoy it. Well, I thought that was that, but soon the area manager came down to listen to the song, and the next thing was that I was asked by the company's musical supervisor, Ernest Grimshaw, to write it out as sheet music. After a while I heard that it was being played and sung in other Gaumont cinemas, which I was pleased about, except that it did not have my name on as author. Some people seemed to think that Grimshaw had written it himself.

Some years later, during the war, when I was serving with the RAF

ODEON REG. MICKEY MOUSE CLUB SONG.

(1) Ev - 'ry Sat - ur - day
(3) For the poor and

morn·ing Where do we go Get - ting in - to mis - chief
need - y a gift we'll al - ways share For oth - er peo - ple's trou - bles

oh dear no! To the Mickey Mouse Club With our bad - ges
have a care, To the sick and suffering our sym - pa - thies be —

on. Ev - 'ry Saturday morning}
-long, We're taught to think of oth - ers} At the O - DE - ON!

8. *Verses one and three of the Official Song for all Odeon Mickey Mouse Clubs, as extended and copyrighted in 1937 after Odeon abandoned the name Odeon Children's Circle*

in India, Grimshaw sent a letter informing me that the song, with four lines changed by him, had been chosen as the official anthem for all the clubs in the GB circuit. This time I got a credit, with Grimshaw, on the sheet music that was circulated to all Gaumont Junior clubs. After that the song remained unchanged for the rest of its life, except for a one-word substitution in 1948. Despite the song's longevity, however, I never made a penny out of it, since it was registered in Grimshaw's name, not mine.

Sidney Parsons got a slightly better deal from the Odeons. In the autumn of 1937, the attempt to keep Mickey Mouse at bay was abandoned, and all Odeon matinees were unified under the title Odeon Mickey Mouse clubs, with the children getting new badges shaped like the O in the company logo. Parsons' song, with the extra verses, was issued to each of the over one hundred participating cinemas as the Official Song for all Odeon Mickey Mouse clubs. On the song-sheet Parsons got a credit as writer and composer, but since he had written it as a company employee, Odeon retained the copyright. The new verses stressed the altruistic activities and road safety that played a major part in Odeon Mickey Mouse club life at the end of the thirties. Coming between the two older verses, the new ones ran:

> *Before we cross a busy road, we know it pays*
> *To think of motor cars and look both ways;*
> *If a car's approaching we wait until it's gone,*
> *Safety first they teach us at the O - DE - ON!*
>
> *For the poor and needy, a gift we'll always share*
> *For other people's troubles have a care.*
> *To the sick and suffering our sympathies belong,*
> *We're taught to think of others at the O - DE - ON!*

Overall, the attempts to inculcate altruism and loyalty by means of creeds, rules and virtuous verses in songs almost certainly had no transformative effect whatever on the children. In their perception, the tune was either an easy one to sing, or it was not; if it was, and the words were not too much of a mouthful (as, I imagine, the line 'To the sick and suffering our sympathies belong' may have been for some sibilant Saturday singers) then it could be fun. Overall, whether or not the children entirely understood the words, in most cases they found the songs perfectly acceptable as part of a general sing-song.

In any case, these exhortatory trappings and trimmings were not directed mainly at them. Parents, teachers, local authorities, MPs – these were the real target, which explains why the lyrics and creeds to some extent went over the children's heads. The idiom 'play the game', for example, occurred in both the Odeon Mickey Mouse club and the Granadiers' song. In the latter, children who cared about the meaning of what they were singing had not only to ponder the phrase 'play the game', but also had to work out how they could play the game while 'at work'. The expression invoked an Edwardian public-school cricketing ethos with which the children who attended matinees would have been totally unfamiliar. The writers of the songs might just as well have retained the words 'I will be a square-shooter' from the American Mickey Mouse clubs: given the popularity of westerns, that sentence would have been as likely to be understood as was 'play the game'.

In the end, however, it was not enhanced public esteem or club songs or creeds or badges or even Mickey Mouse cartoons which reversed the pattern of dwindling attendance and financial loss which Bernstein had suffered at the end of the twenties when he experimented with specialised programming for children. It was *The Clutching Hand*.

5 To Be Continued Next Week

My experience of matinees began in 1933, and from the beginning I was annoyed by exhibitor cheating. The manager often used to save a pound or two by shoving in a film from his regular programme, which I'd already seen. I tried to cultivate a friendship with him, and recommended certain titles. This, coming from a child of five, he didn't take too seriously.

(William K. Everson, film historian, in letter to the author, 1995)

When the circuits took up the challenge of running viable matinees, the premiss from which they operated was that films shown to children could defensibly offer entertainment only: edification and respectability could be left to the club activities. This brought a substantial change in programming style. In all the commercially run clubs and matinees, westerns and serials were from now on staple ingredients. They were not absolutely the only types of film shown, but they easily predominated. Their existence in quantity was a happy accident. The British matinee movement did nothing to call them forth – it was too small to have such clout – and yet in the the thirties it could not have existed without them.

The westerns were made in the first place for the general American market, their purpose being to back up the main feature and thereby provide the public with the double bill they had come to expect. This status as support gave them the name B westerns and determined that they would be short. Around 1,000 of them were produced during the thirties. (John Wayne starred in B westerns for several years and was one of the top ten favourites with Odeon club audiences before *Stagecoach*, in 1939, established him in main features. When he visited matinees in person a decade later, he was rarely seen on matinee screens.) B westerns were usually made in blocks of eight, back to back, a star having been signed up to appear in all eight within one year. With a budget of only about half a million dollars for a whole series, B western directors had to keep it simple. They made extensive use of stock footage of anything that would have been expensive to stage, such as cattle stampedes; and characterisation had to be one-dimensional because there was no time for complexity. Their lack of sophistication meant that many of the B westerns never made it to the major circuit cinemas in big towns. However, audiences in small-town movie-houses accepted them willingly.

In the UK this simplistic presentation of good and bad was one of the aspects that recommended them for children's matinees. It came to be exemplified by the films of William Boyd, the supreme exponent of unwavering righteousness. In 1937 he created for the screen the character of Hopalong Cassidy, an inflexible moralist, a medieval knight transposed to the western range. Between 1937 and 1948 Boyd made sixty-six Cassidy films, never playing any other character during that time. His and the other western heroes' customary uprightness meant that their films were virtually guaranteed the essential U certificate.

As important as morality was plentiful availability. If all the B westerns ever made had come to Britain, there would have been enough titles for a cinema to show a different one every Saturday for twenty years. Major distributors handled the relatively few B westerns which were judged to have general appeal as supporting features, and in such cases there would be a delay before the film was available for the matinee market. However, as the matinee movement grew, there were also small distributors which acquired films specifically for that market, and maintained a special department to deal with it. B westerns therefore seemed to offer a combination of brevity, morality and long-term availability. As far as most UK managers were concerned, whether they were running a club or just a simple performance with no trimmings, it was an offer that could not be refused.

Other European countries in the thirties objected to the idea of showing children films centred around gunshot and violent deaths. Within the UK these objections were echoed in various quarters (such as the parents of the Junior Academy children), but the industry retorted that westerns were the most suitable product available. Speaking in Geneva at a meeting of the Child Welfare Commission of the League of Nations, Oliver Bell, director of the British Film Institute (BFI), summed up the British position:

> It is a mistake to take too narrow a view of what a child may or may not see. British psychologists have come to the conclusion that violent death on the films is not necessarily bad. To this extent they would disagree with the censors in certain other countries. They hold that, provided there is no brutality or cruelty – both of which offend the child's sense of fitness – the shooting of the villain in a western is a 'mopping-up' operation comparable to the rubbing out of a dirty mark in a book or the removal of refuse from the parlour to the ash can. (Bell, 1938)

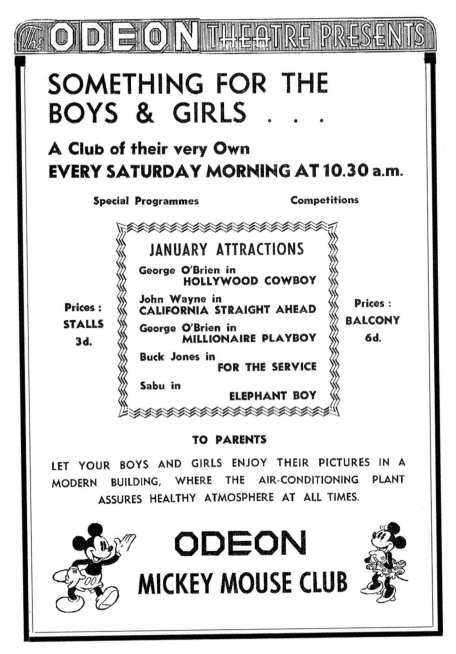

9. Page from the January 1939 brochure of the Odeon, Bournemouth

Ignorant of such national and international adult worries, in the actual cinemas children came to know and take pleasure in not only the individual cowboys, but their horses as well. In the silents, Tom Mix had had Tony. In the thirties, children knew that Ken Maynard would be able to rely on his half-Arabian horse Tarzan; Buck Jones would ride to the rescue at top speed on his white steed Silver; Hopalong Cassidy's all-black outfit would contrast with his horse Topper; Gene Autry would sing while riding Champion; Tex Ritter would be astride White Flash; Allan Lane would be looked after by Blackjack; and Roy Rogers would bestow at least as much affection on his horse Trigger as on Dale Evans, who in her turn would devote some attention to Buttermilk. And when a film gave one of these horses a pro-active role in the plot, the audience's yells of encouragement would be unbounded. Indeed, some of these partnerships became so popular and familiar with matinee audiences that western stories involving Buck Jones, Tim McCoy, Ken Maynard and their horses all appeared inside *Film Fun*.

In one respect only were westerns as a genre unsatisfactory from the audience point of view. Since they were not primarily aimed at children – though the producers and stars came to be well aware that that was where some of their most loyal followers were to be found – they often stuck to a standard Hollywood formula and included a woman as 'love interest'. In the Buck Jones films particularly – and he made sixty of them – there was always an element of romance. This was acceptable in providing the hero with motivation at the beginning of the story, but if it finally resulted in kissing, the matinee audience was likely to greet this with whistles, booing, catcalls and noisy movement. The memories of people who attended matinees in the thirties illustrate this and many other aspects of audience response, both male and female, to these westerns:

> In the Southend Ritz the main feature was almost always a cowboy, Ken Maynard and Roy Rogers being the favourites. Like all the cowboy heroes, these chaps wore white hats; the baddies always had black hats, bristly chins, sombre-looking shirts and evil faces.

> The main feature at the Regal, Golders Green, was invariably a cowboy film starring Ken Maynard, Tim McCoy or my hero Buck Jones. Audience participation was very vocal especially in the fight scenes, except for the final minutes when, as the hero always won the girl and the soppy bit came on, there was a general stampede to the toilets: the faster you got there, the more chance you had to queue for an ice-cream before the lights dimmed again.

> In the Gateshead Ritz, if the big film was a 'cowboy' it went down great, unless there were lots of sloppy scenes and dialogue in it. If that happened we lost interest and threw sweet papers and ice-cream cartons at each other. Roy Rogers, Buck Jones, Hopalong Cassidy were all popular. The kids loved a good cowboy film, especially with Indians to

fight. We all shouted for our hero, and rode our horses (rocking back and forth on the cinema seats), shooting our guns. Very noisy, but we loved it – girls as well as boys. A very good tanner's worth on a Saturday morning.

At the Walpole, Ealing, there must have been a varied programme, but I only remember the westerns. There were dozens of western stars in the thirties. Among the different ones I saw were: Hoot Gibson, George O'Brien, Tim McCoy, Tom Keen, Johnny Mack Brown, Jack Randall, Charles Starrett, Gene Autry, Buck Jones, William Boyd, Dick Foran, Buster Crabbe, Kermit Maynard and his brother Ken. The plots were not important. The action was the thing, and so long as there was fast riding, quick-draw shooting and a good punch-up, I for one was content.

In the Roxy, Edinburgh, the programme followed a regular pattern, almost invariably ending with a western. Only when I became about fifteen did I realise that they were all the same. To younger kids the identification with the stock characters was such that each film became an epic! We would cheer the heroes, boo the villains (who always wore black hats) and drum our feet on the floor during the chases. It was a great release.

In Buckinghamshire we (a group of three or four girls) regularly saw cowboy films, and we thought of the characters, such as Hopalong Cassidy, as friends. In the country, acting out those characters and their stories formed the mainstay of our free play as we 'rode' about in the fields, stalking each other.

I was a very timid, nervous child, and my Saturday mornings with the Mickey Mouse Club at the Synod Hall, Edinburgh, have left me with an abiding fear of North American Indians. All westerns seemed to be anti-Indian. I came to associate Red Indians, as we called them then, with torture, even though nothing explicit was ever shown. When there were Red Indians in the film, I was always slightly on edge as to what might happen. The merest suggestion of torture would send me fleeing to the toilets. However, none of this stopped me going back for more the next week.

 At the Odeon, Harlesden, we saw lots of films with Gene Autry, the singing cowboy. We all shouted and booed – it was bedlam at times. We even had a personal appearance of Gene Autry himself one Easter.

It was marvellous. I can see him now riding his white horse, Champion, down the central aisle of the cinema.

The other major programming change was the reintroduction of the serial. Serials were, and continued to be, regarded by most critics as a very lowly form of cinematic life. They were rarely reviewed by critics. The essential justification for showing them was purely pragmatic: they helped the cinemas to achieve regularity of attendance. This importance of this audience-building role is demonstrated by the fact that in most cases a cinema was prepared to pay as much for a serial episode of around twenty minutes as for a western or other feature three times as long.

Like westerns, serials were made in the first place for an unsophisticated small-town American market. After a lull towards the end of the twenties, serials had been revitalised by the coming of sound, which added greatly to a film's ability to create excitement and tension. During the thirties and forties the three major serial-producing companies turned out nearly 200. Since each one had at least twelve episodes, sometimes as many as fifteen, there were eventually around 2,500 episodes available, so as the thirties progressed, serials – like feature westerns – were sufficiently plentiful to be able to satisfy matinee managers' desire for more or less endless repeatability of a successful pattern. About one-third of them were westerns (with Buck Jones, Ken Maynard, etc.). The others were jungle serials, space exploration serials, police serials, motor-racing serials, super-hero serials, swashbuckling serials and more. There were even serials about serial killers.

The moral justification for showing serials to children was questioned frequenty during the thirties and forties. The basic argument in their favour was that they presented uncomplicated black-and-white characterisation similar to that prevalent in westerns, with good always triumphant at the end. However, this proved hard to sustain in detail. The effect of a serial on an audience was not accepted as likely to be the same as that of a feature western, because a serial could take up to fifteen weeks before showing evil routed and good triumphant. For the first fourteen weeks, evil had to be resourceful enough to get the upper hand and leave good facing imminent destruction. Some adults worried about the effect that each week of tension might have on the audience. And what if a child saw all or most of the first fourteen episodes, and then somehow missed the resolution, showing right resurgent and justice reimposed?

Most managers did not bother with such questions, but some people were certainly a bit shame-faced about showing serials to children. From 1937 onwards the BFI sought to promote special matinees and to help organisers by publishing lists of films recommended for children. Shorts, cartoons, comedies and feature films, including westerns, were all included in these lists – but serials were ignored. Likewise, when Bell gave his 1938 Geneva address he ended by showing a selection of films intended to exemplify a typical British matinee. The programme contained a documentary about a giant liner docking; the Laurel and Hardy Oscar-winning *The Music Box*; the Disney cartoon *Little Hiawatha*; extracts from five features (including a Buck Jones western); but no serial episode.

In most cases the serials that were chosen for the Saturday repertory did what was expected of them. They worked their way into children's imagination, kept them guessing, stimulated play and argument, and strengthened motivation to attend week after week. An aid to speculation was noting the title – often alliterative, always evocative – of the next episode. In the case of one serial that everyone who was there remembers – the 1936 *Flash Gordon* – these separate chapter titles were: The Planet of Peril, The Tunnel of Terror, Captured by Shark Men, Battling the Sea Beast, The Destroying Ray, Flaming Fortune, Shattering Doom, Tournament of Death, Fighting the Fire Dragon, The Unseen Peril, In the Claws of the Tigron, Trapped in the Turret, and Rocketing to Earth. Even more memorable was the major malefactor – Ming the Merciless of Mongo.

Another serial lodged in the psyche of those who saw it is *The Clutching Hand*, which is about a succession of mysterious murders. Odeon managers in the thirties reported that various aspects of it seemed to frighten audiences. The 'apparently disembodied hand appearing from the wall' was one. The 'screams in the dark' was another. Memoirs contributed to this book indicate that over half a century later, the hand still has a strong grip. One sums it up:

10. *Saturday matinee queue, with at least one babe-on-shoulders, outside a cinema in Plaistow, east London, 1937. The programme which they are going to see –* Tarzan, Flash Gordon *and some shorts – is the one that has been screened for evening audiences for the past two days* (British Film Institute)

As well as the feature films, at the Highbury Picture Palace in the late thirties there was a serial with the sinister title *The Clutching Hand*. When the manager was trying to make announcements before the show began, we drowned him out with a chorus of: 'We want the Clutching Hand!' It was a mystery thriller of blood-curdling dimension. In each weekly episode another victim would be strangled at the hand of the assassin – whose identity was not revealed until the final instalment. Audience participation took the form of frantic screams and shouts of 'Look out – it's behind you!' as a hand reached out from behind a curtain towards the throat of the next unsuspecting victim. The action on the screen was accompanied by spine-chilling music. The theatre throbbed with excitement as the tension mounted, and my younger sister, aged nine, would crouch, terrified, behind the seats in front.

Other serials are remembered no less vividly, even though the effect they produced at the time may have been less dramatic. Excitement and anticipation were standard: fright relatively rare. Everyone knew that the hero or heroine would win in the end; everyone knew when that end would come. The question to talk about was not, 'Will they escape?', but 'How will they escape?' The following memoirs evoke something of the atmosphere:

After we had queued up for an ice-cream the lights dimmed again and the climax of the morning, the serial, came on. The one I remember best was *Radio Patrol*, about a New York police car and its team – Grant Withers and his humorous side-kick. It had cliff-hanging endings each week, one being a huge rock hurtling down on to the police car. The film stopped as the rock was a foot above the car roof. Oh, the suspense of having to wait a week to find out how they escaped!

Zorro at the Wealdstone Granada caused us all to erupt into the High Street with our jackets draped over our shoulders like Zorro capes, having imaginary sword fights and smacking our bottoms as we galloped imaginary horses.

My most vivid memory of my first visit to a kids' matinee was the film that came at the end. The loud cheer that heralded it obviously indicated that this was the moment everyone had been waiting for – another thrilling chapter of the serial *Burn 'em up Barnes*, the story of a racing driver and his youthful assistant trying to thwart a gang of crooks anxious to buy a piece of land they knew contained oil.

The only titles I remember are *Tarzan* and *Flash Gordon*, but I remember vividly that they all stopped each week at the most exciting moment when everyone was in danger so we could hardly wait the week out to find out how they came through. The camaraderie of discussing how the hero would escape that week's perils occupied a lot of children, and made school more bearable.

The identity of the villain was frequently the crux on which the plot turned. A film's deliberate laying of false trails could have a whole cinema full of children shouting out in unison 'It's him!' when they thought they had finally penetrated the villain's disguise. A serial that captured audiences in this way during the thirties and forties was *Mystery Mountain*. Since it featured Ken Maynard and Tarzan, already familiar as western stars, it travelled well:

> I don't remember in detail what *Mystery Mountain* was about, even though I saw it twice, except that Maynard was called in to solve some murders that were occurring at a mine. It was probably to do with mining rights, or maybe hidden gold. The villain was The Rattler, a master of disguise who had a cupboard full of face-masks of the rest of the characters, including Maynard, so you never quite knew who was for real or if it was The Rattler himself behind a false face, black hat and swirling cape. But if you heard the sound of a rattlesnake then you knew that The Rattler was about to strike. He was finally unmasked by Maynard's horse, Tarzan, who sniffed him out in a line-up. I saw this serial first in Kemp Town. When I saw it again in Ealing, where it had not been shown before, because I knew the ending I was able to win a few chocolate bars in bets on the identity of The Rattler.

The western, the serial and the cartoon were the eternal triangle of matinee programming. Booking them was relatively easy. However, once a cinema or circuit organiser wanted or needed to go outside the big three, there arose complications resulting from the matinees' position at the bottom of the distribution hierarchy. At the top was the new release, during which films were shown from Monday to Saturday, both afternoons and evenings. In that situation the distributor was able contractually to require from the cinema a proportion, sometimes as high as 50 per cent, of the whole net takings during the time the film was showing. The cinemas that charged most for their seats were thus more attractive to distributors than those that charged least. Next, in the second-run houses, which tended to show films for three days only, when the film was not such a big draw, distributors specified a flat rate, which was dependent on the size of the cinema, and on the number of shows it ran. This flat rate could be anything between £150 and £5, but even £5 was higher than a matinee charging its customers only threepence – and with other films, staff and overheads to pay for – could possibly afford. There was still another outlet which was more profitable than renting to a matinee – the Sunday slot.

A film on its third run would normally be booked for two Sunday screenings. Again the distributors charged a flat rate, and still it was higher than would have been economical for a matinee screening.

Only after these three possibilities had been totally exhausted – which could take some years – were some distributors willing to deal with the matinee market, able as it was to pay only about one pound for one screening. Other distributors were not prepared to bother with matinees at all, arguing that it would cost them more to do the paper-work than they would get in revenue. The most serious result of this situation, as far as the children of the thirties were concerned, was that their overall top favourite film star could almost never be seen on Saturday mornings, because she was too good for them. This was child-star Shirley Temple. In various polls, when children were invited to name the star they liked best of all, not restricting their choice to favourites of the Saturday morning screen, they voted overwhelmingly for Shirley Temple. A newspaper used her name to harness pester power when it told children in 1936 that it was forming a branch of the Shirley Temple League, and that it was sure that she would like them all to join: 'It costs you nothing; all you have to do is ask your father and mother to order a copy of the *Sunday Referee* next Sunday. We will send you a certificate of enrolment, and a lovely blue and gold enamel badge, in the centre of which is a portrait of Shirley Temple.' In one poll of children taken around 1938 she got more than double the number of votes given to Buck Jones, who came second, and Donald Duck who, a close third, had by then taken over from Mickey Mouse as top Disney character.   Her name was to be seen on a vast range of products, including Shirley Temple dolls, the Shirley Temple Book of Fairy Tales, Puffed Wheat ('This is *my* Cereal') and Quaker Rice ('I love Quaker Rice too'). In 1934 she, like Mickey Mouse, had won a Special Oscar not for one particular film, but for her 'outstanding contribution to screen entertainment'. Her films therefore had a very long shelf life, so that by 1939 even the earliest, then five or more years old, had not fallen so low as to be available for threepence.

The result was that matinee-goers who liked to see children on screen, and enjoyed some of the pleasures of identification even when the child on screen was placed in situations far removed from their own daily experience, saw aspirant princesses rather than Queen Shirley herself. Of these the main one was Jane Withers. By her own admission, she was 'plain compared to Shirley and all the other little girls with lots of curls'. She was a talented dancer and impressionist with a round face, innumerable freckles, tremendous vitality – but no curls. She got into films by impressing a producer with her imitation of a machine gun. For the Temple film *Bright Eyes* the story required another orphan, a non-heroine type, to play opposite her. The director reportedly took one look at her and said: 'Ugh! That's the one.' The film was a resounding success, and gave Withers a launch pad for her own career. For the rest of the decade she starred in an average of four films a year, always cast as the pudgy tomboy type, wide-eyed and mischievous. The titles of two of her films – *The Holy Terror* and *Always in Trouble* – sum up the image by which she was promoted. When her films became available at a price that matinees could afford, they were snapped up, and since there were so many of them, with more coming out each year, she became a familiar and popular character with the Saturday morning crowd.

After child-stars, cartoon characters and westerners, the best-liked film actors were comedians. Easily at the top in that category were Laurel and Hardy. Their films were not made for the matinee market, and retained commercial value for many years after their release. In the thirties their feature films rarely reached Saturday screens, but the shorts – such as *The Chimp, Me and my Pal, The Fixer Uppers, Them Thar Hills* – had enormous matinee success. With Laurel and Hardy, the essential communication of emotion and intention is done by facial expression. When the dialogue does come, it's child-like, and delivered slowly (unlike the vaudeville patter of their successors, Abbott and Costello). On top of that, Stan and Ollie were so easy to tell apart. You could simply say 'the fat one', or 'the thin one', and be sure of being understood.

Among other comedians seen and enjoyed on the Saturday screen in the thirties was one who provided most of the very few occasions when matinee children saw British films. The man who filled the gap was a teacher, known variously as Dr Benjamin Twist, or Dr Alexander Smart. As played by Will Hay in *Boys Will Be Boys, Where There's a Will, Good Morning Boys, Convict 99, The Ghost of St Michael's* and *Old Bones of the River*, this Doctor was a shady, seedy, bumbling, incompetent schoolmaster, desperately trying to cover up his ignorance by bluster and deceit, always in the wrong but never admitting it. Even though he existed within a boarding school context there was enough for matinee audiences to recognise and enjoy. After five days of real school, Hay's comic version was a welcome deflation of authority. Up there on the screen the children saw flashes of their own culture, and heard a version of their own language. In Graham Moffat's 'Albert' – an impertinent fat boy – there was a character they could begin to identify with. In Hay's films they may even have heard the phrase 'play the game' – but it would not have helped them to understand it because 'playing the game' was the last thing that Dr Twist/Smart would ever do.

Rivalling Will Hay in popularity was American comedian Joe E. Brown, whose trademark grin was immortalised twenty years later, for a different generation, in the closing shot of *Some Like it Hot*. With a background in circus and vaudeville he had a muscular body, small eyes, an elastic face and a mouth reputed to be big enough to fit in half a dozen golf balls. Unlike Hay, he did not play the same character all the time. In one film he might be a swaggering braggart, in another a timid simpleton. Whatever the character, it was usually

one with formidable athletic ability in baseball, swimming, cycling, polo, boxing or wrestling. In one story he invented an unsinkable bathing suit; in another he entered a six-day cycling contest in the hope of impressing a girl; in a third he was a firefighter who wanted to be a baseball pitcher; in *The Gladiator* he's injected with a serum which enables him to lift ten times his own weight, and jump five times his own height. According to Ford (1939), a manager had only to announce that next week's film would star Joe E. Brown, and he could be certain of an answering roar of approval.

Chaplin, however, had lost his pull. When the decade opened he was still a

11. Saturday morning crowd outside Kemp Town Odeon, Brighton, around 1938, illustrating the line: 'Safety first they teach us at the O - DE - ON'
(British Film Institute)

big matinee attraction, but within a few years silent cinema became not merely unfashionable, but positively unshowable, because most cinemas had equipment that could run only at the sound speed of twenty-four frames per second, not at the slower speed required by silent films. In any case, managers would not want to incur the expense of paying a pianist to accompany a silent film.

In the last half of the decade some Chaplin shorts with added soundtracks were available, but they were not received with universal matinee acclaim. A fair number of managers never showed Chaplin at all, finding that children just could not get used to the conventions of silent screen acting. For many he remained just a name that adults invoked from time to time. And there was at least one manager (quoted by Ford, 1939) who decided that the commentary on a Chaplin soundtrack was 'too suggestive', and stopped the screening of the film before it had finished.

Another situation in which managerial discretion came into play was in regard to the showing of the current newsreel. Because of their topicality newsreels were not certificated. They could therefore all be shown to children without infringing any licence conditions. To some managers, the attraction of showing a newsreel was that it cost absolutely nothing over and above the flat rate fee which would have to be paid anyway, and it could be a useful filler. There were others who thought it educationally desirable for children to have some knowledge of national and international events. For either type of manager, there were occasional sequences – incidents of violence, such as the Japanese invasion of China, or the assassination of King Alexander of Yugoslavia – on which a judgement of suitability had to be made quickly.

Many aspects of thirties' matinees are encapsulated in a memoir about a unique animal movie, long awaited and much heralded. This was Flaherty and Korda's *Elephant Boy* – combining a child character to identify with, and plenty of animal life. Playing the title role, Sabu was the only international child-star that the British cinema produced in the thirties, and after only a few films he began to appear in children's lists of their favourite actors. A contributor recalls:

One Saturday morning at the Regent, Holloway, Mr Black came on to the stage and told us that we were going to see a jungle film with Sabu in it. He told us that we were to take great notice of the film and then go home, and draw a picture of an elephant, and hand it in next week. The prizes were three pairs of cowboy guns and gun belts for the three best boys' drawings, and three nurses' uniforms for the girls. I was only seven, and could not draw a thing, but I wanted one of the guns so bad. I was mad on cowboys and we used to play out on the streets every night for hours after coming home from school, so when I got home I asked my uncle to draw me an elephant. He was a very good artist, and he drew me a right smasher – only it was too smashing. Along came next Saturday, and off we all went to the cinema. We handed in our drawings and at half-time Mr Black came out on to the stage with a small table. On the table were the three pairs of guns with white handles, and the belts even had bullets all around. My eyes nearly fell out, along with those of the rest of the kids.

He picked up three of the drawings and said 'Will Jimmy Brown come up on to the stage, and also Freddie Jones and William Riefe' (that was me). He said to the first kid, 'Did you draw this?'

The boy said 'Yes'.

'Very good, here's your guns', and off the stage the kid went. Mr Black then said the same to the second one, and got the same answer. Off the boy went, all smiles with his guns.

He left me till last. 'Did you draw this?' he said.

I said 'Yes'.

He then said: 'Here's a pencil and paper. Now draw me another one.'

I jumped off the stage and ran out crying all the way home. Not only did I not get my guns, but I also missed my films as well.

6   *Uplift with a Smile*

We may be sure that these Club members will soon be growing into fine little citizens; it will not be they who trouble the police or are run over by motor-cars, or go slouching through the world like ignorant good-for-nothings.

(*The Children's Newspaper*, April 1943)

There are some people who, despite having been devotedly regular in their attendance at a Saturday matinee, never found out the identity of The Rattler. There are others who still wonder to whose body The Clutching Hand was attached. People born early in September are still liable to remember with bitterness the birthday-present complimentary tickets which they should have received for the show of Saturday 9 September 1939 – but never did. Such were the effects of Chamberlain's declaration of war with Germany on 3 September.

Next day all cinemas were closed down because the government feared the possibility of hundreds of deaths being caused if a German bomb hit a crowded cinema. The ban lasted for only two weeks, so matinees could have reopened on 23 September, but in most cases they did not. In the cities, where the largest attendances were, thousands of Minnies and Mickeys and Granadiers and Minors and GB Juniors were on the move as part of the government's scheme of evacuating centres of dense population. The country was divided into areas judged to be 'safe' or 'unsafe', and even schools were initially not allowed to open if they were in an 'unsafe' area. In these circumstances, there were restrictions that children could fall foul of even at ordinary screenings. This memoir relates an incident that occurred in Wallasey, on the very first day of the cinemas' reopening:

Because of the local schools being still closed, it came as a great relief to us all when the cinemas were open again on that Monday two weeks after the outbreak of war. My mother was only too glad to give me the necessary money to join a couple of friends bound for our local Gaumont, where the film was *Trouble Brewing*, a U starring George Formby. At the cinema there was already a long queue waiting for the doors to open, and it wasn't till we got close to the entrance that we became aware of a large board announcing that: 'Due to the present emergency no children will be admitted unless accompanied by a parent or bonafide guardian'. Standing by the board was a smartly uniformed doorman obviously intent on preventing any youngster from asking an adult to 'Take me in, please'. So we had to return home, where my mother was dismayed to have me once again under her feet. At first she didn't believe me, but a phone call to the Gaumont manager confirmed what I had told her. He was acting under instructions from head office who feared that children would panic in the event of an air raid.

Another wartime hazard caused a problem in Leven, Fife, where children found themselves not properly equipped for seeing a Disney release:

In the early spring of 1942 *Dumbo* was shown at the Regent. It was more than a mile away, but my parents allowed my twin brother and me to set off on our own on a Saturday afternoon. It was an ordinary showing, with normal prices and plenty of adults around. Outside the Regent we found crowds of children and parents milling about, and wondered why they were all carrying small cardboard boxes. Being an unassertive pair it took us a very long time to get to the box office. There, standing by the ticket desk was a commissionaire dressed entirely in chocolate brown trimmed with gold braid. He grabbed hold of my brother and me. 'You two can't go in', he said, 'you're not carrying your gas-masks.' He just wouldn't let us through, and we traipsed back home in tears.

That same year two events occurred which were to shape the matinee situation for decades to come. First, J. Arthur Rank acquired control of Gaumont-British, the company which owned the 300 Gaumont cinemas (not all of them named Gaumont). By so doing he became president of all the clubs in which children sang 'We come along on Saturday morning . . . .' Second, Oscar Deutsch died. Deutsch had spent the thirties building up the Odeon chain, and realised the value of children's matinees as a way of raising the Odeon name in public perception. At the time of his death, the Odeon chain was roughly the same size as the Gaumont chain: about 230 cinemas actually called Odeons, with another sixty or so from recently acquired groups still using their old names. Once again it was Rank who stepped in, bringing the total of cinemas under his control to around 600. His nearest rival, the ABC chain, owned around 500. This emergence of Rank as film supremo was remarkable because he had been in the business for only nine years. A millionaire miller from Yorkshire, and a devout Methodist, his first contact with the cinema had come in 1933 when he gave financial aid to Methodist Sunday schools which wanted film projectors for use in religious instruction. From there Rank got involved in financing religious films, and then steadily advanced towards the heart of British film production, distribution and exhibition.

For a year he hardly noticed the clubs that he now controlled. More and more of these, in other chains and independents too, had started operating again after the Battle of Britain had significantly diminished Germany's power to conduct daylight bombing raids. There had also been a drift back to the towns of evacuees unable to adapt to life in the country. The cinematic menu provided for them was much the same as in the thirties, except that the news-reel was better enjoyed than before. One Odeon report states: 'At matinees there is a strong response to the newsreels when they are shown these days, and the Fascist leaders receive their fair share of boos, whilst the sight of even *one* Spitfire against the sky calls forth wild cheering.' In addition, the programme frequently included a short Ministry of Information 'filler'. These were films of information and persuasion designed to promote good wartime habits of thrift, hygiene and discretion (for example, *Salvage with a Smile*, *We've Got to Get Rid of the Rats*, *Careless Talk Costs Lives*). The inclusion of this type of item in children's shows was soon to lead to a significant extension of Gaumont-British Instructional's production.

But it was still westerns that held the predominant place in children's imag-inations. The way cowboy heroes behaved could sometimes inspire something close to idolatry. Such influence would on occasion be noticed even by teachers, hostile to the cinema as many of them still were:

When you were sitting downstairs in the cinema you would often get some missile from upstairs falling on your head, but it didn't seem to bother us because if Johnny Mack Brown was on the screen nothing else mattered. To see Johnny Mack Brown in a cowboy film was to me the be-all and end-all of everything. It was absolutely stupendous, and had such a big influence on me. We used to imitate him as we came out, hitting our backsides with our hands and pretending to ride horses as we galloped over bomb sites and derelict land. In our minds, we were in Arizona or somewhere like that. In the early forties they were god-like, these cowboy stars. One thing I noticed was that the singing cowboys, such as Gene Autry, always seemed to put their heads on one side when they sang. As a result, whenever I sang, I put my head on one side, and once got told off at school about it. The teacher asked me why I always did that when I sang. I didn't dare tell her that I was imitating Gene Autry singing something like *South of the Border*. She definitely would not have approved my choice of role model.

It was conduct of a rather more reprehensible kind that in early 1943 drew Rank's attention to the smallest corners of his £20,000,000 empire. In the middle of the Second World War, just as in the middle of the First, there was perceived to be a rise in anti-social behaviour among the young. The phrase 'juvenile delinquency' came into common use. This time, however, it was not particularly the cinema that was blamed. Rather, it was lack of adequate parental control, due to so many parents being engaged in war work. Schools likewise were judged to be overstretched and ineffective in instilling discipline. In this context Rank had the idea that cinema should do something more than simply escape blame. Instead of being content with the negative virtue of being 'not bad', it should aim to achieve positive good by making a contribution to character-building, by looking ahead to post-war peace. This could be done under the guise of entertainment. The aim was summed up by the four words which became the motto of the new Odeon National Cinema Club (ONCC) for Boys and Girls – 'Uplift with a Smile'.

The differences between the old and the new were more a matter of presentation than substance. The existing Odeon Mickey Mouse club network was used as a foundation, and on the screen there was little change, except that a Disney cartoon was no longer obligatory – since the name Mickey Mouse was not being used – and there was more stress on the instructional shorts. The only entirely new element on the screen was a still image. The ONCC believed that some simple messages could be got across most effectively by means of a coloured drawing and a memorable slogan or verse on a slide. 'It is rude and very silly/To push and shove, says Odeon Billy' was one. Another featured two cherubic children saying to the audience: 'We are going to Sunday School tomorrow. Are you?' (Rank himself was a Sunday School teacher, and regularly cycled three miles each way on Sundays for that purpose.) A more elaborate combination of rhyme, reason and reproof was this one:

> *Tommy Tinker is a sight*
> *Exactly like a trout.*
> *He never, never cleans his teeth*
> *And now they've all dropped out.*

It was in front of the screen, and in some cases outside the cinema completely, that the more significant changes were apparently introduced. For the ONCC, Saturday morning was no longer just a film show. What the children turned up for was a 'meeting', the implication being that watching films was

Under the spreading Chestnut Tree
Poor Mopey Mickey stands
They won't let him stroke the wee white lamb
'COS HE HASN'T WASHED HIS HANDS!

12. One of the admonitory slides in use within the ONCC *at the time of its launch in 1943*
(redrawn)

just one of various activities which occurred or were initiated then. Such activities would need a committee to arrange salvage collection, to organise visits to sick club members, to keep the other children in order, and to advise on choice of film. After seeing the instructional short, members were to be invited to write an essay on the topic it covered, the normal prize for winning being National Savings stamps. In fact, none of this, not even the use of the word 'meeting', was actually new; it had been the recommended standard practice in Odeon Mickey Mouse clubs before the war.

There was also a set of pledges which, printed on the black, red and green membership cards, certainly looked new. There were seven promises, broken down into three sentences. In essence, however, they were the old pre-war Mickey Mouse club creed, rejigged. The difference was the ritual by which they were promulgated: each week the cinema manager, known as the club chief, read them out, and then the refrain 'I promise' was required to be intoned by all present:

- ❏ I promise to tell the truth, to help others, and to obey my parents.
- ❏ I promise to be thoughtful to old folks, to be kind to animals, and always to play the game.
- ❏ I promise to try to make this great country of ours a better place to live in.

The only aspect of the ONCC that was totally new was the song. Gone was 'Every Saturday morning . . . .' Now, to a tune reminiscent of *Oh I do like to be beside the seaside*, the children twice each week were enjoined to 'Let it rip', and sang these words, aided by a bouncing ball on screen:

> *Is everybody happy? YES!*
> *Do we ever worry? NO!*
> *To the Odeon we have come*
> *Now we're all together*
> *We can have some fun, Oi!*
> *Do we ask for favours? NO!*
> *Do we help our neighbours? YES!*
> *We're a hundred thousand strong*
> *So how can we all be wrong?*
> *As members of the OCC we stress*
> *Is everybody happy? YES!*

This song seems to have been intended to be free of ideology, to evoke instead a kind of collective holiday-camp jollity. Though written and sung in the middle of the war, it contains no patriotic sentiments and little civic virtue. It was meant to be pure jam, concealing nothing. The pill was to be found elsewhere, in the promise. By all accounts this new song was sung lustily enough. One memoir says: 'I remember only two lines. "Is everybody happy? YES!", we would roar. "Do we ever worry? NO!", we would roar again. The rest of the words have vanished, but at the time we sang them as enthusiastically and proudly as *Rule Britannia* or *Land of Hope and Glory*.'

The date chosen for the launch of this new package was 17 April 1943. On that day, in 150 of the 170 cinemas where there had been matinees before the war, the Odeon Mickey Mouse club died, and the ONCC was born, to a mighty fanfare, the event being widely reported in both the local and national papers. Virtually all press comment was supportive of Rank's endeavour, and more than once, the ONCC was described as 'an indoor Boy Scouts' Association'. Rank himself spearheaded the publicity campaign. As national president of the new club, he went to the Odeon, Morden, to inaugurate that branch, with a key convert, Derek McCulloch ('Uncle Mac'), then head of BBC children's radio. The BBC's rule of impartiality would not have allowed McCulloch to plug the ONCC explicitly on air; but by thus associating himself publicly with the club he was sending his endorsement to the radio millions.

McCulloch represented established virtues – the uplift. However, the ONCC needed someone else as well, someone who symbolised fun. Filling this role at the Morden was Arthur Askey, a radio and film comedian who was then one of the biggest names in British light entertainment. His drawn likeness

The Gaumont British Junior Club's Song.

Words and Music by

GRIMSHAW & DOCHERTY.

('Big-Hearted Arthur') had featured in *Radio Fun* since its inception in 1938. One of his specialities was the singing of Silly Songs such as *The Worm*, *The Seagull* and *The Bee* ('Oh what a glorious thing to be, A healthy grown-up busy busy bee'). The final thing that made him right for the slot was that he had already, in various fillers, taken on the task of making hygiene enjoyable.

13. For the 1943 relaunch Con Docherty's song – with lines about 'good citizens' and 'champions of the free' added by Ernest Grimshaw – was copyrighted and officially adopted for all Gaumont British Junior clubs

Together, Rank, McCulloch and Askey must have been an impressive trio (though not in physical stature, since the top of Askey's head did not reach as high as Rank's shoulder). The 1,500-seater cinema was full to capacity, with another thousand or so, unable to get in, waiting around on the pavement to get a glimpse of the celebrities. A guard of honour, comprising the members of the Morden ONCC children's committee, greeted the guests. Inside, the audience, feeling privileged to have got in, joined in a boisterous bout of community singing, including patriotic songs as well as the new club anthem. In his capacity as president of the ONCC, Rank then swore in the manager as local club chief. Turning to the children, he told them what a grand experience it was to see and hear them singing, and to know that they were happy. He recited the club promise, and waited for their affirmative response. Next Uncle Mac welcomed the club to the family of organisations concerned with children's welfare, and introduced the first film of the morning – *The Nose Has It*. This was a six-minute Askey filler about the dangers of unrestricted sneezing.

Finally, to general enthusiasm, Askey appeared on stage in person and sang a silly song. Under the cloak of doing a comic turn, he stressed the lesson of the film, and the general importance of personal hygiene, perhaps making good use of one of his familiar catch-phrases – 'Oh, don't be filthy!' – and being careful not to use another – 'Doesn't it make you want to spit!' The climax of this on-stage presentation neatly epitomised the ONCC's attempt to harness the attraction of the cinema as a force for good. One lucky boy or girl in the audience, Askey told them, could soon be the proud owner of something which they had seen on the screen many times, worn by somebody whose little horse they had cheered till they themselves were a little hoarse. For the writer of the best essay on personal hygiene, the prize would be – Gene Autry's hat.

In the other 150 or so Odeons where the ONCC opened a branch that morning, the prizes may have been less prestigious, and the visitors less celebrated, but they all made an effort to signal to the children, and to the community, that something new and different had arrived. In Gillingham a long column of naval cadets, army cadets, Sea Scouts and Air Scouts, headed by the Chatham Division of the Seamen's Band, marched round the town to mark the club's inauguration. In Wales the members of the Colwyn Bay ONCC set up a Cot Fund, in the hope of soon collecting enough to pay for an Odeon Children's Cot at the West Denbighshire Hospital. In Dundee there were two branches of the ONCC, one functioning at the Odeon on Saturday mornings, and another at the Dundee Empire (also owned by Rank) in the afternoons. The largest branch of the new club was that formed in Luton, where over 2,000 children signed up. On the stage that morning was a vast uniformed array of members of the Women's Voluntary Service, the Air Training Corps, the St John's Ambulance Brigade, the Boys' Brigade, the Army Cadet Corps, the Girl Guides, the Boy Scouts, the Land Army, the Girls' Junior Training Corps, the Royal Air

Force, the Air Cadets, the Sea Cadets and the British Red Cross. In Bury, according to the *Bury Times*, the Director of Education there wished the ONCC every success, and told the members that he hoped they would enjoy 'good hearing, good listening, good filming and – most important of all – good thinking'. Such massive endorsement by establishment organisations and individuals was certainly something that the old Mickey Mouse Club had never achieved.

What the children made of this attempt at turning them into better young people is difficult to establish. The Bury report says that the children 'groaned when the cinema manager told them they must forget about their old favourite, Mickey Mouse, but soon brightened when they heard the new attractions in store for them – the competitions centred round the educational films, and the Children's Committee that would be appointed'. However, people who were members of the wartime ONCC remember nothing of this 'club' aspect, and certainly did not think of the Saturday mornings as 'meetings'. Rather, they were, as ever, film-shows and social occasions. *A Hendon Times* reporter who attended the ONCC opening day wrote: 'I watched the children enjoying themselves booing the villain and cheering the hero of the western serial.' A commissionaire, interviewed, said that there was an unfortunate aspect to having a large number of excited children together, 'in the fact that the wear and tear on seats and fittings is enormous'. One of his jobs was 'to go round and tighten up all the seats after the children had left'. It seems likely that it was the western serial, rather than the prospect of having a committee or writing an esay, that caused the seats to become loose.

The serial in question may well have been *Riders of Death Valley*, which enjoyed enormous popularity in the forties. Of the five Riders, two were Buck Jones and Dick Foran. Another who got star billing was Leo Carillo, as a Mexican comrade, Pancho, who speaks broken English. At least once in each of the fifteen episodes he says, 'Let's went'. More important than the dialogue, broken or whole, is the non-stop action centred on greedy conflict over possession of an Aztec gold mine which Mary Morgan has inherited from her murdered uncle. When the Riders take on the job of protecting her against the murderers, caves are dynamited, wild horses stampede and avalanches descend. Episodes end with Dick Foran staggering against a sandstorm and finally being overcome by it; with Mary falling from her horse into the path of fast-approaching wagons; with lightning striking a bridge just as Foran and Jones are galloping full tilt across it. And each one began with a song which preached the simple morality thought to be ample justification for inclusion of westerns in matinee programmes: 'Ride along, ride along, let us fight for law and order till the wrong is right . . . Fight for the right to ride along.'

Another serial, even newer, had just appeared when the ONCC opened. *Don Winslow of the Navy* gave matinee-goers, for the second time, a maritime hero to cheer for. This time the hero's rank was not specified, presumably so that he could get promoted without necessitating a title-change. Created for an American radio serial in 1937, he was transferred to film before the USA entered the war as a result of the Japanese bombing of Pearl Harbor in December 1941. On his cruiser in the Pacific Ocean, Winslow's skirmishes were against Scorpia, an enemy agent of unspecified origin. Even more than the *Riders of Death Valley*, Winslow had a philosophy which must have appealed to the ONCC controllers. In the radio serial, Winslow had invited listeners to join his Squadron of Peace, and subscribe to a creed quite close at certain points to the ONCC promise: 'Love your country, its flags and all the things for which it stands. Follow the advice of your parents and superiors and help someone every day.' Among the memoirs that describe *Don Winslow* as the favourite serial, this one sums up the mood:

> The biggest cheers of the morning were reserved for the final part of the programme – the serial. It invariably seemed to be *Don Winslow of the Navy*. Not the Royal Navy, of course. Nevertheless, Don Winslow was our hero. As soon as the theme music – *Anchors Aweigh* – filled the cinema, we knew that Don was back and the cheers rang out for the next fifteen minutes. Finally, it was all over, with Don facing certain death for the thirty-second time. We slowly emerged, blinking, into the Saturday sunlight. Since those days I've often wondered what happened to Don Winslow. I hope he made Admiral . . . .

Don Winslow and the westerns, plus the cartoons and fillers, must have taken up at least 95 per cent of Saturday matinee screen time; but here and there, from 1943 onwards, something different would occasionally be shown – a Russian fairy-tale. Early in the thirties, the USSR had believed it was necessary to produce films specially for children, and set up a Children's Film Studio in Moscow. Some of the Studio's pre-war realist dramas – such as *Lone White Sail*, about two boys who in the Russia of 1905 help an escaped Potemkin sailor in his armed fight against Tsarist authority – were available in the UK but were regarded as too propagandistic to be suitable for matinees. Now, in 1942–3, things were different. After two years of going it alone against Nazism, the Commonwealth countries had acquired a powerful new ally. Hitler launched an invasion of the USSR in June 1941, and for six months the Germans made significant gains till, in December, the Red Army finally engaged and repulsed them. A film record of this Soviet victory was shown in both the UK and the USA, where it won an Oscar. For the rest of the war Soviet films, many of them documentaries, were being released in the UK at the rate of more than one a month; and British films were in return making the trip to Moscow and beyond. One Edinburgh contributor to the researches for this book remembers both the Soviet films he saw in 1943 (not in children's matinees) and the practical action which such films helped to inspire:

> There was one film in which a Russian soldier fell tumbling down a vast shell crater, equipment falling from him. There were others of huge and ferocious tank battles, and of Nazi atrocities, such as children's dead bodies, with ropes around their necks, hanging from trees in Russian villages. I have vivid memories of later going knocking on doors in the tenements of Gorgie with my pals. Wearing crimson headbands, we asked people to put money for 'Comforts For the Red Army' into our collecting tins.

In this climate of mutual support and cultural exchange between London, Moscow and Washington, a distribution company named Anglo-American took the lead in finding Russian children's films that could swim in the stream of goodwill. As well as the films which the West was likely to find too didactic or too culturally specific, the Moscow Children's Film Studio had produced some virtually propaganda-free fairy-tale films espousing the values of the secular humanist tradition in Western thought. In the view of Mary Field (soon to become doyenne of the UK children's film movement): 'The Russian films deal with patience, hard work, collaboration, kindness and good temper.'

The first such film to be distributed in this country – one which Uncle Mac was associated with – was *The Magic Fish*, made in Moscow before the war. When Yemelya catches a talking pike it pleads to be put back in the water. Yemelya agrees, and the fish thanks him by promising to grant any wish. In a palace nearby lives a tsar whose beautiful but bad-tempered daughter refuses ever to smile. The tsar announces that he will marry her to the first man who makes her laugh. With the help of the magic fish, Yemelya succeeds; but the tsar then reneges. By now the princess loves Yemelya, so they run away together, the pursuers sent by the tsar being easily outwitted by Yemelya and the pike.

According to contemporary reviews, this satisfying fifty-minute tale is made all the more entertaining by the comic characterisation of the tsar and his courtiers, the clever trick photography which creates magical transformations, and the introduction of three pantomime-style bears. It was released in the UK just before Christmas 1942, targeted initially to be available as the second feature in festive family double bills, but expected soon to find a more lasting home in matinees. Accordingly, the method of adaptation of this film for UK audiences was simple, inexpensive and, apparently, effective. There was no subtitling or dubbing. Instead a newly overlaid soundtrack provided a commentary, spoken by the voice of Children's Hour, which explained the gist of the dialogue while it was going on.

Two more fairy tales from Moscow soon followed, coming into distribution around the time of the ONCC launch. The shorter one, *The Land of Toys*, concerns two children who are very careless and destructive with their playthings, until one night they both dream that they themselves are turned into toys and taken to Toyland. There they learn to see the error of their ways, and are made to atone for their misdeeds. The last and longest of this trio of films was one of the first colour features ever shown at a children's matinee. *The Little Humpback Horse* belongs to Ivan, a shepherd, who becomes chief groom to the tsar. When the tsar hears of the existence of a beautiful princess called Silver Morning, Ivan is ordered, on pain of death, to find the princess and bring her back for the tsar to marry. Ivan and his talking horse have many adventures on their quest: they meet bandits and wolves, they go up to the moon, they go down to the bottom of the sea. When they finally return with Silver Morning, the tsar throws Ivan into jail and turns his attention to the princess, but she rejects him and rescues Ivan with the help of the humpback horse and a magic flower. Again, there is reportedly a deal of skilful camerawork and some pictorially excellent landscapes, which produce the flying horse, the land of giants, a whale big enough to swallow a fleet of ships, the Kingdom of the Moon, and King Neptune's domain. Reviewers found the film charming, colourful, attractive and entertaining. Like the others, it has an English narrative added.

I have not been able to view any of these films, nor does any contributor remember them. For children in wartime and post-war Saturday matinees they must have taken some getting used to, so different were they from anything that had been shown before. They were perhaps preceded in some places by Don Duck, and followed by Don Winslow. Expecting to whoop and whistle, the children may have taken some time to accept that the humpback horse was not going to be ridden by Gene Autry. In the smaller cinemas they may have gradually settled down, soothed by the voice of Uncle Mac, and relaxed into enjoyment, but in larger audiences, despite the novelty of the colour in *The Little Humpback Horse*, Russian films may well have been unable to overcome the exhibition context and gain the sustained attention that they needed. In matinees, all through the decades, particularly when a film was different from what had become the established norm, much depended on the manager's rapport with the children.

It was managers who initiated the train of events that led to the next major development. Within the Odeon circuit, there were committees representing the cinemas within each particular region. From one such committee, in the summer of 1943, came the idea that, in order to combat the petty stealing that was believed to be rife among children at that time, the clubs should show a special film designed to get across the simple idea that thieving was always wrong. The managers' request was very modest: all they were asking for was a shorter-than-usual filler. Something like the MoI one-minute 'food flashes', all exhortation and no dramatisation, was what they envisaged. It might have been thought initially that such a simple message could be conveyed by the still slide images that the ONCC was using; but the managers knew that that method had severe limitations. (The slide asking the audience whether they were going to Sunday School next day invariably received the gleefully shouted reply: 'NO!!!') At the same time, Rank himself was thinking about whether the ONCC was doing all it could to help make children better citizens. He may have been aware that the Edinburgh report ten years earlier had pointed to special production of films for children as the logical way to go. He called in the controller of the ONCC and asked him whether the films shown at the clubs were such as would 'do the children good'. According to one account (Wood, 1952), he received the guarded reply:

'Well, they don't do the children any harm'.
'H'mm,' said Rank, 'why not show them films that would do them good?'
'Because there aren't any.'
'Very well, then,' said Rank, 'we must make some.'

7   *Parables in Pictures*

The financial aspect means that there is very little likelihood for many years to come (if ever) of films being produced specially for exhibition at children's matinees. Such a policy is only capable of realisation if the children's matinees were subsidised by the state, by the voluntary social organisations interested in children's welfare, or by princely donations from multi-millionaire philanthropists, none of which seem likely to happen.

(Oliver Bell, 1938)

The combination of war, money and Methodism had finally cut the knot. A multi-millionaire philanthropist had turned up to subsidise special production of films for children within little more than five years of Bell's assessment that it was unlikely ever to happen. It was as if a magic fish had granted someone's wish.

Fairy-tales, however, were not what Rank had in mind. He wanted something more explicit, more didactic, more rooted in the here and now. He announced that his plan was to produce one ten-minute film, containing a direct moral, each week, to be shown in all Rank clubs. In the middle of the war there were problems standing in the way of putting flesh on the bones of this plan. All Rank studios were committed to making films directly connected to the requirements of wartime; there was a shortage of film stock and petrol, priority for the use of what there was being given to projects that aided the war effort; furthermore, none of Rank's staff claimed to have any idea of what such a film might look like. Most importantly, there was a limitation imposed by the Children and Young Persons Act of 1933 which made it illegal to employ children of school age in film-making, except under such restrictions as made it impracticable. 'School age' at that time meant under fourteen, but the Education Act of 1944 envisaged it as being raised to fifteen, and eventually sixteen. It was to be many years before that clause was repealed.

These factors and others meant that there was never any real chance of Rank's one-a-week rate of production being achieved in 1943; but they did not prevent a start being made. One of the units that Rank now owned was Gaumont-British Instructional, and it was to GBI that Rank gave the task of making his series of films that would 'do the children good'. A staff script-writer named Mary Cathcart Borer picked up the controllers' request for a film with an anti-stealing moral, and developed round it a ten-minute scenario called *The Bicycle*. At the controllers' insistence, it initially contained a maximum of moral exhortation, and a minimum of dramatic action. When an experienced GBI director, Darrell Catling, was given *The Bicycle* to turn into a film, he must have been widely regarded by his colleagues as having drawn the short straw. Perhaps he was the only GBI director who had children of his own. An able writer himself, he was dismayed by the lack of dramatisation in the approved script, and asked the controllers to consent to its being amended so as to include a chase. Negotiations followed; agreement was finally reached. The title was changed to *Tom's Ride*, both because it had more implied action in it than the static *The Bicycle*, and because it allowed for the possibility of a sequel called *Tom Rides Again*.

During the foggy days of September and October 1943, in various locations near North London, and one-and-a-half days in a studio, the first version of *Tom's Ride* was filmed. Finding a brand-new bicycle for Tom to yearn for was a typical wartime problem that had to be solved. The two principal child actors in it, playing Tom and his sister, were of necessity fourteen or more, but they were chosen for being smallish and looking younger than they were. Clothes helped too: Tom is shown as wearing short trousers, which signified him as being eleven or twelve. Another factor which places him for the matinee audience is that he is seen going to an ONCC show – actually at the Southgate Odeon, but not named in the film – just like the one in which they are looking at him on the screen.

A more detailed account of *Tom's Ride* will illuminate the trail that it blazed, the problems inherent in the idea of a children's film, and what Saturday matinees were like in 1943. It opens with jolly music, evocative of Laurel and Hardy. In the first shot, two children, a boy and his sister, who seems younger, are seen walking along together. The girl has a bicycle but is pushing it so that she can stay with her brother, Tom. Two other children on a bike, one of them sitting astride the carrier, whizz past. The sister comments that they'll have an accident, riding two on a bike like that, to which Tom replies: 'Why can't I have a bike?' His sister explains that, as he well knows, 'Daddy can't afford it'. At that moment they pass a shop displaying on its forecourt a new boy's bike, priced £5. Tom looks at it covetously, and passes on. Soon they arrive at their local Odeon and join the long, lively ONCC queue. A poster outside advertises the feature film as being *The Rangers Ride at Dawn*, starring

Allan Lane and Blackjack. Once inside, they all, except Tom, happily sing the new ONCC song. Tom broods about the bike that he has not got. On the screen appears a slide showing a boy riding a bike with a girl on the back carrier. The accompanying caption is: 'The most dangerous thing a cyclist can do!' Tom barely notices this. All through the western too he sits miserable and unmoved. The others are yelling encouragement at the hero on the screen, but all Tom can see is the bike in the shop. Next comes a newsreel showing wounded soldiers arriving back in Britain. At this, Tom starts to take an interest, and hears the commentator say: 'These men are only here because they are no longer able to fight in the war; and that means they won't be able to fight in the peace either.'

14. Production still taken in the studio, on the set of Tom's Ride. *The incident depicted does not actually occur in the version that was finally released. Tom is played by Colin Simpson; his sister by Angela Glynne*

Outside once more, Tom and his sister are on their way home when he spots a notecase on the ground. Inside is a £5 note. Immediately he thinks of the bike he could buy with that money, but the sight of a policeman makes him hesitate, and his sister tells him that to use it would be stealing.

TOM: Is it really stealing if you find something?
SISTER: Of course it is - and you don't want to be a thief, do you?
TOM: Of course not.
SISTER: Then you must take it to the police station.
TOM (*still hesitating*): It takes too long to save up. I want to use *this* money.
TOM: They won't want you in the Club, you know, if you do that.
TOM (*finally convinced*): OK.

At the police station a policeman looks inside it, finds that it belongs to Mrs Britain, and gives it to Tom to take back to her. However, she has just left on a bus for the railway station, on her way to London to see her son – recently repatriated because of his injuries – receive a military decoration at Buckingham Palace. But without the money in her note case, how will she be able to buy her train ticket? And if she misses that train, she'll be too late. That's when Tom's ride begins. He borrows his sister's bike and pedals off to get to the station in time to return the notecase to Mrs Britain. On a lonely road, two bigger boys jeer at him because the bike he's riding has no crossbar – 'What's the rush, cissy?' They get in his way, and pull him off. A rough-and-tumble fight ensues, in which Tom stands up to them, and finally escapes, only to encounter another obstacle – the level-crossing gates near the station. He has to dismount and push the bike through the pedestrian gateway. Despite these hindrances he arrives at the station booking office just in time. Mrs Britain, trying to buy a ticket to Kings Cross, with a queue muttering impatiently behind her, has found that she has lost her notecase. Tom returns it to her. In gratitude, she offers him a coin, saying: 'Take this and get yourself something.'

The direction of the narrative up to this point seems to have been more or less agreed by everyone before shooting began. The ending, however, proved problematical. The first version, in which Tom accepted the money from Mrs Britain, was ready by the end of November, and soon previewed by Rank. Probably Borer and Catling were there as well. It provoked a long discussion on whether the morality of that ending was the type that the ONCC wished to promote. Should the club members be taught to expect an immediate and tangible return for being honest? Or should virtue be its own reward? There must have been ready agreement that Tom should not be rewarded simply for not stealing. By that logic, most children would receive several rewards every day.

But Tom had done rather more than just overcome the temptation to steal – he had suffered the indignity of being seen riding a girl's bike, fought with bullies and got to the station in time despite the level-crossing gates. After an hour's discussion the final ruling, which obviously had Rank's approval, was that Tom should not profit materially from his action in handing in the notecase. His efforts to get it back to Mrs Britain might be seen as a sort of atonement for letting himself be tempted in the first place.

In the version that was finally accepted, and shown in all the Odeon and Gaumont clubs in the summer of 1944, Tom says to Mrs Britain, in response to her offer of money: 'No thanks, I couldn't do that. It was nothing, honestly.' Tom then helps her to get safely on to the train to Kings Cross, his face displaying a mixture of emotions as he does so. A final sequence drives home the point in the way that the controllers originally wanted. Tom's sister tells their father what has happened. The father asks Tom what he is looking so glum about, and says that he ought to be very pleased with himself, after doing a good job like that. After hearing the full story, he then delivers a moralising conclusion for Tom and the audience:

> If you'd kept that money in the notecase, it would have been a very mean action. And even if you'd bought the bike, do you think you would have got any pleasure out of it? Of course you wouldn't! You would always have been thinking, 'This isn't my bike'. And even though the bike wore out and disappeared, the memory of that mean action would have been with you always.

The sight and sound of the father speaking these words was probably thought by some to be the right place to end the film, but Catling managed to bring the focus back to Tom as he remembers and tells his father and sister about the fun of the race to the railway station and the bullies that he overcame. In the final scene of the film he grabs a chair, turns it round the wrong way and sits astride it, pedalling and punching furiously to illustrate his words.

Again, none of the contributors to my research remembers seeing *Tom's Ride* during the war, but contemporary accounts suggest that it made a great impact on children, and one can easily imagine why. It offered something that no film had ever offered them before – child characters with whom they could identify in a social and urban context that was indisputably contemporary England. Children had long been known to respond well to seeing other children on the screen but the background had virtually always been American or historical, and the child-stars glamorous and multi-talented. Tom and his sister were unmistakably ordinary and of the here and now. The stage-school quality of their diction might have been expected to alienate working-class English children (the bulk of the matinee audience); and their Englishness must have put them at one remove from children in Scotland and Wales. But in 1944 those aspects were unimportant compared with the familiarity of the clothes, buses, trains, streets, bikes, bullies, level-crossing gates, policemen – and, above all, the Saturday matinee to which Tom and his sister went. In Southgate, the children quite literally saw themselves up there on the screen; and in other places, the effect cannot have been much less dramatic. Mary Field saw *Tom's Ride* with a wartime matinee audience and noted an incident which dramatised for her the necessity of having children in children's films (Field, 1952):

> I remember, at Birkenhead, a little boy of about seven dashing for the gentleman's lavatory when the opening titles of *Tom's Ride* appeared on the screen. He was half way through the door when he saw Tom. There he stood, like a statue, all through the ten minutes of the story, even to the end of the concluding moral speech. Then, to my great relief, he disappeared through the door. What a tribute to the compelling interest of one child in another child!

This is not to say that all children accepted the film wholeheartedly, totally without criticism. The converse of their responding to the fact that it presented a recognisable world was that they picked holes in it where it got details wrong. Field quotes one boy as saying to her, authoritatively: 'Police stations are not like that.' In Leeds it was found unconvincing that Tom's sister should have a bike while Tom did not. 'The house seemed very posh to say they hadn't much money', was one reservation. Again: 'If his parents could not afford a new bike for Tom, they could have got him one on the instalment plan.'

But the main problem that children had with *Tom's Ride* was nothing to do with verisimilitude. It was to do with natural justice. Many cinema managers reported that children had complained that the ending simply was not fair. Their attitude was summed up as: 'How mean not to give Tom anything!' Tom's actions should have earned him a bicycle, believed some, perhaps influenced by the ethos of *The Magic Fish* and *The Little Humpback Horse*.

Rank himself was satisfied with *Tom's Ride* as a start, but only as a start. His goal of one such film per week may have been shown to be impracticable, but he still wanted to move in that direction. Specialisation was obviously needed, so he called in Field (who had no children of her own, and had virtually nothing to do with the making of *Tom's Ride*) and asked her to take on the job of heading a Children's Film Department (CFD) within GBI. In her perception, he was 'influenced no doubt by the popular fallacy that women understand children better than men do'. She was not keen to take it on, but could not find a satisfactory way out, so for six years, from the spring of 1944 to the spring of 1950, she wrestled with the problem of how to edify without alienating.

One of the things learned from *Tom's Ride* was that it is impossible for characters to have any depth if they are on the screen for only ten minutes. That may not matter if you only want to preach; but if you want drama as well, it does. There was also a fresh dawning of the realisation that ten minutes of 'doing them good' was apt to get dwarfed when located within a two-hour programme of the standard matinee fare. The CFD needed therefore to aim to supply cartoons and serials, and ultimately features, if it was to make a real difference to Saturday mornings. In this developing situation, *Tom's Ride* turned out to be not just the first, but also the only, ten-minute live-action drama made according to Rank's prescription. There were cartoons and nature films and documentaries lasting for only one reel, but drama could not be thus strait-jacketed.

One of the documentaries was a series called *Our Club Magazine* (OCM). Made fairly quickly and cheaply once a month for over six years by a non-Rank company, (Wallace Productions), for CFD, this was intended to give the clubs a sense of identity and of participation in a wider fellowship. Each edition contained five or six two-minute items, one of them usually being about the non-cinema activities of ONCC or Gaumont club members. The intention was that they should enjoy feeling that this magazine had been made especially for them; that they were not simply being allowed to listen in on something that was really meant for their parents. There is very little on-the-spot sound in any of the items – it's almost entirely chirpy music and exhortatory commentary. A typical wartime edition of OCM starts with an item called *On the River*. The commentary explains: 'We're going on the river to Henley – not for the races, but to see a little sporting rivalry between the Henley and Slough clubs.' Two teams of girls engage in a skipping contest, in pairs. The girl who does more skips in one minute is the winner of her pair. 'It was good happy fun for spectators as well as skippers.' Shot of some children up a tree. 'Those in the tree-grandstand could see another contest as well – a tug-of-war between some very young club members.' The tuggers are all boys. 'In a tug-of-war, it can truly be said that the best team wins – the team that pulls together. Why don't you try to arrange some sort of contest in your town? It's grand fun.' The next item, *Monarchs of the Air*, is about eagles. Close-up of an eagle in the zoo. 'These talons, as you can see, are very big and powerful . . . .' Then, to meet The Spotters, the magazine goes to London's Waterloo Station, where a gang of children armed with notebooks and pencils is found. 'The engine-drivers are always helpful, and how the spotters envy them, for being in charge of their powerful giants, that can be whisked along at such high speeds . . . It's an interesting hobby for those who live near a mainline station, so now, boys and girls, who wants to be a spotter?'

The fourth item, *Say it with Strings*, features child violinists at the Children's Art School in Moscow. 'As you can see, these boys and girls are about the same age as you club members. And, as you can hear, they play wonderfully well. By the way, in another number of *Our Club Magazine* we're going to film a club orchestra.' Another bought-in item, entitled *Picking a Lock*, is not about felonious entry. Instead, it's about boys offering their services to water-craft. 'Now we're slipping over to Canada to meet a group of boys who have appointed themselves lock-keepers. Why? To turn an honest penny. Then, at the end of the day, it's all shared out fairly between everybody. You know the system – one for you, one for me . . . .' Finally, the magazine comes back home for *Happy Days*, an item about Belgian children, exiled because of the war, going to a special school in Kingston upon Thames. 'Here they receive the same education as they would have got in Belgium, but they learn English as well.' Shot of Belgian children playing games in the playground. 'School is quite a serious matter, as you club members know, but when it's over, they know how to enjoy themselves. Well, members, on this jolly note, we'll close this number of your magazine. So long!'

The next CFD story-film set out, like its forerunner, with a specific moral lesson to teach – in this case that cruelty to animals is wrong. This may have been inspired by the second part of the third of the ONCC promises, rather than by a sudden rash of animal maltreatment. The script – a school story – was again by Borer, and again there was a boy called Tom, with a sister, at the centre of it. This time the sister has a name – Peggy – and is played by Jean Simmons, in an early screen appearance. *Sports Day*, as this second short film was called, was shot in the autumn of 1944, one year after *Tom's Ride*. Like its forerunner, it was to incur initial rejection, but this time not from Rank himself. It begins with a scene at a swimming pool to which Tom and Peggy have gone together. Tom is in training, hoping to do well at the forthcoming school sports day. Peggy gets pushed off the side into the water as a group of boys goes past her. Was it an accident, or malice? Tom takes Peggy's side, and a skirmish breaks out between him and two or three boys, which results in Tom being punched and ending up in the pool. Next day, as Tom goes to school, he finds a dog with a tin can tied to its tail. In the distance he sees the culprits running off, and recognises them as the boys he fought with at the pool the day before. Untying the tin can, Tom is spotted by a passing adult who jumps to the conclusion that Tom is the perpetrator of the mischief. The adult comes to the school, reports the incident, and identifies Tom as the culprit. Tom protests his innocence, but is not believed. He could exculpate himself by naming the real offenders, but refuses to do so. That would be 'sneaking'. Peggy tells other children that, in any case, he has 'thrashed the culprit already'. Tom's punishment is detention during Sports Day, which will mean not being able to take part in the swimming. Despite this bitter blow, Tom refuses to tell what he knows. Sports Day starts, the contest being between the 'Blacks' and the 'Whites'. It looks as if Tom's team will have to do without him, when Peggy goes to see the headmaster. She loyally insists that Tom is innocent, and gives some clues as to the identity of the real culprit. The Head tells her: 'Tom's a very lucky boy to have a sister like you', then confronts the real offender and gets a confession out of him. 'We were only playing with the dog', is the excuse offered. The Head will have none of it. 'You ought to be ashamed of yourself. See me after prayers tomorrow!' Released from detention, Tom is just in time to win the swimming competition for his team. In a speech to the whole school, the Head singles out Tom for special mention, and hands out not only the trophies but also the moral lesson: 'Tom has done a great deal more than win a cup. He has set an excellent example to all of us.'

The problem with this film is that it's actually not at all clear what the 'excellent example' is that Tom has set. The dilemma over 'to sneak or not to sneak' has rather taken over from the cruelty-to-animals theme which was the film's starting point. The writer and director seem to have become more interested in that question, because it is less clear cut, than in whether or not one should be kind to animals. The moral message as delivered by the Head comes across as being about the rightness of not sneaking, which is certainly not what the film set out to promote. This confusion over the film's purpose is also a result of the trouble it ran into with the BBFC. As originally shot, the film had shown in some detail the incident of the 'silly bullies' (as Tom calls them) catching the dog and tying the tin can to its tail. Cruelty to animals has, however, not been allowed to be shown on British screens since the formation of the BBFC. An animal must never be made to suffer just to suit the purposes of a screen fiction. In this case, the cruelty incurred the extra objection of being easy to copy. As a result, the BBFC refused to pass the film in that version. It was not just a question of refusing to give it a 'U' certificate. They would not give it a certificate of any kind unless cuts were made. Thus an incident that was supposed to be central and essential was practically deleted.

For the Odeon and Gaumont audiences, the film had a recognisable milieu in its favour (like *Tom's Ride*) – a British state school. For that reason alone, it must have given a lot of pleasure to matinee audiences. Further, Tom and Peggy are both spirited characters, with Peggy having a more positive part to play than the other Tom's sister had had. On that level, it was thrilling and enjoyable. Over and above that, though, Jean Simmons and Peter Jeffrey (playing Tom) are quite obviously too old for their roles, and both have plummy middle-class accents. This last factor must have been in the minds of girls who (as reported by Field) complained that Peggy was a 'show-off'. But the more serious criticisms – serious because they touched on mistakes that the film-makers knew they could and should have avoided – related to what was presented as happening in the swimming pool. First, in a real pool there would have been attendants present, and they would have intervened to stop the pushing and fighting of the first scene. Secondly, a serious inaccuracy that must have been noticed by many children was pointed out by a boy who wrote: 'This is a silly film. The schoolmaster said the race would be three lengths of the baths, but they finished up the end they started.'

The final notable aspect of *Sports Day* is that within it there is no reference whatsoever to the war. Made at a time when the Allies were beginning to feel victory within their grasp, and in the same year as the Education Act, it is, by implication, looking forward to post-war reconstruction. The same was true of the film's makers. Even before *Sports Day* had got very far in its tour of the Saturday morning circuit, Field was protesting about one of its limiting factors – the law that kept children of school age off the screen – and thinking of ways of getting round it. In interviews given in 1945 and 1946 she said:

> I am often asked why British films do not show happy home life. We can show British children family life abroad, but we are not allowed to show children abroad family life in Britain. It is not legal to employ any child under fourteen in a British film studio. Educationalists have asked us to film certain classics which would make excellent pictures. But if we attempt to make films about children in this country the youngest has to be fourteen in order to be old enough to be filmed. That makes the eldest child, say, eighteen. To show 'children' of eighteen playing in a childish way would be ridiculous. We are missing a lot in prestige that we could build up. We are therefore making plans to produce in Europe as soon as we can. France, Sweden, Czechoslovakia, Poland and Russia are all possibilities. Films with children in can be produced in the USA and Canada, with careful safeguards. There's also South Africa, and Australia, where I am hoping to do a serial. Some of the films that we are planning to make abroad we would certainly make in this country – if we could.

Equally bullish at this time was her boss. He regarded the ONCC as a success, and was already planning to develop it after the war. He was full of optimism as to what Field and the CFD might be expected to accomplish within five years. What few criticisms of his monopolistic position had been voiced, he regarded as misguided. In an interview for an American film trade magazine he exuded righteous confidence:

> Our great experiment is passing through the inevitable perod of trial by error. Child welfare authorities, students of juvenile delinquency, leaders of diverse religious denominations, have been kind enough to express their approval of our endeavours . . . . My team of chosen producers sets out to make little pictures which will entertain the youngsters and at the same time – without the children realising it – implant some seed of decent citizenship in their fertile minds. The aim is to make parables

in pictures. We have so far succeeded that I propose now to make full-length feature films for children. Within five years we plan to have produced enough features and shorts to fill the Saturday morning screens for two hours every week . . . I have heard it said that grave danger exists in the work I am trying to do with the highest motives. It has been said that I may, in the execution of my plans, affect the whole range of thought of the nation's young people. I appreciate fully the sincerity of those fears. I maintain, nevertheless, that what I am striving to achieve is the improvement of a child's outlook on life during its most receptive period, without relation to any particular political or religious creed. Our one concern is to assist them to grow into better men or women.

Not all of these ambitions were to be realised. The commercial and political realities of the post-war period – the coming down of the Iron Curtain, the sterling exchange rate, the American film industry's resistance to the idea that children's films are different from family films, the government's over-full legislative programme – got in the way. The rate of production that Rank envisaged was so unrealistic that even thirty-five years later it had still not been achieved.

But 1945 was a year for dreaming. While the war was still being fought, and in its immediate aftermath, few adult voices were raised against the clubs or the films shown in them. They were a contribution to the war effort, and they were costing the tax-payer nothing. Whether or not they were not doing the good which they aspired to, they certainly seemed to be doing no harm. Even where they were not positively welcomed, they were at least uncritically accepted.

This was soon to change. Though he did not know it, Rank was nurturing a viper in his bosom. In his magnanimous way, he had allowed an eminent academic Marxist sociologist, J. P. Mayer, to visit Odeon and Gaumont clubs freely as part of his research for a book on the role of film in British life. Between August 1944 and June 1945 Mayer and two research assistants spent around twenty Saturday mornings sitting with the children in ONCC and Gaumont clubs in three of the Home Counties and in the West Country. Mayer's findings, when published in preliminary form in January 1946, re-ignited public and parliamentary concern over the 'poison' that pictures could inject into children's minds.

8 *Poisoning their Daydreams*

I resent the cinema being made a whipping-boy for children who are badly behaved. There was the 'penny dreadful' when I was young. Sanctimonious people then wanted those stories banned. At another time it was considered a fearful thing if people went to a theatre. I do not want to attack the Christian Church but at one time it was suggested that any child who went to see one of Shakespeare's plays was taking a ticket for a warmer place.

(Earl Winterton, MP for Horsham, House of Commons, November 1946)

When Rank launched the ONCC in 1943, his target was one million children. By the end of the decade, across England, Scotland and Wales, that target had been achieved – but not by Rank's Odeons and Gaumonts alone. In fact, their 400 clubs accounted for only about three-tenths of the million. The ABC chain revived their Minors, and opened up branches with blitzes of local publicity from October 1945, reaching by 1950 a total weekly attendance, in their 175 matinees, of around 150,000. Another 50,000 attended cinemas belonging to the smaller, regional circuits – Granada (London area), Shipman and King (South of England), Southan and Morris (North of England), Caledonian Association (Scotland), Clifton (Midlands). The other half million were associated either with the multitude of even smaller regional circuits; or, in greater numbers (approaching 300,000), with the 700 independent exhibitors whose cinemas tended to be smaller than the circuits', and who frequently carried on the thirties' tradition of using the afternoon screening for children, rather than incur the extra cost of opening in the morning.

In these years the number of children in Britain between the ages of five and fifteen was reckoned to be just over seven million. However, that did not mean that only one-seventh of the child population was attending a Saturday show, because it was essentially the seven-to ten-year-olds who went. In some places, under-sevens were discouraged from attending; and increasingly, as the decade progressed, children gave up going to matinees when they transferred from a junior to a secondary school. Therefore the proportion going at any one time, out of those who were of an age to consider it as a possibility, was around one-third.

It was against the background of this rapid expansion of the matinee habit that the establishment knives came out again in 1946, when *The Times* published a condensed version of the chapter about cinema clubs from Mayer's forthcoming book, in the guise of an article from 'a special correspondent'. In it he suggested that his twenty visits to matinees had given him enough evidence to draw conclusions for the whole nation, since the clubs were under central control. At the same time he pointed out that local controllers – that is, managers – were not all alike. Some he had found satisfactory in their rapport with children, while 'others prefer to be orderly and extinguish any child-like atmosphere in the proceedings'.

Turning his attention to the screen, he disparaged the 'crude' coloured slides bearing such admonitions as 'It pays if you say thank you and please' and 'Odeon Billy wishes you not to push when you are waiting in a queue'. Four lines of the ONCC 'hymn' were then misquoted: 'To the Odeon we have come/To have our fun . . . /We are thousands strong/So we can't be wrong.' The rest of it, said Mayer, was 'in similar vein'. In parenthesis he added that the Gaumont clubs had no song, not having discovered that they had been singing 'We come along . . .' since the thirties. The club promise was to Meyer 'obtrusive moralizing'.

Then he commented on the films: 'First, an animal cartoon picture, usually not a genuine Walt Disney product, but one of those plagiarisms which copy Disney's technique but lack his taste.' As to the features: 'Occasionally good films like *My Friend Flicka* are shown, but it appears that westerns or comic pictures of ten or fifteen years ago are usually considered appropriate for children.' Finally, he condemned the suspense-mechanism of the third item:

> Last comes the serial story of American origin, such as *Don Winslow of the Navy*. These films seem to have no coherent plot. A considerable amount of shooting goes on, with nerve-wracking persecutions of the bad men who have kidnapped the beautiful innocent blonde secretary. To the children the serials are the high spot of the programme, but their psychological effects are deplored by psychological experts. As the writer sees it, the children are left at a high pitch of expectation for next week's show, with their day-dreams poisoned and their play influenced by an utterly artificial unreality.

The main general point developed by the article is a charge that the British film industry did not recognise the existence of child psychologists who, if asked, could give so much guidance both in running cinema clubs for children and in making films for them. Mayer believed that the age of the enthusiastic showman had gone and the age of the expert had arrived. Education authorities should employ only properly qualified people to supervise matinees. The BBFC should apply child psychology in their awarding of U certificates. Only the best producers and directors should be allowed to make children's films, 'as is the practice in, notably, Russia, from which there is much to be learnt'. The need and urge for entertainment could and must go together with education. Given good film material, available in sufficient quantities, and intelligent and responsible managements, the clubs could eventually become a valuable auxiliary instrument in education.

Mayer also had more pragmatic objections. He reported conversations with club controllers, in which one admitted that he did not have time to view every film before sending it round the circuit, and the other agreed that there was not a sufficient supply of suitable films. As to the specially-made CFD films which were intended to remedy this deficiency, Mayer was dismissive: 'The new films so far produced are unsatisfactory and insignificant.' His conclusion was: 'Many local managers would, I believe, share in the request for a speedy and far-reaching reform of the present state of affairs.'

Much of this was not new. Anyone who remembered 1917, or the early thirties, would have heard it before. But the war had obliterated many memories; those that survived were regarded as irrelevant to the new mood of social reconstruction that had created a landslide victory for the Labour Party in the general election of 1945. Moreover, the emphasis on the club aspects and the production of special films were indeed new. Mayer's implication that the words of the ONCC song proclaimed that numerical might is necessarily right was bound, in a country that had just spent six years fighting totalitarian Nazism, to touch a raw nerve. The simple fact was that, until now, very few adults outside the relevant cinema organisations had had any idea of what went on at matinees. Adults were not barred from Odeon and Gaumont club meetings, but very few went, and those that did were either satisfied or not in a position to get their thoughts published in *The Times*. What Mayer's article did was to put the 'problem' of Saturday matinees on the national agenda for the rest of the year and beyond.

The argument rumbled on way above the heads of the children concerned, who carried on riding through Death Valley and cheering Don Winslow. The J. Arthur Rank Organisation (JARO) on the other hand was understandably put out by Mayer's strictures, especially as they appeared in such a prestigious forum as *The Times*. Five days later the paper printed the first of several letters which Mayer's comments provoked. In it John Davis, the second most powerful man after Rank himself within JARO, tackled some of Mayer's criticisms and ignored others. He began with the most sensitive point, declaring: 'This is no attempt at mass education in the Nazi manner, but simply a plan to provide healthy cinema entertainment for the young and at the same time to inculcate a spirit of good citizenship and help build character.' If the correspondent objected to the club promise, then surely he must also object to the Boy Scouts' law. Davis rejected Mayer's call for only the best directors and producers to be invited to work on films for children, on the ground that the screenplay, rather than its direction, was the all-important factor in determining the quality of a film for children, and that the screenplays were already being overseen by just such experts as Mayer was calling for. Davis was referring to the independent Advisory Council for children's films which CFD had set up in 1944; it consisted of representatives from the Ministry of Education, the Home Office, the Scottish Office, the BBC, the National Union of Teachers, the National Associations of Girls' Clubs and Boys' Clubs, the Christian Cinema Council, the Library Association, the National Union of Townswomen's Guilds, the National Federation of Women's Institutes, the Association of Education Committees and the British Film Institute. Davis finished by listing some of the activities, designed to teach elementary standards of behaviour, which went on in clubs, and which these experts found acceptable: 'talks on road safety, book collection schemes, savings groups, first-aid groups, salvage campaigns, orchestras, dramatic societies, art and handicraft exhibitions, sports sections, service as traffic stewards, and visiting sick members'.

Mayer was supported by a documentary film producer, Ralph Bond, who said that he too had attended a number of matinee performances. He thought that Mayer perhaps exaggerated the harmful effects of westerns: 'It is perhaps a tribute to the healthy good sense and vigour of the children that they cheer lustily when their favourite cowboy or serial star appears, and boo the coloured slide asking them if they intend going to Sunday school the next day.' What concerned him was not this aspect, but 'the sanctimonious halo of "goodness" over what is largely a straightforward commercial proposition'. Further, he objected to the 'facade of democracy' embodied in the claim that each club had an elected children's committee to work with the manager. 'In some cinemas, at least, these committees are appointed and not elected, and at one performance I attended the appearance of the committee on the stage was the signal for catcalls and boos.'

The chairman of the Advisory Council that Davis had referred to, Lady Allen of Hurtwood, gave figures to back up her assertion that, far from making a profit out of children, 'Mr Rank is financing an important pioneer experiment'. Another council member, Oliver Bell of the BFI, urged parents and teachers to visit matinees and see for themselves. There would then be some informed opinion available to a conference on the subject which the BFI was planning. Ultimately, said Bell, the solution lay in the teaching of film appreciation. Only thus could children be weaned away from their enthusiastic support of 'second-rate Hollywood films' and learn to enjoy British features and documentaries.

A letter from the Petroleum Films Bureau drew a distinction between film entertainment and entertainment films. Film entertainment could be derived from factual films. Anything in the world, suitably treated, could be made entertaining. Films of fact should therefore be included in every children's programme, because they stimulated the mind 'while giving a much-needed rest to the emotions'. On the last day of the correspondence, 28 January, the paper printed a letter from Field in which she agreed that films of fact could also be films of fun 'if treated in an imaginative manner'. In her thinking, all children's films should have a factual background, and to illustrate this she detailed both current and forthcoming CFD productions. In addition to OCM, there was *The Magic Globe*, which 'shows children the lives of their contemporaries in other lands'. In the area of drama 'an adventure film, almost completed, gives the audience a revealing picture of life on a canal barge, and of the working of the locks'. Abroad, a modern fantasy film called *The Boy who Stopped Niagara*, being produced in Canada, was 'in reality an explanation of how much of our daily life is dependent on electricity'. Also in production were two serials, one set in the London docks, and the other in the Blue Mountains of Australia. Finally, there was to be a feature called *The Little Ballerina*, which 'aims at showing the ballet as a living part of our cultural life'. For Field, this list of locations was not just another way of saying that everything has to have *somewhere* to happen; she believed the background (the 'fact') to be as important as the characters and action in the foreground (the 'fun').

The concluding editorial comment perceived a bottom line of agreement. This was that 'outside the home and the school, the cinema is almost certainly the most potent single agency influencing the behaviour and habits of the town child; and that this influence is too great to permit indifference'. Yet again the Hitler Youth movement was invoked. 'What must concern the public, and especially parents, is that character formation through mass suggestion conducted by a commercial undertaking may be a dangerous venture, however good the intention, unless it is carried through with great skill and restraint.' The special correspondent had been especially concerned with the younger children, and had proposed that seven should be the youngest age of admission to the cinema; no one had offered any argument against that. Equally, no one had taken issue with the charge that the quality of most of the films being shown in the clubs was low; or with the appraisal of the CFD films as 'unsatisfactory and insignificant'. The conclusion to be drawn from the debate was that it was essential for disinterested inquiry into the problem of children and cinema to be conducted as rapidly and effectively as possible.

Several such inquiries did indeed follow rapidly. In Middlesbrough, the local association of head teachers set about gathering data from the children in their schools; in London thirty-three students of Camden Teacher Training College arranged with the ONCC to visit various matinees in England and Scotland as an exercise in child observation, and to investigate Mayer's criticisms; in Leeds it was again a training college that heeded the call, but in this case it was lecturers rather than students, and the observations were confined to one cinema.

Before any of these inquiries were finished, the conference that Bell had trailed in *The Times* took place, organised jointly by the BFI and the National Council of Women. On 9 April in London, 400 people – including representatives from the Home Office, the Ministry of Education and the Scottish Office – gathered to discuss 'Children and the Cinema'. Before the speeches, three films were shown: a wartime edition of OCM; a 1938 British feature called *Scruffy*, about an orphan boy, a dog, a rich but unloving foster-mother and a young burglar; and – unprecedentedly – the first episode from a western serial. The overall tone of the conference echoed Mayer. Indeed, one of the invited speakers was Ralph Bond. Most speeches were overwhelmingly critical, the word 'mass' being used frequently. Some of them went so far as to call on local authorities to close the clubs down completely. The rest in the main reiterated, or expanded on, what had been said in *The Times*. A headmaster attacked the singing, the promise and a programme he had seen:

> You get this community singing – the standards are dreadful – community screeching and shouting. Then you have all that appeal from this poor man, the manager, shouting at these children, asking them to answer questions, yes or no, working all the time on mass emotion . . . The show I saw I should think had fifteen violent deaths in it during the morning and most of them built right up at the last. That was the children's final impression as they went out into the sunshine.

The call for children's films to be based on the classics of children's literature was heard again too. The strong attraction of this idea to parents and teachers derived from four things. First, such films seemed to be guaranteed to be safe and suitable, since the original books had survived the rigours of critical scrutiny and entered the established canon. Second, their very status as classics promised an inbuilt element of 'improvement'. Third, there was widespread trust in the notion that seeing the film of a book would lead children back to the written source, and to an understanding that books are better than films. The final important point about literary classics was that, with a few exceptions, they were not American. The linguistic/patriotic objection, widely shared since the late twenties, was voiced by a delegate who said: 'We have an extremely beautiful language which we share with no other nation whatsoever... It is deplorable that our children should learn to speak American before they have learned to speak our own glorious language.' A corollary was a request that some films for children should be based on the lives of 'good and famous people' – by which was meant English people.

Mayer himself was not there but some experts of the kind he was calling for were. One was a Dr. Loewenfeld, who described himself as a 'children's psycho-therapeutist'. He began by thanking Rank for starting the children's clubs, saying that members of the community ought to be ashamed that they had left it to private commercial interests and not done it themselves. Loewenfeld then added the standard warning against mass-suggestion, but brought in a new note by stressing the gender element. 'Speaking as a psycho-therapeutist, this question of having thousands of children together with a single male person in charge is a dangerous situation. We have seen sufficiently in the past years what can happen in a country where that kind of arrangement becomes dangerous.' He also jumped up later to express 'unhesitating condemnation' of the ONCC promise when he heard it, even though the Odeon representative tried to head off criticism by giving the conference a shorter and sweeter version of the promise than was actually being recited in the clubs. He reduced it from seven components to three – and of those three, only two were authentic. The one specially minted for the occasion was presumably offered as a sop to the National Council of Women (NCW). According to the Odeon representative, the ONCC promise was simply: 'I promise to tell the truth, to help mother, and to try to make this great country of ours a better place to live in.'

The ONCC song came off even worse. There was a widespread accusation that it was a hymn in praise of mob rule. People quoted Mayer's (not quite accurate) couplet – 'We are thousands strong/So we can't be wrong' – and demanded to know whether it was still being sung in the clubs. Again, the JARO had anticipated this, and in the two months since the correspondence in *The Times* had decided to do something about the two offending lines. Dismissively, the Odeon representative told the persistent critics that the song had already been completely removed from the cinemas. This was a considerable exaggeration of the truth. In fact, all that the ONCC management did in the short term was simply to rewrite the two lines that had provoked the outrage. Thus 'We are a hundred thousand strong/How can we all be wrong?' became 'We're a quarter million strong/And full of mirth and song'.

(Two years later, the ONCC song was indeed completely removed from cinemas. An internal reorganisation of JARO brought about the merging of the management structures of the Odeon and Gaumont chains in 1948, under the umbrella of the Circuits Management Association. John Davis, who by then had operational control of the whole of JARO, was an ex-Gaumont man, and he took the opportunity to divert criticism and at the same time unify the clubs by abolishing the ONCC song and replacing it with the Gaumont song. The only change necessary was the substitution of the word 'Odeon' for 'Gaumont', so that the fifth and sixth lines became: 'As members of the Odeon Club/We all intend to be . . . .' This spread of Docherty's song from Gaumonts to Odeons meant that it became one of the two best-remembered today.)

A further reason for getting rid of the original ONCC song, in addition to the criticisms of the ideological implications of its words, had come from three west London ONCC members interviewed at the 1946 conference. Their evidence made it plain that the distinction ONCC members were interested in was not between political and non-political song-words, but between those they could easily subvert and those that were more resistant. A song with questions and answers in was certainly fair game. Barry and George, at thirteen, were rather older than the generality of ONCC members; Sheila, aged eleven and still at a junior school, was more representative. Barry was attending a secondary modern (non-selective) school, while George was at a technical school (described by the Chair as 'a new school connected with the building trade'). They were introduced by the Chair as all being on the committees of their clubs. For George and Sheila this was not actually true, though they would have liked it to be. All three seem to have found the experience of being questioned publicly both unnerving and exciting. There certainly seems to be, in the published transcript, an element of 'telling them what they want to hear'. Some of the answers (for example 'Great Expectations') do not relate to club viewing at all. Barry was given a round of applause after his fourth answer, and may have been hungry for more. Nevertheless the combined testimony of these three brought to the conference the view from a Saturday morning cinema seat, and provided some children's reality to set beside the 'corporate piety' which one critic had said he perceived in the ONCC. At the same time, the questions from the chairman (the president of the NCW) and the floor illustrate succinctly the attitudes and concerns of the well-meaning, but not always well-informed, middle classes:

> CHAIR: What I would like to ask first is what type of picture you like best?
> BARRY: Most of the children like Abbot and Costello, westerns and thrillers and comical things, but I prefer one of the novels, such as *Great Expectations*.
> CHAIR: What other classical ones have you seen like *Great Expectations*? Did you see *Wuthering Heights*? What did you like there?
> BARRY: It was fairly good. I did not enjoy it much.
> CHAIR: And *Nicholas Nickleby*?
> BARRY: I haven't seen the film.
> CHAIR: Do you like to see the film and read the story afterwards?
> BARRY: Oh, I don't know really, because the book is always much better

than the film. [At this point the audience applauded, and were asked by the Chair to desist, and let her and the children get on with it.]

CHAIR: Sheila, what sort of things do you like best?

SHEILA: I like adventure.

CHAIR: Do you remember one now which you like?

SHEILA: *The Adventures of Tom Sawyer*.

CHAIR: And have you read the book, too?

SHEILA: No. My next favourite is a cowboy.

CHAIR: You like it when they go over a dangerous precipice and when you get them shooting at each other?

SHEILA: Not very much.

CHAIR: What about those with animals in them?

SHEILA: I only like ones with dogs in them.

CHAIR: Did you see *Laddie Come Back*? [She presumably meant *Lassie Come Home*.]

SHEILA: Yes.

CHAIR: What about you boys?

BARRY: I like ones that are not impossible. In some cowboys you see the hero making a horse jump over a precipice that has never been done before. I like Tarzan best, to see him swimming along. You even get tired of that. He is swimming along a river that has a fast current. Suddenly a crocodile comes behind him and he gets to the bank just before it snaps his head off.

CHAIR: Do you like scientific films?

GEORGE: Yes. Whenever there is a film on a scientist, I try to get to the front.

CHAIR: There is a gentleman here from the Scientific Society. Would you like to join that when you grow up?

GEORGE: Yes, especially if there are experiments.

CHAIR: How many committee members have you?

BARRY: Three boys and three girls. We generally have two of each at a meeting.

CHAIR: Do you check up in your committee work what things other kids like?

BARRY: Yes, because that is how we have our choice.

CHAIR: Do you have a vote, calling for hands?

BARRY: No, some of the committee members go round to their houses and get their opinion of the films they like and dislike.

CHAIR: When do you do your calling?

BARRY: On Saturday evening. It is not a habit. We might even ask them at school.

CHAIR: What do you find your committee people do, George?

GEORGE: I am not on a committee yet. I would not mind being on one, because you get in for nothing.

CHAIR: Sheila, are you on a committee?

SHEILA: No.

CHAIR: As a committee member, Barry, you have something to do with keeping order. What do you find on the whole? I am told sometimes seats in cinemas get cut up and nobody knows who cut them up.

BARRY: I don't know. We don't notice them cut before the children come in. The only time they notice them is after.

CHAIR: Have you noticed any indiscipline you would not approve of in school?

BARRY: Sometimes in the middle of the pictures they start changing around seats, and the committee members have to run around and put them back again.

CHAIR: Another thing I have been told to ask you is this. It is all right to sing and to sing in tune. On the whole do you think the singing is well done?

SHEILA: We have a special song.

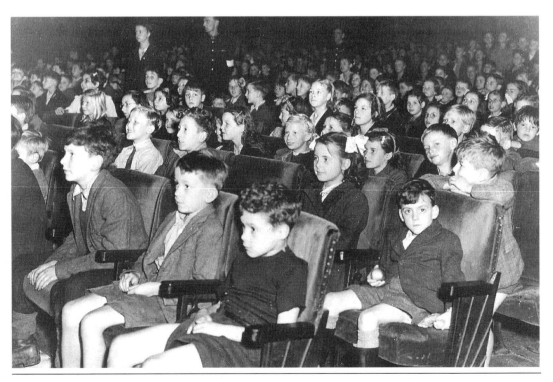

15. *A Rank club audience in 1946, the year of letters to* The Times

CHAIR: You sing that at the Odeon? What is the song? 'We are thousands strong . . .' Can you give more of the words?

BARRY: It starts: 'Do we ever worry? No! Do we love our neighbours? Yes!' But about twenty-five per cent of the children sing it in the negative. 'Do we ever worry? Yes! Do we love our neighbours? No!'

CHAIR: On the whole, is the singing too loud or boisterous or is it fairly good?

BARRY: On the whole, the singing is fairly good. We take it the more we shout, the more they like it. [The Odeon representative had earlier said that the purpose of the singing was 'to get rid of the children's animal spirits'.]

CHAIR: I wonder now, if other people here today would like to give me the questions which I have not yet asked? [Various questions then came from the floor.] Now, the first question is: How old are the children in the Clubs?

BARRY: They run from seven to fourteen, although sometimes you see toddlers coming in the charge of an older one.

CHAIR: How is the committee elected?

BARRY: In some theatres there is a ballot box and the members dealing with these fill in a quantity of members' names and put a cross against them and the members are elected who get most votes.

CHAIR: How do they get hold of the list of names? Supposing I want to get on a committee, do I offer to do jobs until I get on that list?

BARRY: When members join the club we have records of their names and I think that is how the election goes. They put on the ballot paper those they want.

CHAIR: How?

GEORGE: I am not on the committee. I know little about it. I think it is the ones who first join. The first ones that come in, if they are old enough, their names are put down on the committee and when they leave the next ones come on.

CHAIR: When you are on the committee and do these jobs, do you get a free pass?

BARRY: We go in free on the Saturday mornings, but not in the week.

CHAIR: Is it the same in yours, Sheila?

SHEILA: Yes, that's why I want to be on the committee.

CHAIR: What about outside activities? Is there anything else connected with it, such as football? Do the boys of the committee take charge of it?

BARRY: We put out an announcement after taking the Promise and the boys of the football team see the manager after the show. We take their names and test them.

CHAIR: Is there a similar club to yours, or would you not want to be in
any other?

BARRY: There was one boy who wanted to join and had been in the
Gaumont Club as well. When he does not like their things he comes
to ours.

CHAIR: What about other films? Do you think on the whole the kids of
the Saturday morning shows go to other films during the week?

BARRY: Yes.

CHAIR: Do you think on the whole they go to very late ones?

BARRY: I do.

GEORGE: I am generally home about quarter past ten. I go in there
about six.

CHAIR: We have, I think, asked all the questions we wanted to, and are
very glad you children have come. We do all feel that it is something
that can be a very useful thing in your lives, if it is kept nice, which
is what we all like.

This moderate tone did not sum up the overall mood of the conference,
which was on the whole Mayerish, but it did anticipate the findings and recommendations of the various reports which were soon to appear. These amplified
some of the things said at the conference, contradicted others, and put forward
recommendations not previously aired. The Leeds report (Parnaby and Woodhouse, 1947) in particular, based on observations in Bradford Odeon, received
wide circulation through being published and distributed by the BFI, as part of
its director's call for the building up of a body of literature relating to children's
cinema clubs.

All three reports expressed concern over the language that children heard
in the cinema, though none of them produced any detailed evidence to substan-
tiate or clarify their claims. The Middlesbrough report (1946), summarising
the replies sent in by fifty-six head teachers, said the majority of them regretted
that 'so little good English speech' was heard in cinemas, and believed that
cinema-going (not specifically Saturday matinees) led to 'the acquisition of an
appalling vocabulary'. Some of the thirty-three Camden Training College students who fanned out across England and Wales encountered an unexpected
language problem – that they found the dialogue in cartoons unintelligible,
while the children appeared to have no difficulty whatsoever. In relation to the
other films, the students subscribed to the general view, lamenting 'the absence
of a good English accent'. Reporting on thirteen consecutive weeks of matinee
attendance and observation at the Bradford Odeon, the two Leeds Training
College lecturers were concerned about speech only as part of the totality of
human behaviour. Their fear was that 'unfortunately, the great majority of films

seen are of poor aesthetic quality, and may have a deleterious effect on manners, speech and standards in general'.

The reason the Bradford Odeon survey lasted thirteen weeks, neither more nor less, was that that was the length of the serial showing there in the autumn of 1946. Every Saturday from 28 September to 21 December the two lecturers, Mary Parnaby and Maurice Woodhouse, sat with the children and watched an episode of *Jungle Queen*. They had presumably decided to do that because it was against the serial in particular that Mayer had directed his fiercest criticisms. (At the BFI/NCW Conference, even the controller of the ONCC had made no attempt to defend serials, saying that they were all much the same as each other, and that 'We do not like them any more than you do'.) Despite the centrality of serials in the perceived 'problem' of children's cinema clubs, Parnaby and Woodhouse were the only adult investigators who saw a serial right through in one place.

Released earlier that year, *Jungle Queen* would have been fresh to all the children, as well as to the two lecturers. Moreover, the print was probably in reasonable condition. Though an American production, like all serials up to that time, it is about British agents in 1939 waging a struggle with Nazi spies for control of the African continent. The main narrative line shows Nazis attempting to instigate an African revolt against British rule. In this they are thwarted by Lothel, Queen of the Jungle, described in the publicity as 'a mysterious girl who exerts a powerful influence over the natives, and who is blessed with supernatural gifts which enable her to walk unharmed through roaring flames'. By means of her special powers, she 'appears at crucial moments and is feared and obeyed by all the natives'. When British and American agents are sent to investigate the disturbances, their plane crashes in the jungle. Having narrowly escaped from the burning plane, they are captured by natives who decide to offer one of the British agents, the beautiful Pamela Courtney, as a sacrifice to their gods . . . . Together with the children, Parnaby and Woodhouse received an Invitation to Danger in episode one, then saw a Jungle Sacrifice (2), became caught up in a Wild Cat Stampede (4), escaped from a Burning Jungle (5), witnessed a Trip Wire Murder (7), suffered the devastation caused by a Mortar Bomb (8), followed the Trail to Doom (11), got Dragged Under (12) and finally discovered, just before Christmas, The Secret of the Sword. Their judgement on this serial as an aesthetic experience was not favourable:

We have witnessed the whole of *Jungle Queen*. The plot is at times involved and the photography poor. The story is crude and sensational, and evidently designed for adult audiences of low intelligence . . . There are scenes of mere talk and sentiment which bore the children . . . Each episode ends, characteristically, with the heroes and/or heroines in an apparently impossible impasse. The following week there is a slight alteration in the timing, which allows them to extricate themselves. This is a crude artifice.

Nonetheless, they did not go along with Mayer's implication that children should not be shown such films. They saw no evidence of daydreams being poisoned. Rather, they saw in the serial many elements which rightly appealed to children – 'fast-moving action, excitement, pictures of animal and jungle life, and repetitive incidents for which they look from week to week'. The boring scenes of talk and sentiment did not last long and were not that frequent. Parnaby and Woodhouse were, moreover, impressed by the children's ability to see that the film cheated each week at the beginning of the episode, presenting a cliff-hanging sequence differently from the way it had been shown at the end of the previous episode: 'The children detected this, and occasionally expressed disappointment and annoyance that such unfair technique had been employed.'

Parnaby and Woodhouse stood out among commentators in urging the retention of the serial 'because of its appeal to the natural interests of children – weekly familiarity with screen personalities and settings, suspense, and anticipation'. They thus staked a claim to be regarded as the children's champions, Don's defenders, the friends of Flash, the only investigators who did the job thoroughly and did not demonise Hollywood – but at the end they added the rider that they would nonetheless prefer to see 'more suitable' stories used as the basis for serials. By this they meant that they thought it would be better if the serial format were imported and applied to British literary material such as *Treasure Island*, the Robin Hood legends, the Just William stories and the novels of Arthur Ransome (*Pigeon Post*, *Swallows and Amazons*, *Peter Duck*). Whether they would have been happy to retain the 'crude artifice' of the certain-doom ending one week and miraculous escape the next week, they did not make clear.

Something else which only people with their kind of direct participatory experience would have noticed was the nonsense of the two prices of admission. At the turn of the century, in Mickleover, seats had been the same price in all parts of the school room; but in Bradford Odeon forty-six years later, and in most other Odeons and Gaumonts, there was a caste system in operation. Some children paid ninepence and sat in a cluster at the back. Others paid six-pence and sat in a cluster at the front. Between these two blocks of children there was a gap of empty seats, to separate the clean from the unclean. Parnaby and Woodhouse were the first to point out in print that it was ridiculously illogical to call an organisation a 'club' if it had that kind of discrimination operating within it. The notion of a club implied equality; without that it was meaningless. Dual pricing was 'a big obstacle to unity and cohesion'. As long as it was retained, then the matinees could not seriously be regarded as anything other than commercial film shows, and the use of the term 'club' should be dropped. Here again Parnaby and Woodhouse were seeing things more clearly than anyone else had, as a result of putting themselves in the children's position. And this time they did not add a rider.

A different kind of bifurcation of the audience was noted in the Camden report (1946). The contributing students observed that with an age range of 7–14 there was no way that any one film could possibly satisfy all the children. When the younger ones were on the whole enjoying an animated feature such as *Hoppity Goes To Town*, the older ones felt it to be childish. Younger ones tended to regard each shot as an entity in itself, rather than as part of a sequence. For that reason, when a film contained prolonged dialogue, they showed no interest in it, got bored, and started chatting. Indeed all feature films, of whatever genre, seemed too long for under-tens. One of the recommendations of the Camden report therefore was that there should be two types of club – Junior Clubs for primary children, and Senior Clubs for secondary. The ONCC and Gaumont controllers might well have accepted this in principle but would have declared it to be totally impracticable on the ground that they were having enough difficulty servicing the clubs that existed, and could not possibly find the films needed to supply a second tier. In any case the problem was solving itself, as secondary-school pupils increasingly came to regard the clubs as childish things, to be put away along with short trousers and ankle socks.

The Camden and Bradford reports differed on the question of whether it was justifiable for the clubs to concern themselves with activities not directly connected with the screening of films. The Camden students suggested that the other recreational activities were adequately provided for by other youth organisations; consequently nothing was gained by asking an untrained and overstretched cinema manager to organise the setting up of an orchestra. Parnaby and Woodhouse did not have quite the same experience in Bradford. As a result of their thirteen weeks of observation and discussions with children and cinema staff they recognised that managers were being expected to do the work of a youth leader 'without the time to devote to the job, or the training that would equip them for it'. Nonetheless, because their survey showed that a large number of ONCC members were not associated at all with any other kinds of clubs or play centres, they concluded that the extra activities should be retained, but not left to the manager to run. Instead, the local education authority should be induced to send experts to help out. One particular activity – committee membership – came in for unqualified commendation from Parnaby and Woodhouse, though, as they noted, it was one that most children could never benefit from.

Overall, the verdict of the three reports was: 'Must do better'. After blaming habitual cinema attendance for 'lack of concentration at school, creation of false standards, extreme pallor, lethargy, nightmares, and a tendency towards roughness and gangster games in play', the Middlesbrough head teachers conceded that: 'Cinema clubs are an undoubted attraction and have pleasing features'. Parnaby and Woodhouse concluded that if the clubs were to be a force for good, then much greater use of experts must be made, both in the running of the matinees, and in the making of the films to be shown there. Otherwise, they warned, 'there is a real danger that the clubs will, at best, encourage children in the habit of seeking ready-made entertainment which involves no effort and, at worst, MAY be used to instill false values and low standards of thought and morals'.

The *Times* correspondence, BFI/NCW Conference and three small-scale investigations were by no means the only manifestations of the debate. At all levels, except among children, it was one of the talking points of the year. There was distrust of Rank's motivation: he could not be as altruistic as he claimed. If he was not after becoming a dictator, then he must ultimately be driven by the profit motive. He had been widely quoted in the press as saying that his aim was to help make children good citizens able to appreciate good films; if he could not achieve that, well, at least he could turn them into habitual cinema-goers and make money out of them in five years' time. Despite JARO's insistence that the second half of that statement was a joke, it achieved wide circulation and notoriety. Field was later to write that: 'For a couple of years, in our efforts to improve films for children, we became the demons of the piece, with Mr Rank as chief demon . . . To own, in 1947, that one was associated with the children's film movement often made the social temperature drop several degrees.'

This disquiet reached its apogee on Wednesday, 27 November, 1946, at 5.38 p.m. when, for the first and only time, 'children's cinema clubs', as a subject for debate rather than just for questions to a minister, reached the floor of the House of Commons. For just under two hours that evening, Members discussed what the initiator described as 'a matter affecting the mental and spiritual welfare of many hundreds of thousands of our children'. It was, in one sense, 'only' an adjournment debate. (That is, a debate at which a backbench MP, chosen by ballot, is entitled to raise, and speak for about fifteen minutes on, a topic of which he or she has given prior notice. There is no party line, no Whip. The appropriate minister, or a deputy, is obliged to be there and respond on behalf of the government. The MP can explain and press the case for government action, but may not ask for legislation.) Most of what was said in it was either old, or irrelevant. Several speakers made reference to the BFI/NCW Conference, a verbatim transcript having been published soon after it took place. The Bradford investigation (Parnaby and Woodhouse, 1947) was at that time only two-thirds completed, so the view from the front stalls offered by Parnaby and Woodhouse was not available to the MPs. (The two lecturers had seen episode nine – *Death Watch* – on the preceding Saturday, and were less than three days away from *The Execution Chamber*.) Another source was the Mayer correspondence. The major new perspective introduced by some of the older MPs was that there had been matinee life before Rank. Overall, the debate's importance lay not in what was said but in where it was said, and the action that resulted.

The debate was initiated by Cyril Dumpleton, Labour MP for St Albans since the 1945 general election. A Quaker, he had visited several Odeon cinema clubs to see for himself what the argument was about. He now sought to convince those present that the matter was one to which the House should give some attention. His main request was simply that there should be an inquiry into this 'interesting experiment', because of the widespread concern which had been voiced. As evidence of this concern, he quoted a letter written to him by a headmistress in his constituency who had visited a Saturday morning show. He did not himself agree with it, but it was an expert opinion and should be heard:

> No factual film was shown. The singing at the beginning was designed to loosen any self-control that they might have gained during the week, and any taste or judgement. No really good standards of behaviour were shown. The gangster serial was definitely harmful and distorted facts. Instead of provoking thought and criticism, they encouraged escapism; instead of healthy adventure an uncritical reception of ideas, so preparing the youngsters of this country for mass suggestion and exploitation.

Dumpleton's conclusion was that if such an inquiry as he was asking for were implemented, he would want there to be on it 'people who know something about children's welfare, child psychology, and the influence of the films upon children and upon juvenile delinquency'. He was backed up by Thomas Skeffington-Lodge, Labour MP for Bedford, and a member of the Central Council of the Socialist Christian League, who spoke far less temperately than Dumpleton. His analysis of the situation was that 'Nearly 500,000 children are subjected to what at present amounts very largely to their leisure hours being exploited by private enterprise on a purely commercial basis.' He hoped that improved social conditions would do something to counter 'the present inclination on the part of parents to look upon the pictures as a ready-made chance of keeping the children occupied for an afternoon'. He wanted more than just an inquiry; he wanted a promise that the government would subsidise the production of suitable films.

16. J. Arthur Rank with children of JARO *staff at a party in 1947*

There was no outright opposition to Dumpleton's call for an inquiry at any stage of the debate, but Earl Winterton, Conservative MP for Horsham, even though he presented himself as a defender of the film industry and a friend of J. Arthur Rank, pointed out that there was nothing new about Saturday cinema: 'In the years before the war, children poured into the cinemas on Saturdays. I resent the suggestion that the children of this generation are worse than those of the previous generation.' This view was backed by William Blyton, Labour MP for Houghton-le-Spring: 'I agree with the noble Lord that there was too much talk by the elders of past generations about the mischief which youth can do. When I was young, there was nothing we enjoyed better than going to a Saturday matinee and shouting as loud as we could until the pictures came on.'

Another aspect was illumined by Kenneth Lindsay MP, who showed himself well informed about the restrictions governing children's employment in front of the camera. A few weeks previously, he said, he had seen an exceptionally brilliant Czech film, a fantasy featuring a child. He commented: 'I am not in favour of child labour. In fact, I have spent a certain amount of my life fighting against child labour, but that film could not have been made in this country because a child of that age could never be employed.'

Dr Hyacinth Morgan, MP for Rochdale and a member of the Council of the British Medical Association, professed to be just such an expert in child psychology as Mayer was calling for. He disparaged what had been produced for children so far as 'made for pure sensual pleasure'. He would prefer such films to have an educational purpose. As an example of the sort of subject he favoured, he mentioned 'the human hand and foot, and the different uses of the fingers'. They, he said, 'would command the pleasure of a child, and he would come out of the cinema asking questions and wanting to know more'. A second proposal for what a children's film should be about came from John Mack, MP for Newcastle-under-Lyme. Recalling that once when he had visited a boys' school in his constituency the children had asked him all sorts of questions about the House of Commons, he recommended that a film be made about how Parliament works – the Mace, the Serjeant at Arms, Mr Speaker. 'If they could be educated at an earlier age in the subject of Parliamentary institutions, we should have better representatives in the future Parliaments of England.'

Replying for the government, George Oliver, under-secretary at the Home Office, gave an assurance that either his department, or the Ministry of Education, or the two combined, would take the matter further. There could, however, be no question of the government intervening in the production of films for children. His main comment was on the inculcation of the habit of picture-going, which many Members had referred to. He recalled that people of his generation had liked to go to the cinema thirty years before: 'We were not stimulated by cinema clubs. It is something which appeals to the people of this country. So I do not think it is necessary to create an appetite for the pictures. I think it is already there.'

Thirteen months later, a Departmental Committee on Children and the Cinema was indeed set up, on behalf of not just the Home Office and the Ministry of Education, but also the Scottish Office. Its terms of reference were:

1. To consider the effects of attendance at the cinema on children under the age of sixteen, with special reference to attendance at cinema clubs.
2. To consider whether, in the light of these effects, any modification is desirable in the existing system of film classification, the existing position with regard to the admission of children to cinemas, or in the organisation, conduct and management of children's cinema clubs.

That was what Dumpleton had asked for, but he did not sit back and wait. He now added his voice to those demanding a fresh look at the law governing child actors. So strong was the case that in June 1948 the Home Secretary, Chuter Ede, informed Dumpleton, without promising an early change in the law, that he had just appointed a small Committee 'to consider under what safeguards as to health, welfare and education the employment of children as film actors could properly be allowed'.

9   *Stinkers and Smashers*

For Neza Saunders, the Aboriginal boy in the film, 'witchety-grubs' figured on the menu. These rather repulsive creatures are white, hairless grubs, about three inches long, highly esteemed as food by some of the tribes. In the film, the boy is supposed to eat them with relish when he is wandering, lost and foodless, with the other children. Unfortunately, Neza came from a part of Queensland where the grubs were unknown and so, to encourage him, director Ralph Smart ate one first. 'It was not too pleasant', says Smart, 'and I noticed that Neza got rid of his too, as soon as the shot was taken.'

(Publicity notes for Bush Christmas, 1947).

The children in the clubs may have been unaware of the adult debate, but the people who staffed CFD were not. The blasts of disapproval may have been ill-informed, as Field believed, but they nonetheless caused confusion and dismay. Until May 1945, public projects were judged in terms of whether or not they sought to make a contribution to the war effort – as the coverage of the ONCC launch in 1943 had shown. But after VE Day, normal critical services were resumed.

During the war, no press show had been held of CFD product. Any reviewer could have arranged to see the films at an Odeon or Gaumont on a Saturday morning with a club audience, as Mayer had. However, Saturday morning was not a normal time of work for film reviewers; and cinemas away from the centre of town were not the regular place to go. The CFD therefore arranged a press show in the Leicester Square Odeon, three weeks after VE Day, of the previous twenty months' product. It was a normal Thursday afternoon. The audience consisted entirely of adults – critics, educationalists and others professionally concerned with children. In her introduction, Field warned them that they might not like all five films, because they were not the intended audience. The gathering first saw *Tom's Ride, Sports Day* and OCM3, featuring penguins at the zoo, a children's art school in Moscow, the wartime work of a village blacksmith and a visit to an exhibition about toys.

Then came two films which both showed that CFD's thinking, under the pressure of combining morality and entertainment, had become even woollier since *Sports Day*. *Sally the Sparrow* used the device of following a foraging sparrow round a zoo from cage to cage in order to show the contrast in size between her and bigger animals such as lions and pandas. The commentary, in rhyming couplets, admonished Sally for taking the other animals' food, saying that that was stealing; the right thing for her to do was to wait to be fed by children visiting the zoo. In the black and white cartoon *Robbie Finds a Gun* a rabbit is having fun with a catapult. When he finds a gun he uses that instead, and tries to shoot a crow, but the crow carries him off, and drops him into a pond.

According to Field, it was apparent while the films were being shown that the Thursday afternoon adults were not responding warmly; and the printed reviews confirmed this impression. One particularly dismissive writer, in the *Documentary News Letter* (volume 5, 1945), said: 'This programme suggests that it is high time that adults, particularly teachers, considered not only whether there is any point in making such films, but whether they are not positively harmful.' What was found especially objectionable was the element of 'snob morality' in *Tom's Ride* and *Sports Day*. An ex-education officer (Llewellyn) also had strong reservations. The association of Uncle Mac with the Advisory Council was to him no guarantee of success with a very problematic project: 'To write especially for children is one of the most difficult tasks if one is to avoid condescension, that insufferable patronising tone we sometimes hear in *Children's Hour* . . . The script for *Sports Day* is feeble. It is a goody-goody story.' Even some of Field's fellow-members of the Association of Cine Technicians joined in the attack on the CFD films at their 1946 conference (*Kinematograph Weekly*, 2 May). One claimed that the films for production were selected 'on a moral basis that is 60 years out of date'. Another summed up the CFD films as 'real stinkers'. *The Manchester Guardian* and *The Scotsman* were milder in tone; they concentrated on welcoming the principle of special films for children, even if the results so far were not perfect.

Faced with such a reception, the CFD saw the necessity of working out a consistent, well-reasoned policy to guide future production. In this rethinking, the most important element – which even Rank himself accepted – was that the moral teaching of each film should be less obtrusive, though there was no question of abandoning it altogether. Somehow the films had to satisfy that requirement, because that was what Rank was paying for. The problem was: how to make films that would 'do the children good' and yet escape being labelled 'goody-goody'.

A new line of thought, summarised in Field's letter to *The Times*, was that the background setting for each film should be chosen with care, and recorded in documentary style. It would thus incorporate an element of education. Fresh input came also from the voice of the children. What Field really wanted was a way of gauging children's spontaneous responses, but for the moment she had to be content with managers' reports and occasional children's letters. In particular, Field had been convinced by the children that Rank was wrong not to allow Tom to have any reward for his heroic ride to the station, and she was prepared to be not so mean in future. A further guideline adduced from audience response was that children tended to regard western and serial narratives as taking place in a fantasy world whose improbabilities they did not question. However, as the response to the two Toms had shown, when a film dealt with children like themselves, in a milieu they recognised, then they demanded complete accuracy and realism.

The first film finished in this new climate of thought was *Jean's Plan*, as the film featuring life on a canal barge came to be called. It opens with Jean, played by fourteen-year-old Vivien Pickles, repairing a teddy-bear that she has become too old for, in the spirit of the national slogan 'Make Do and Mend'. She's going to give it to a cousin. When her father, a jeweller, shows her a valuable heirloom bracelet that he's working on, a man enters the shop and sees it. To a dismissive reference that he makes to Jean's old toy, she replies: 'Never judge a teddy by the stitches in his tummy.' Later the necklace is stolen, and Jean, still carrying the teddy, is soon on the trail, hitching a ride on a canal barge in pursuit of the thieves. There are shots of the countryside, and Jean calls attention to it by saying, 'It is pretty down here'. As the barge goes through a lock, there are close-up shots showing how the procedure works. Having regained the bracelet, Jean has to think of a good place to hide it. She phones the police for help from a call box, but before they arrive she is spotted by the thieves, who want the necklace back. She escapes, and there's a frantic chase along the towpath. Seeing her run into an old dilapidated farmhouse, they are certain that they have her cornered, but they hunt in vain. When they go outside, Jean emerges: she has been hiding under a pile of sacks. The thieves look for her in the cellar, but Jean locks them in, then waits for the police and her father to show up. Back home, in the final scene, she reveals that the necklace has been hidden inside her teddy all the time. Told that she's in for a surprise in recognition of her courage and cleverness, she replies: 'I hope it's a new pair of socks.' It is in fact a puppy. There is no concluding moral.

As originally filmed, *Jean's Plan* ran into trouble with the BBFC, but for a different reason from *Sports Day*. The censors were concerned about shots of Jean fleeing the thieves along the towpath. In these shots, Jean looked frightened. It was not desirable, in the censors' view, to let children in the audience see a child on screen looking frightened. The fear would be communicated from screen to cinema seat. If the producers insisted on those shots being left in, then the film would have to carry an A certificate. CFD therefore had to agree to re-edit the towpath chase. This BBFC stance had long-lasting ramifications, and conditioned CFD's thinking about child protagonists. On the one hand, according to Field: 'We found our audiences preferred to see the main parts in a film played by ordinary types of children like themselves, and not by the "sweet" little girls and waif-like little boys that enthral adult film-goers.' On the other hand, they could not present these ordinary children as showing the ordinary emotion of fear.

This concentration on ordinary children, and on factual backgrounds, meant that Russian fairy-tales no longer found favour. At Christmas 1945, *The Magic Seed* was released in the UK, in a version with the narrative explained by broadcaster Wilfred Pickles. Made by the best-known of all Russian directors, Sergei Eisenstein, this was an archetypal presentation of the battle between good and evil. What was more, it had child characters as protagonists. A boy and a girl, Andreyka and Maryka, are presented by a blacksmith with a casket containing a magic seed. There is only one other in the world, and that is held by Karamur, a wicked ogre, who keeps it locked up to prevent it from spreading happiness. Karamur has heard about the seed which the children hold, and plans to capture and destroy it by means of his army of Longnoses. However, with the aid of Dr Knowall, a magic flute and a little black slave, the children defeat Karamur, find the other magic seed and set about spreading happiness everywhere.

The BBFC gave it a U certificate, though it contained scenes which some adults, including Field, thought children might find frightening. The argument was over whether or not a few unpleasant images – described by Field as 'monsters with horrible hands and faces' – nullified a story which ultimately showed right triumphing. At the BFI/NCW conference, one speaker said she was not impressed by either *Tom's Ride* or *Sports Day*. Her children preferred *The Wizard of Oz* and *The Magic Seed*. She explained: 'These films are gruesome in parts, but I have never found children worried by them. Children can look at something and be quite callous towards it. I do not think you can condemn *The Magic Seed* because there are parts in it which we think they should find gruesome.' Nonetheless, Field did condemn *The Magic Seed*, and it was not shown in Rank clubs.

It must therefore have been particularly satisfying for CFD when they had reason to feel that they were beginning to hit the target with their own realist productions. These started with *Jean's Plan*, which in the spring of 1946 began to go round the Rank matinee circuit, and in the summer was shown to reviewers. The response from both sectors was strongly favourable; and in the case of the critics markedly different from what it had been before. The *Monthly Film Bulletin* wrote: 'It has no moral axe to grind, and no child could help enjoying it. The heroine is a normal child full of sense and courage. The story is full of thrills and incidents; the country scenes are summery and pleasant.'

Kine Weekly approved the high quota of action, 'including a canal jump, a tussle with the thieves, and a car chase', and the 'good acting by the juvenile star'. The film did not play at Bradford Odeon while Parnaby and Woodhouse were there, but they made a point of seeing it before finishing their report, and commented that it was 'a good film, revealing a genuine appreciation of children's needs and interests'. Their praise was not unqualified – they also said it left too little to the imagination – but it contributed to the development of the view that maybe the CFD were starting to get it right.

The other films detailed in Field's *Times* letter all crossed the finishing line during 1946 or 1947. (One of them was not in the shape that had been intended for it, but turned out to be none the worse for its transformation.) The serial set in the London docks was called *Dusty Bates*. Directed in five two-reel episodes by Darrel Catling, who had done more than most to enable Tom to take his ride, it featured Antony Newley, who later played the Artful Dodger in Lean's *Oliver Twist*. The three-reel *Boy who Stopped Niagara*, having been shot in Canada by the National Film Board, had the great advantage of having young actors of about six and eight in it. The boy, Tommy, dreams that he has pulled off a handle while visiting Niagara Falls power station and that, as a result, all electricity has stopped running. It was favourably reviewed by critics, and received a strongly positive response from 65 per cent of the children, but Field thought that it did not work as well as it could have done because Niagara was not a sufficiently familiar reference point for British children. In *The Little Ballerina*, Margot Fonteyn made a guest appearance as herself, encouraging a working-class girl who was struggling to make the grade.

At the same time, a range of short non-fiction films continued to be produced. OCM rarely missed a month, and sometimes got outside the Home Counties, as when in 1947 Edinburgh Gaumont club members participated in such items as the washing of animals at the Scottish Zoological Park, Mary Queen of Scots' associations with the Royal Mile, repair work on the Forth Bridge, ship-building on the Tay and the landing of the herring catch at Anstruther. In each two-reel episode of another series, *The Magic Globe*, two English children found themselves transported to Lapland, Poland, Czechoslovakia, the Canadian Rockies or Alberta. And, in an attempt to counter the criticism that matinees began with 'community screeching', CFD commissioned six one-reel films called *Let's Sing Together*, based on folk-songs such as *The Raggle Taggle Gipsies*, *Bound for the Rio Grande*, and *Dashing away with the Smoothing Iron*. They were made by six different production companies, each being encouraged to explore new techniques, as CFD wanted to know what worked best.

Some of this documentary stuff was made rather more hurriedly than the showcase fiction. Even so, the rate of production was not fast enough to hit the target of one reel per week. To eke out the supply of specially written CFD product, Field instituted a policy of buying material that had been shot for another audience, and getting it adapted for British children. Thus out of *Before the Raid*, an adult feature with a child character in it – about the struggles of a Norwegian fishing village against German invaders – came the three-reel *Escape from Norway*. A Swedish film made for young children became a one-reeler called *The House Goblin*, with rhyming commentary added. Rank's original dictum had been 'Then we will make some', not 'Then we will re-edit some', but according to Field he never objected to any of the directions in which CFD was finding it necessary to go.

Meanwhile, in Australia, *Bush Christmas* had turned from the serial which Field had commissioned into the first full-length feature to be produced in English specially for children. If it had been made a few years later it would have been regarded as too long and cut down by 25 per cent, but in 1946–47 there were fewer rules. This was fortunate, because *Bush Christmas* turned out to be CFD's finest hour (and twenty minutes). In production terms, it was a spin-off from *The Overlanders*, a successful 1946 Ealing film about a stockman (Chips Rafferty) taking a huge herd of cattle 2,000 miles across wartime Australia to keep them out of the hands of the Japanese. This had been pro-duced by Ralph Smart, a writer born in London of Australian parents, who had previously worked in the documentary field for GBI. Having heard of the CFD and the problems posed by the illegality of using school-age children in the UK, he wrote an outline story about children surviving in the Blue Mountains of Australia and sent it to Field. It must have been received with rapture by CFD, since as well as being a rattling good adventure it included children of varying ages, a beautiful background, an Aboriginal boy, British currency and dialogue in English. Furthermore, Smart was proposing to get Chips Rafferty to appear in it as one of the thieves.

The story begins at the start of the Christmas holidays in the remote little town of Mara Mara, during the war. Five children are riding four ponies home from school. They are Helen, John and Snow Thompson (three white Australian children), Michael (an English evacuee who lives with them), and Neza (son of an aboriginal stockman who works for the Thompsons' father). Against Helen's wishes and Neza's advice, they decide to go home by Heavy Tree Gap, where three of them come across two strangers who have just finished paint-ing out a white mark on a stolen horse. When John and Snow boast about their father's mare Lucy and her new foal, the strangers give them two shillings each on condition that they promise not to tell anyone of their meeting. They rejoin Helen, who is angry with them, saying 'We promised that we wouldn't ever take money from strangers'. When she insists that it must be given back, Snow says he's already spent it. Helen prevails, however, only to find when they go back that the two suspicious-looking strangers, who had looked as if they were settled for the night, have decamped.

Unable to give the money back, the children feel obliged to keep their promise not to tell anyone about the encounter. By next morning, however, Lucy and her foal have been stolen. Feeling that it's all their fault, they own up, making Mr Thompson so angry that he cancels the Christmas arrangements. John has a hunch that the thieves have gone into the Warrigal Ranges, so Helen asks for permission for all of them to go camping for a few days at Bellbird Ford, not far away. Neza is to go too, to make sure that they don't get lost. All five set off into the Warrigal, searching in vain for a trail. After three days all their food is finished; their Christmas dinner consists of boiled snake – killed by Neza, cooked by Helen. Finally Snow, peering over a cliff, sees the thieves camping in the valley below.

In the long, central section of the film, the children resourcefully harry the thieves, who are now three in number, without ever letting themselves be seen. Adopting an Aboriginal trick, they tie leaves under their feet to disguise their tracks. In the middle of the night, they recover Lucy and her foal, steal the thieves' boots and hide their food. By means of a well-aimed dart, Neza destroys their water supply too. At the climax the children are at last outwitted by the thieves in a deserted mining village. Captured, they are all hung up, by their clothing, on a row of meat hooks in an old butcher's shop. Even in this situation they remain fearless and refuse to give any information. Enraged by all the indignity and pain they have suffered, the thieves are all set to ride off, leaving the children dangling, when Mr Thompson, Neza's father and a police search party arrive.

In the middle of 1947, *Bush Christmas* started the first of its triumphal tours of the Rank circuit. Only four months earlier, CFD had changed its name to Children's Entertainment Films (CEF), and must have felt vindicated in that decision by the success of *Bush Christmas*. Supportive reviews came from all quarters. *The Manchester Guardian*, for example, wrote (16 June 1947):

> The greatest advantage of this film over the normal cowboy picture is that it is made with due respect for child psychology. At the Kensington cinema about a thousand children cheered and jumped up and down in their seats as the clever Australian child actors baffled and defeated three horse-thieves after a long chase through the bush. In comparison with an ordinary serial shown in the same programme this specially designed and excellently directed film was worth far more in entertainment value. Its only shortcoming as a film for children is likely to be the difficulty of keeping grown-ups out of the audience. This is the first of many such films, and there seems to be a hope that within a few years children's cinema clubs will be able to show no films except those made specially for them.

17. *Publicity still from* Bush Christmas, 1947. *From left to right the children are Helen (Helen Grieve), Michael (Michael Yardley), Snow (Nicky Yardley), Neza (Neza Saunders) and John (Morris Unicomb)*

There is a mass of evidence that millions of children – not only in the UK but in other countries as well, especially Germany and Australia – were as enthusiastic about *Bush Christmas* as the critics and the thousand children in the Kensington Odeon, and that its appeal lasted. The CEF report of 1950 refers to a case of one boy in Lancashire who was known to have seen the film five times. When in 1949 a group of children taking part in film-study sessions conducted by Maurice Woodhouse were shown it, a boy, who had previously said that he liked only thrillers and westerns, summed up their feelings: 'This was the best of all because it had more truth in it than the others.' Neza was particularly liked by the group 'because he provided all the ideas'; and the other four children were appreciated for the way the expressions on their faces communicated vividly their rejection of one of Neza's ideas – eating witchety grubs to stay alive. The camerawork was praised, as when it revealed the thrilling panoramic view from the ridge overlooking the valley; the music too was judged to be part of the pleasure of it all, since it was 'exciting' when the children were stealing the thieves' boots, and 'sad' when Helen told her parents a lie about their camping plans. The only serious criticism from this group was that Michael, the English evacuee, was weedy and did not contribute much to the children's overall effort – all he did was hold things up and endanger the others by losing his glasses. Nobody asked why the children did not look frightened when they were dangling from meat hooks.

Field was proud of *Bush Christmas* for many reasons, one of them being that it 'introduces the colour problem indirectly'. That is, it showed black and white children living together peacefully, without that fact being the crux of the

18. ONCC *audience at Swiss Cottage Odeon, November 1948. Bush Christmas is being shown for the second time in eighteen months. This is the fifth of the eight flash photographs taken before audience resistance put a stop to the project (see Chapter 12). On screen, the children's bad luck has finally changed: Neza has found the footprints of the stolen horses.* (British Film Institute)

story. Writer/director/producer Smart has a similar view. It was, he told me, 'a statement about the need for equality. It was about how things could be, and indeed should be.' This being one of the aims, it is unfortunate that the commentary (written by CEF, not Smart) which accompanies the opening sequences of the film, introducing the characters and explaining to British children that in Australia Christmas falls in the middle of summer, is discriminatory. Over a shot of John and Neza together on one pony, the commentary explains: 'This is John.'

In one way, *Bush Christmas* was too successful. JARO very early took the hint that it could appeal not just to the Saturday matinee crowds but to general (higher-price-paying) audiences as well. One among many attractions was that it could be promoted as having the same star as *The Overlanders*. The idea of gaining widespead attention by putting *Bush Christmas* out on the commercial circuit at the same time as it was doing its first tour of the club circuit must have been irresistible. In the summer and autumn of 1947 *Bush Christmas* played all round Britain in regular Odeon programmes, including that of Leicester Square, where two years earlier critics had panned *Tom's Ride* and *Sports Day*. It was the thirties' Shirley Temple situation in reverse. Temple had been too good to show to children, and now *Bush Christmas* was too good to be shown only to children. Such considerations did not trouble two boys in Edinburgh, where the parallel releases of *Bush Christmas* resulted in the following conversation during a Saturday morning Gaumont screening of it:

(Boy of twelve, to boy of nine in front): 'It's a smasher. I saw it last night in the Playhouse.'
(Boy in front, ten minutes later): 'Is it a serial? Oh, I hope it's a serial!'

Fortunately for CEF, this twin-track exhibition did not render *Bush Christmas* ineligible for entry in competitions. The idea of special production, inspired by the UK rather than the USSR, had taken root in post-war Europe so rapidly that in 1947 the Venice Biennale organised the first competitive international festival of children's films. In Britain, the Wheare Committee had not even been appointed when in Italy *Bush Christmas* won gold.

Buoyed by such critical and audience success, CEF kept up its rate of production for the next three years, until after the Wheare report (1950) was published, but even then, six years after Rank first asked Field to take on the task, the difference that special production had made to the clubs' screens was relatively slight. The hope, reported in *The Manchester Guardian*, that there would be a Bush Christmas for everyone all the time 'within a few years' was very far from being realised. Out of 104 screen hours, in the twelve months from May 1949 to May 1950, the ONCC Dudley received only enough special films to fill six. There was still a long way to go.

10 *Roped and Badly Mutilated*

My first visit alone to a Saturday matinee took place at the Queen's, just off the docks in Whitehaven, next to the Quay Street Roman Catholic chapel and infant school I attended. In the serial, Superman was left in the final frames pushing desperately with his outstretched arms at the sides of a tunnel melting into a hot, dangerous, black treacle-like substance which threatened to engulf him. The image was awesome and utterly seductive.

(Michael O'Pray, 1990)

In the clubs and matinees themselves, the overwhelming majority of children did not experience any of those six hours. They knew nothing of *Jean's Plan* or OCM or *With Uncle Bill at the Zoo* or *Dashing Away with the Smoothing Iron* or any other CFD/CEF productions, except possibly *Bush Christmas* or *Little Ballerina* which they could have seen at an evening show with their parents. The fact was that most matinee children were not members of a Rank club. Rather, they went to a cinema belonging to ABC (well over 500 throughout the UK), the King Circuit (over 100 in Scotland), Granada (36 around London), Clifton (32 in the Midlands and the West Country), one of the even smaller circuits, or, in the greatest numbers, to an independent cinema the owner/manager of which had complete autonomy and was more likely to operate shows for children in the afternoon than in the morning. In principle these circuits and independents were free to hire CFD/CEF product after it had been round the Rank clubs, but very few of them did. In the forties there was an element of suspicion and distrust between JARO Saturday cinema and non-JARO Saturday cinema. Thinking particularly of the ABC chain, Field (1952) wrote dismissively: 'Our aim was gradually to accustom children to specially made story films that were "good" for them; theirs was to excite the children for the passing moment by means of any adult film that had enough action to catch visual attention.'

It was certainly true that the ABC chain were always careful never to profess any do-gooding intentions. Nor did they use the word 'club' to describe their Saturday morning arrangements. They ran matinees, not clubs; the children were Minors, not members; the performances were shows, not meetings. After the war, the general rule relating to age of admission in Rank clubs, especially Gaumonts, was that members had to be at least seven. Since ABCs did not claim to be running a club, they imposed fewer restrictions. In general, where local regulations allowed, they admitted children from the start of school attendance. As a corollary of not being a club and therefore not much concerned with activities outside the cinema, ABC concentrated on making sure that what went on inside the cinema ran as happily and safely as possible. Managers who wanted to run matinees had first to get approval, by satisfying the overall controller – a woman known as 'Aunty Andy' – of their rapport with children. After that, they had to set up and publicise the forthcoming Minors' matinees, making the opening into a newsworthy local event. Part of the build-up was the establishment of a Minors' Corner in the main foyer, in which would be posted publicity regarding films to be shown. There had also to be a suggestions box, by means of which Minors could communicate with Aunty Andy. The aim was to get as many children enrolled as there were seats in a particular cinema before the opening date. When everything was in place, then head office would supply a quota of badges showing the ABC logo in white inside a red triangle, which itself was superimposed on two blue triangles. Additionally, even though the ABCs had deliberately eschewed the term 'club', they nonetheless did issue membership cards in some cinemas. This enabled Aunty Andy to send a birthday card and a free ticket from head office to each Minor once a year. More importantly, from the manager's point of view, the purpose of membership cards was to serve as a record of the holder's seat number. Expecting each child to sit in a particular seat each week and, if possible, having no unallocated seats, was a way of avoiding the 'sixpenny rush' that otherwise might have revived the pre-war tradition of running and fighting for the best seats. It was a different approach to the problem that the ONCC was trying to tackle by means of exhortation and slides.

The ABC's system of having children sit in the same place each week was reinforced and made possible by a system of Block Monitors. These were children not less than twelve years old, who were put in charge of a block of around fifty seats. Their tasks were to discourage unruly behaviour or running around in the cinema, and to keep the block clean and tidy. In theory each monitor was elected by the children of that block, and served for only twelve weeks before being either re-elected or replaced by somebody else. In addition to the Block Monitors, there could be a Lost Property Monitor, a First-Aid Monitor, a Directions Monitor, a Welfare Monitor, a Queue Monitor. All of them would be invited to meet once a week, have tea with the manager, and

19. *Announcement of the start of ABC Minors' matinees at the Palace Theatre, Erdington, Birmingham in 1946. 'Enrol now and obtain your badge and membership card'* (The Allen Eyles Collection)

discuss ideas for improving the matinees. If a non-screening activity was suggested, then managers were free to agree and to help make it happen if they personally wanted to, but there was no central policy directive telling them that this was an essential part of their job. There was thus a certain amount of stamp-collecting, forming sports teams, organising choirs, and fund-raising to buy toys for children in hospital, but it was limited. There were also occasional one-off events such as a Minors' march through Bradford carrying a banner in support of national savings.

The most widespread ongoing Minors' activity in the post-war period was participation in pen-friend schemes, something which schools and churches too were keen to promote. One year, Aunty Andy ran a national Minors competition for designing and painting a calendar, the prize for the winner in each age group being a bike. On a more local and informal level, it became common in ABC cinemas to have contests and performances as part of the pre-screening warm-up. It could be a snatch of ballet, or a burst of particularly talented whistling. Someone who could sing a popular song well – *The Bells of St Mary's* became a frequent choice – would be especially appreciated. In the Glasgow Ritz, Allister McAllister (an under-sixteens' national champion accordionist) entertained Minors one morning, while at the Chatham Ritz ten girls in sailor suits danced the hornpipe.

Just like the Rank club committee members (as revealed by the children at the BFI/NCW conference), ABC Monitors received tangible rewards for performing their tasks. This was not something that either JARO or ABC mentioned in the evidence they gave to Wheare. They would have preferred not to have to do it. They would have liked children to accept the precept that public service is its own reward. However, they gave in. This is a composite Monitor memoir:

> I was a member of the ABC Minors just after the war, and during my last year at school in 1948 I became a Monitor. By then I was covered in badges. Some I had got for being 'good' (not standing up on the seat) and then there was an extra big one for being a Monitor. As well as being in charge of the children in a block of seats, I had to look after part of the queue before we went into the cinema; then I had to keep the older boys from destroying the seats. There were four perks for this job. Firstly, I did not have to pay sixpence to go in. Secondly, there was a Monitors' tea-party with the manager on Friday evenings immediately after school, where we talked a bit about Minors who had birthdays coming up, before having to clean up the plates and get out quick, at about five o'clock. Thirdly, depending on what was showing, we were sometimes allowed into the auditorium free to see the feature film that

the cinema was playing that week. Finally, once a year, after Christmas, there would be a special New Year Party for Monitors only.

Some of the independents modelled themselves partially on the clubs and matinees of the major circuits, while others just took the money and ran the films. Edinburgh in the late forties had three cinemas running clubs (Barclay, 1951.) Two of them, the New Victoria and the Capitol, were Gaumont cinemas, so they followed the guidelines laid down by JARO, and showed films booked and approved by the Gaumont club controller. There the children took the Club promise each week, sang 'We come along on Saturday morning . . .', saw the CFD/CEF productions, and were supposed to be at least seven. The third club in Edinburgh was at the Roxy Cinema, independently owned and managed by the Poole family. There no age-restriction was imposed. Similarly, the choice of activities and films was entirely up to James Poole. Being in Scotland, he could have shown A-certificate films if he had chosen to. In fact, before and during the war, the Roxy event had been run as a Mickey Mouse Club, and when Poole restarted it in 1946, its internal organisation was similar to that of the Gaumont clubs. Like them it had membership cards and free admission for birthdays. Poole was 'Chief', and the matinees he ran at the Roxy are remembered like this:

> The cinema would fill up with hundreds of kids, causing absolute chaos and cacophony. Then the younger Mr Poole would appear on the stage before the screen. He was a tall thin man in his forties with a moustache – in fact he looked very like Walt Disney. He would hold up his hands for silence, and when the row subsided he would shout, into a mike, 'Hi Ya Members!', to which the appropriate response was 'Hi Ya Chief! R - O - X - Y, Roxy, Hurrah! Hurrah! Hurrah!'

After that, at the Roxy, slides illustrating an aspect of road safety were shown and explained. This solemnity would be leavened by a draw of four lucky numbers from the stubs of the admission tickets, the winners each receiving half-a-crown in cash or savings stamps. Occasionally, the Chief would issue a 'command', just as he had done before the war, by which each child might be asked to donate one penny the following week in order to buy a gift for someone ill or needy. On rare occasions Chief Poole found it necessary to expel a member from the Roxy Club; this he did by publicly tearing up the child's membership card. Finally there was community singing, and this brought a major change from circuit practice because the Roxy, like most independents, had no organ. The children had therefore to sing unaccompanied, or follow a words-and-music film (probably American).

The actual programme of films was much the same in the three cinemas except that CFD/CEF shorts and features were replaced at the Roxy by Buster Keaton and the Three Stooges. In the summer of 1947, the all-important serial was the same at the Roxy as it was at the New Victoria – *The Royal Mounted Rides Again*. The highlights of this were 'an avalanche, a raging forest fire, and a canoe carrying the heroine tossed along a rockstrewn torrent and finally over a waterfall'. Likewise Pluto and Donald Duck were to be found everywhere. The features were mainly interchangeable westerns – *The Eagle's Brood*, *Whirlwind Horseman*, *Texas Kid*. The Gaumonts were able to get away from this standard fixture when it was their turn to show Helen, Snow, Neza, John and Michael enjoying their *Bush Christmas*, but the Roxy riposted with *The Five Little Peppers*, a family film about 'vigorous, lovable American children in reduced circumstances befriended by a mining magnate through contacts made by his lonely grandson' (Barclay, 1951).

A final significant difference between major circuit clubs and independents was revealed in the school summer holidays. The Roxy's club closed down for the duration because experience had shown that the attendance would be too low to make it commercially viable. The Gaumont clubs on the other hand had no choice. Being part of JARO with its sense of mission, they had to carry on for fifty-two weeks a year despite the summer slump in attendance.

Birthday Greetings

As members of the G.B. Club
we all intend to be...
Good citizens when we grow up
And champions of the free.

BIRTHDAY GREETINGS

The Legend of the White Knight

"I pass this way but ONCE.
If there is any good I can do,
let me do it NOW – for I
shall not pass this way again."

20. *Two Gaumont Junior Club birthday cards. The white knight card, in use in 1945, said on the other side: 'We wish you a very happy birthday and invite you and a friend to be our guests next Saturday.' It was signed in facsimile by J. Arthur Rank as national president, and in person by the local cinema manager as Club Leader. The other card, also dating from the forties, bore a similar message*

For children in the small town of Chard, Somerset, the choice was not between an independent and a circuit cinema, but between one independent and another. Actually, choice was not essential, because their shows did not clash. The Regent, showing in the morning, was organised as a club; the Cerdic, showing in the afternoon, was not. The Chard Regent even had something which the much bigger Edinburgh Roxy did not – its own unique club song. To a tune which the children knew well because it introduced every episode of *Don Winslow*, they sang their own special words. As in the Roxy, there was no organ, so they sang unaccompanied. Those cinemas are recalled by two sisters in this composite memoir:

Early in the morning we had to go down to the gasworks pulling a hand-cart and fetch back a hessian sack of coke before our parents would give us the money for cinema-going. Then we got to the Regent by ten o'clock. It was the smaller of the two cinemas, with only about 250 seats, and we more or less all knew each other in there. It cost 6d. in the front rows, and 9d. in the back. We had badges and membership cards, which were stamped every week. Before the films started, the owner-manager made a little speech, and read out the names of all the children who had a birthday that week. However, they didn't get a free admission – all they got was the rest of us singing *Happy Birthday* to them. Sometimes there was live entertainment. We had a magician one week, and another time it was a lady playing tunes by rubbing her index finger around the rims of glasses that had different levels of water in them. Before the films started we sang our own special song, to the tune of *Anchors Aweigh*. The words went like this:

> *We are the boys and girls*
> *Who've joined the Regent Club.*
> *We meet on Saturdays to see good films that make us gay,*
> *And when we all sing our song*
> *You'll hear it for a mile*
> *So here's to the Regent Club*
> *So smile you boys and girls of Chard, all smile.*

Among the films we saw were Roy Rogers, Old Mother Riley, Hop-along Cassidy, the Lone Ranger, Tarzan, Ma and Pa Kettle and cartoons. But best of all were the serials, such as *Flash Gordon, Buck Rogers, The Cisco Kid, King of the Rocket Men* and *Batman*, which we particularly looked forward to. All the children used to take part in them, cheering and booing like mad. Lots of dodging about went on as well. For most of those films, it's impossible now to remember in which cinema we saw them, because like most kids of our age in Chard we went to both.

The Cerdic operated from 2.00 till 4.00, and showed exactly the same kind of films as the Regent, yet their programmes never seemed to duplicate each other. Films, however, were the only thing the Cerdic did have. It was nothing like a club at all. There was no club song, no introduction from the manager. It was simply not as friendly as the Regent. This was partly because it was bigger – it held around 400 – and the seats were more luxurious. There was even a balcony, and it had some double seats for courting couples. Again, the prices were 6d. at the front and 9d. in the more luxurious ones further back, and there was a visible gap between the sixpennies and the ninepennies, because the cinema was not full.

One Saturday morning one of us somehow got the job of looking after a younger girl from a wealthy family, one and sixpence being provided for two ninepenny seats. That meant sitting apart from your friends, who were all in the sixpennies, jeering. But it was worth it, because when the young girl was safely taken home, her mother brought out coconut pyramid cakes for tea. At school each week we talked about the films, especially the serials. We read Roy Rogers annuals, and copies of *Film Fun*. Some people read the Tarzan comic, and even went so far as to write off and join the Tarzan Club. For us at that time, outside school, those two cinemas were definitely the hub of the town.

The same county provides also an example of the kind of club run by one of the regional circuits, Clifton, which in 1947 owned twenty-four cinemas and controlled another eight:

I learned in 1949 that one of my local cinemas, the Regal, Wells, part of the small Clifton chain, was going to start a children's club after the summer holidays. Application forms were available in advance, and I soon got one, filled it in and returned it. I remember well the opening day of the new club. It was Saturday the 17th of September, and film star Jane Hylton was in attendance. She was presented with membership card number one of the Wells branch of the Clifton Children's Cinema Club, and later the rest of us got one too. There was also a very distinctive badge – oval in shape, rather than round. It had the logo 'CcCc' in the centre, and around the edge were the words 'Clifton Children's Cinema Club'. The colours were maroon and pale blue. There were also special badges for Leaders, for which the colouring was white lettering on a green background.

The film programme that first day included a cartoon, a Laurel and Hardy, a travel film, episode one of the serial *Batman* and a stage performance from a local magician. At the end we were all given an ice-cream as we filed out, plus an autographed photograph of Jane Hylton, presented by her personally. A few days later a picture appeared in the local newspaper showing the throng of children on the front steps of the Regal.

The Club continued to be well supported, and as it progressed the programme often contained, between the films, live items such as dog shows and talent competitions. Every week after the cartoon the manager, 'Uncle Nick', read the list of birthdays from the stage, and the members would eagerly receive their present – a complimentary ticket for two consecutive weeks. They had, however, to wait until *Happy Birthday* had been sung to them, led from the stage by a team of Leaders. Uncle Nick must have regarded this as not very successful, because the Leaders were soon replaced by a filmlet version of *Happy Birthday*, which was fortunate, for it meant that my lack of singing ability would not prevent me from becoming a Leader. My uncle had a shoe repair shop, and shortly after the club had opened, using a magnetic sign board, I placed information about forthcoming attractions in his shop window. This was reported back to the manager, who summoned me to appear with my sign at the Regal, where to my delight I was presented with a Leader's badge.

In the climate of moral concern that pervaded the late forties, another small regional circuit, the Granadas, contributed to the research evidence by including children in the audience questionnaires which they issued that year. It had been Bernstein's practice to solicit audience comments every four years since 1927, the year before he pioneered special matinees, but children had never before been included. In 1947 the 50,000 Granadiers were invited to complete at home a questionnaire specially devised with the guidance of child psychiatrist Dr Emanuel Miller. To encourage maximum participation, Granada turned it into a competition, with Bernstein himself as one of the judges. The criteria would be completion, neatness and the reply to the last question: 'Can you think of anything which would make your Saturday morning shows better than they are?' The other nineteen were partly the standard ones about likes and dislikes in relation to stars, genres and cartoon characters, but there were also some designed to probe a little deeper, such as:

- ❏ Do you like films with children in them?
- ❏ Do you feel that you want to look away or go on watching when someone is getting hurt on the screen?
- ❏ What is the last film you remember dreaming about?
- ❏ Was the dream frightening or unpleasant in any way?
- ❏ Do you like Saturday morning shows better than shows for grown-ups?
- ❏ What is your favourite wireless programme?
- ❏ Do you like community singing?

The thousands of replies were analysed by Miller (1947) with a view to determining whether the Granada programmes could be justly accused of accentuating 'socially undesirable interests which would ultimately end in anti-social behaviour'; he also looked for clues which might guide Granada in future policy. One of his first conclusions was something that cinema managers had known for years, though they might not have phrased it like this: 'Both sexes have put the sex problem into abeyance. As this is due to a necessary psychological repression, it is a clear indication that exhibitors should be encouraged to eliminate sex themes wherever possible . . . because they are of little active interest to the child.' Out of all the Disney characters, most preferred Donald Duck; the report suggested that this was because the aggressive themes of Donald Duck cartoons represented more satisfactorily than any others

'the primitive impulse life of the child'. A finding that Field must have been pleased to read, though she would have said that she knew it already, was that children as an audience overwhelmingly liked to see children and animals on the screen. Ninety-two per cent of the respondents confirmed this.

As a corollary of liking to see themselves on the screen, a similar number preferred having their own Saturday morning show rather than go to adult performances. To be with their peer-group was a primary attraction. This was corroborated strongly by another survey carried out in the same year by a contributor to Mass-Observation, an organisation run and staffed by volunteers, and dedicated to recording the opinions and behaviour of ordinary people. Sixty children aged between nine and eleven, in the south London suburb of Wickham Common, were asked to write about going to Saturday pictures. All sixty went to the same school and lived in close proximity to two different cinema clubs. The investigation revealed that twenty-five of the thirty girls, and twenty-four of the thirty boys, attended one of the clubs regularly. Of the five girls who did not attend, one would have liked to but was unable because it clashed with a dancing class; and one of the boys who absented himself claimed that he never attended any cinema at all. Nine children, for various reasons, preferred to go at other times, sometimes with their family. (A kindred spirit to these nine would have been the contributor who, referring to the same period, comments: 'I found the other kids at matinees rough and noisy. The films I really liked were evening shows. They had Sabu and Dorothy Lamour or Betty Grable, and were in Technicolor. Saturday morning pictures were dull and pale black-and-white.') For the remaining forty-nine in Wickham Common a cinema club was the unquestioned place to go on Saturday mornings, a chance to carry on weekday friendships or enmities, a necessity if you wanted to keep up with what was being talked about and played in the playground, a place to see and be seen. The actual films were relatively unimportant as a motive for going. Illustrating this social aspect, one of the Wickham Common children wrote: 'I like the pictures better than anything else that there is. I like it because we try to do what they have done on the pictures. Sometimes we manage and sometimes we don't.' Another stated: 'When I arrive at the cinema I always look at the people in case I see anybody I know.'

From the responses to the questions about dreams no satisfactory conclusion could be drawn. Most children could not recall having had a film-induced dream of any kind; of those that could, only 19 per cent claimed to have had one that was frightening in any way. Evidence about film-induced nightmares or distress is necessarily anecdotal and idiosyncratic. The memories contributed to this book – memories that have survived many years – suggest that such fear was largely the product of each individual's personal experience, not forming a pattern from which to make social generalisations. An ex-Granadier, who was attending at the time of the survey, recalls: 'I used to worry about certain traps in cliffhangers, such as kids getting sprayed by skunks and smelling badly. This made me worry just in case the person didn't make it through to the next week. I dreamed about the kids and the skunk for ages afterwards.' Another ex-Granadier was very unhappy at a time when all around her were chuckling away: 'Strangely enough it was a Laurel and Hardy film – probably *Pack up your Troubles* – which scared me most. When they were in the trenches in the 1914–18 war, and German tanks were coming towards them, I cried.' An example of highly personal distress that became known to club organisers concerned a girl who had been taken out of a matinee, screaming and greatly upset. The incident which had triggered this response was a scene in which one character threw a custard pie at another.

On the simpler questions of taste, some apparently contradictory answers were received, perhaps because, as already suggested, the actual films were far from being the main reason for going. By an overwhelming majority, Roy Rogers was voted the most popular star with both boys and girls. (The Granadiers of Tooting had communicated their enthusiasm to Roy Rogers himself in Hollywood, and received in reply a golden statuette of his horse, Trigger, which the mayor of Wandsworth took the opportunity of being photographed holding.) Rogers received six times as many votes as the next on the list, yet the type of film he appeared in was liked least of all. Most-liked was 'historical', seemingly because of the serial *Black Arrow*, which was fresh in children's minds as it had recently played at matinees. It is about the efforts of a young seventeenth-century Red Indian brave to prevent bloodshed between his people and the white settlers.

The question on which winning the bike primarily depended – about ways of making the matinees better – produced further evidence that seeing each other, and being seen by each other, was high in children's priorities. The most frequently made request was that there should be more stage shows. By that they meant competitions for singing, quizzes, tap dancing, musical bumps, spelling bees, tugs-of-war, conjuring, acting, acrobatics, clowning, piano-playing, fancy-dress parades, carol-singing, first aid, blowing up paper bags and then bursting them – in short, anything exhibitionistic that they or the manager could think of.

There was indeed an emerging trend at all the clubs and matinees, not just those at the ABCs and Granadas, towards greater use of stage events as a complement or alternative to community-singing as a way of letting off steam before the films started. This, however, was not to reach its full dominance till the fifties. In the forties special guests, like Jane Hylton at Wells, were as common a feature of Saturday mornings as local managers and head offices could make them. Such guests normally represented either fun or uplift, but sometimes there could be an attempt to combine the two. The size of the attendance (well over 1,000 in some places) and its presumed impressionability made it an audience worth engaging with. Some of the larger clubs in the cities netted very big names indeed. A relief manager for Rank moved around a great deal from club to club, and remembers the problems that such visitors could create:

> Nearly all the children's clubs I managed had guests. Lots of them were mayors, MPs and minor celebrities, but there were a few major figures

as well. To name just two – at the Gaumont Hammersmith we had Field Marshal Viscount Montgomery in 1949 and John Wayne in February 1951. [Montgomery was in Hammersmith to receive the Freedom of the Borough, and even-handedly visited the ABC Minors at the nearby Commodore Theatre on the same day. Wayne, who was in England primarily for the première of the film *Rio Grande*, met the Acton Granadiers as well as the Hammersmith Gaumont Juniors during his stay.] Such visiting stars were scheduled to be on stage for only ten minutes, but sometimes they'd still be there after half an hour. Well, within the Rank circuit, managers were forbidden to shorten the children's show. Whatever happened, the whole film programme must be screened; no reels could be omitted. The result was that sometimes, when we had a guest celebrity in the morning, the start of the afternoon adult show was delayed, and then everything ran late for the rest of the day.

22. *When John Wayne came to England in 1951, he visited a range of cinema clubs. In Acton, west London, he presented autographed Stetsons to the two Granadiers, shown here, who had been judged 'best club members of the year'. Later all the other members got a signed photograph of the star*   (Allan Scott)

Another very high-profile club visitor was the England player Stanley Matthews, who autographed a football for the ONCC at Cleveley; but, in general, speakers of that stature were rare. Much more frequently, the stage event would be a talk from someone of more topical, transient fame, national or local. ABC Minors in various places had visits from Jim Leggard, an England Rugby League full-back; Dick Turpin, UK middleweight boxing champion; Geoff Bennett, a Midlands speedway ace; and Victor Birkett, a Channel-swimmer. In one Gaumont cinema Bruce Woodcock, then European and British Empire heavyweight boxing champion, enrolled as a member of the Junior Club; in another, one of Geoff Bennett's speedway rivals, Jack Parker, conducted a road safety quiz.

There was a third group of guests – film actors and actresses. These did not visit; rather, they made personal appearances. When she appeared at Wells CcCc, Jane Hylton had had a succession of small roles, including that of the fishmonger's assistant in *Passport to Pimlico*, and a bigger one as a member of the screen Huggett family in the first of a trio of films. By 1949, in her early twenties, she was no longer under contract to Rank, so could range more widely – and did. In addition to turning up at Wells, she distributed prizes and balloons at the reopening of the Wandsworth Granada, went hospital-visiting with Clapham Granadiers, and returned to Wandsworth to lead the singing of *Auld Lang Syne* on New Year's Eve.

Another Huggett was Petula Clark, who played the youngest daughter, 'Pet'. Unlike Hylton, Clark stuck with Rank and acted in the other two Huggett films as well – *Vote for Huggett* and *The Huggetts Abroad*. One of her earliest roles had been in the 1946 CFD two-reeler *Trouble at Townsend*, which set out to show town children the right way to behave in the country. As a rising star in the late forties, not much older than some of the club members, she made personal appearances at many cinemas, chatting and singing. In the first edition of *The Boys' and Girls' Cinema Club Annual*, published in 1948, she said that several fourteen-year-old boys had written to her proposing marriage after seeing her. However, this sighting was very unlikely to have occurred on a Saturday morning because, with the exception of *Trouble at Townsend*, the films she was in were too new and expensive for the club circuit.

A good male example of the kind of actor who was in demand for personal appearances was Don Stannard. A former swimmer, boxer and commando, he got into acting after the war, and was chosen for the lead role in three films based on the immensely successful BBC radio cliff-hanger *Dick Barton, Special Agent*. The first of them was also made available in serial form, and was shown at matinees. While these films were appearing, Stannard was willing to oblige. He drove to Swiss Cottage Odeon, for example, to talk to club members as part of Hampstead Road Safety Week, 1949.

For the studio to whom such a player was under contract, there was a

23. Don Stannard, star of the three Dick Barton films, with Acton Granadiers in 1950 around the time that Dick Barton at Bay *was released* (Allan Scott)

second point to such visits, beyond that of pleasing or exciting the children. It was that newspapers, especially local ones, could usually be prompted to turn up and take photographs of the star signing autographs, or surrounded by eager young fans, or having a badge pinned on by a club member, or taking a sock on the jaw from the smallest boy in the audience, or in whatever other amusing tableau could be devised. The newspaper story accompanying the picture would of course mention the club, the name of the cinema, and the film the star was currently appearing in. The presence of the children, innocent and enthusiastic, gave extra pictorial value to the situation. For this reason club members were even invited on occasion to lend their photogenic presence to events that took place in a cinema other than their local, on a day other than Saturday. For example, on a Thursday evening in April 1948 a group of children from the Temple Fortune ONCC in north-west London were among the gathering in the foyer of the Leicester Square Odeon (which did not have its own club) for the Royal Première of Olivier's *Hamlet*. From behind a tasselled cordon, standing next to a marble pillar, the spruced-up children watched as King George and Queen Elizabeth, accompanied by their daughters Elizabeth and Margaret, entered the cinema, where The Queen was presented with a bouquet. This conjunction of royalty and Roy Rogers fans was captured in press photographs. Undoubtedly, Rank believed that by giving the children that unique opportunity he was doing them good. They could not be anything other than enriched by proximity to two of the pillars of the nation – the King and the Bard. But it was also a public-relations exercise: the children's presence in the photographs was a symbol of JARO's concern for social welfare, for the future, for democracy. At a time when the Wheare committee had just started its investigations, the children at the *Hamlet* Royal Premiere were part of JARO's campaign to make a distinction in the public mind between their clubs and the rest – in short, to be accepted as not the problem, but the solution.

There is unfortunately no record of whether the children were allowed, or encouraged, to stay to see the film. The case could have been argued both ways. On the one hand, it was Shakespeare, it had a U certificate and it starred CFD graduate Jean Simmons. On the other hand, it did not start till eight, and it was over two and a quarter hours long. The children, who presumably had school next day as usual, would not have got home till around eleven if they stayed to see the whole film. Further, though it had a U certificate, it contained language which provoked outrage from the American Catholic Legion of Decency, and which the ONCC would never have allowed to be heard on a Saturday morning: for example, Hamlet accuses his mother of lying 'in the rank sweat of a lascivious bed', and of having gone 'with such dexterity to incestuous sheets'.

The desire for respectability was surely behind another royal occasion when, in the same year, the King's mother, Queen Mary, visited the Junior Club at the Kilburn Gaumont, flanked by Rank himself and his two club controllers. Whether she stayed to see *Jungle Queen* is unclear. Not to be outdone, the ABC soon afterwards seized the opportunity to seek a connection between matinees and monarchy. From the Minors of Lewisham, who attended a cinema called The Prince of Wales, a letter was sent to the Queen, inviting her to put on their waiting list the name of her infant grandson, Prince Charles. Perhaps they pointed out that as a Minor, rather than a Rank club member, he could start attending at the age of five rather than seven, and would not have to promise to be loyal to his grandfather.

Many of the visitors to clubs and matinees in the forties must have been looked at and listened to with interest, pleasure, excitement or respect. Some were definitely not so welcome, particularly the MPs and mayors who came to preach or reward civic virtue (and hoped to get their picture in the local paper). One memoir recalls a Saturday morning visit at Southgate Odeon (where Tom had yearned for a bike earlier in the decade) from the MP for that constituency:

Goodness knows what made him do it, but our local MP, Sir Beverley Baxter – famous for having been in Parliament the highest number of years and given the lowest number of speeches – was persuaded to turn up and give prizes. There was always a birthday prize and other awards.

He tried to make a speech and was completely howled down. He was very much an 'old general' type, small and tubby. He was very condescending and attempted to ingratiate himself with all of us ten- to twelve-year-olds. It went down very badly. Even then, rather than see him as a figure of authority, I saw him as a fool, an irrelevant Blimp figure.

Amidst all the diversity of practice among the matinees and clubs of the forties, one factor was constant for all children – the condition of the prints that were shown. All through the five years between Mayer first writing his chapter on children's cinema clubs, and the publication of the Wheare report that drew a line under the debate it provoked, nobody ever challenged his claim that the prints – because they did not reach the clubs till every other commercial possibility had been exhausted – were often in a dreadful state. The situation was even worse for the independents than for the big circuits, because the circuits could offer the distributors block booking, which was much more administratively convenient and economical than dealing with individual cinemas one at a time. The circuits therefore generally got priority.

Half of the features, and most of the serials, shown in clubs and matinees in the second half of the forties had been made before the war. Their age did not make them bad films, but it did mean that the prints had travelled extensively. Wartime and post-war films could be equally well-worn. Even the CFD/CEF films, which went round the club circuit only, were soon imperfect because the number of copies that were struck was small, so each one had to work hard every Saturday in a different place for several years. OCM 4 , made during the war, was still doing Saturday morning service in Rank clubs on New Year's Eve 1949.

The chief operator's condition report book for Dudley Odeon, recording the twelve months from May 1949, had a good word to say for only one of the 221 prints which were screened for ONCC members during that period. *Players of Merit, Number Six, Fred Perry* was reported to be in 'fair' condition. Every one of the other 220 prints was, at best, 'roped' (having a scratch on the emulsion going all the way through a reel) and 'strained' (the sprocket holes having been placed under excessive pressure). Many of them were in a far worse state than just that. *The Mighty Tundra*, an Alaskan adventure from 1936, was described as: 'General condition very bad. Leaders and tails missing. Identification of reels difficult. Perforations badly broken. Numerous bad joins.' Made ten years later, *Old Mother Riley Overseas* was no better: 'Very dry and brittle condition. Edges of film mutilated. Numerous very bad joins. Perforations badly broken. Half-way reel one joined wrong side up.' Other words and phrases that recur in the reports are: 'buckled', 'end badly cut', 'dirty and oily', 'sound-track badly sprocket-marked', 'disgusting condition', 'very loud hum from scored sound track', 'sound track scratched', 'no censor' and 'leaders, ends and sound-track badly mutilated'.

During that twelve-month period in Dudley the American serials – *Burn 'em Up Barnes*, *Law of the Wild* and *Jungle Menace* – were all from the thirties; but new serials were still being made, and now, unlike the situation in the previous decade, were shown very little outside the Saturday morning circuit. Consequently such serials as *Superman*, released in the United States in July 1948, and *King of the Rocket Men*, one year later, reached club and matinee screens in, initially at least, very good condition, and in some cases made a more lasting impression than anything else that was seen in the late forties.

Such moments of clarity were, however, rare. The general run of prints caused problems of all kinds, not just technical and visual, as a contributor – who as a boy went to ABC Saturday shows in Woodford during the two years before the war, and after it got a job as a projectionist with the Rank circuit in Leyton and later Becontree – recalls:

> For projectionists, the Saturday morning shift was terrible. We only got three bob while the organist got ten, and the manager got fifteen – and all he had to do was stand on the stage and sing to the kids! But what made it terrible was not the money. It was the condition of the prints. There was more work in preparing the matinee programme than there was in sorting out the whole of the rest of the week. Now, in those days every cinema had a cat, to keep rats and mice down, and in the Gaumonts there was an allowance of half-a-crown a week to buy meat scraps for it. When we were doing the Saturday morning shift we always used to joke that we were only getting sixpence more than the cat. The condition of the cartoons and the interest films was not so bad – they were often from Disney – but after that came the serial and the feature. Usually their condition was diabolical, absolutely cut to ribbons, not fit to screen. Sometimes they'd be scheduled to run for, say, seventy minutes, but they'd come out at only sixty-two minutes, because of all the cuts.
>
> When the children were coming in there used to be a board outside telling parents what time the show would end, as a lot of them used to come and meet their kids. Also, the police liked to know, as there had been several accidents from children rushing out into the main road. That was why managers liked to finish at the advertised time. So sometimes, when the screening had ended early, they used to just keep the children in there until it was the right time to let them out.
>
> The Gaumont shows were much the same during the forties and fifties as they had been at the ABC when I went as a boy, except for the community-singing. That was new, but some of the films, such as *Flash Gordon*, were the same. In fact I was projecting, in the forties and fifties, films which I'd seen as a boy in the thirties. I bet it was even the same prints in some cases too!

11 *Happy and Wholesome*

The children's cinema show has come to stay . . . Society owes it to the children to see that when they visit the cinema they get the best entertainment possible, without vulgarity on the one hand, or dullness on the other.

(Wheare report, 1950)

The publication of Wheare's Departmental Committee Report on 5 May 1950 was a watershed in the story of Saturday cinema. The culmination of two decades of argument, it was the comprehensive survey that the Birmingham Vigilance Committee had campaigned for nineteen years previously. Sir Charles Grant Robertson, however, would not have welcomed its findings. On the specific issue of Saturday cinema (as opposed to the wider situation which was also part of its remit) its general conclusion was this:

> On our visits we found much to criticise. There were many examples of deplorable films being shown to children. But, when we consider the size and scope of this enterprise in children's entertainment, and the fact that for the most part no particular standards are required of them, our general opinion is that it is admirable that on the whole so many of these exhibitions are run as well as they are. The children undoubtedly feel happy and at ease, even in large cinemas, as evidenced by their self-possessed and purposeful entry, either alone or in small parties, and their quick settling down in their seats . . . We formed the impression that all the evidence offered to us was inspired by a desire that children should enjoy happy and wholesome recreation when attending the cinema and should be wisely safeguarded from any dangers which might result from their attendance . . . Entertainment of this kind seems to us worthy of all the help that can be given it.

The committee of twenty people had started from the assumption that nobody knew anything. Over the course of two years they had thirty-two meetings in London, one in Edinburgh and one in Cardiff. They visited children's cinema exhibitions in London, Edinburgh, Glasgow, Cardiff and the Rhondda Valley (where shows took place under the auspices of the Miners' Welfare Fund). The 270 witnesses they interviewed included representatives from the film trade, the legal profession, Cardiff Corporation, Birmingham University, the Catholic Education Council, the Educational Institute of Scotland, Jewish religious bodies, the Standing Conference of Women's Organisations of Glasgow, the Undeb Cymru Fydd (New Wales Union) and the National Association for Mental Health. Rank represented his organisation in person. Among the individuals who testified on their own behalf were Mayer, Miller, Parnaby and Woodhouse. Written memoranda were received from a further forty-four organisations and individuals, including the Bourneville Film Society, the Feltham and Sunbury-on-Thames Local Joint Road Safety Organisation, the Royal Scottish Society for the Prevention of Cruelty to Children, the Public Morality Council, the Welsh Society of the Institute of Christian Education and the Southend-on-Sea Youth Parliament.

Unlike the NCPM Inquiry of 1917 and the NCW/BFI Conference of 1946, the Wheare Committee did not formally interview children. Mary Field, among others, may well have suggested to them that in a formal interview context children are likely to try to say what they think the questioner wants to hear. Instead, individual members of the Committee, with the help of a free pass, made visits on their own to different cinemas in England, Scotland and Wales. As well as seeing the films, they made a point of chatting informally to the children among whom they were sitting, and to some of the monitors or committee members. Over one hundred such visits were reported on. Additionally, they got information from secondary-school children who had attended clubs or matinees when younger; and from 1,000 mothers.

The fundamental set of figures that the report threw up showed that 90 per cent of schoolchildren in Britain visited a cinema sometimes; and that more than half of them went at least once a week. Broadly, the matinee audiences, totalling around a million, consisted of 25 per cent who went to that show only, and 75 per cent who also went at some other time. The Committee was of the opinion that attendance once a week was enough for anyone, on the ground that extra-curricular interests and school work were liable to be interfered with by excessive cinema-going. Given their general approval of Saturday cinema, their preferred option would obviously have been that the weekly visit should take place within that structure.

There was north–south differentiation in respect of the timing of children's Saturday shows. In London and the South of England they most commonly took place in the morning; in Wales, the North of England and Scotland, the norm was for shows to take place in the afternoon. The ones that took place in the morning almost all provided something apart from the screenings: they were 'clubs' of a kind, whether or not they used that term. Backed in the main by a circuit, they either ran at a loss or, at best, broke even, and they had to apply to their local authority for a special licence in order to be able to operate. The afternoon shows, on the other hand, were predominantly commercial matinees. Their running costs were lower than those of the morning clubs because, since they were opening the cinema only within normal licensing hours, they did not have extra wages to pay. If these shows were not profitable, they closed down. This is not to say that there were no clubs at all in the North or Wales – there were (such as the two Gaumonts and the Roxy in Edinburgh). Equally, it is not to say that none of the afternoon shows were run as clubs – some areas, such as Liverpool, refused to grant Odeons and ABCs a licence to operate in the mornings. But the general pattern was one of morning shows in London, and afternoon shows in Cardiff and Edinburgh. Numerically, there were about 5 per cent more afternoon shows than morning shows, but since they tended to happen in smaller cinemas, the actual attendance figures came out as more or less equal – about half a million each every Saturday.

There was, however, a certain section of people for whom it did not matter whether children's shows took place in the morning or afternoon. What mattered to them was simply that it was always a Saturday. The Committee heard that the religious welfare of Jewish children had been adversely affected in areas where there were popular cinema clubs or matinees. The attraction of sticking with the peer-group meant that some Jewish children were tempted into cinemas and thereby away from synagogue worship or general Sabbath observance. (Gerald Kaufman MP, in his autobiography (1985), recalls that in the thirties his father's devout Jewish orthodoxy meant that he was forbidden to attend Saturday matinees.) The Wheare Committee consequently recommended that, in areas with large Jewish populations, the industry should arrange clubs or special screenings for Jewish children early on Sunday afternoons, before the normal time of opening. This recommendation seems to have come to nothing.

Physical welfare presented problems as well. Overall, the average ratio of children to attendants at clubs and matinees was satisfactory. However, this picture included many cinemas in which 'too much reliance was being placed on child monitors and stewards'. The worst example of this that they came across was a cinema where there were only two adult attendants to supervise over 800 children. Against this were set such cinemas as the one which contained 1,500 children and employed seven retired people as extra stewards. The Committee's general recommendation on this point was that nothing should be left to chance; there should be complete consistency across Britain. All children's shows should need to be specially licensed, whether they took place in the morning or in the afternoon, and the licence should impose adequate precautions. The Committee noted that since the early thirties, within the LCC all licences for special shows had precluded the admission of children under seven; but on balance thought that unnecessarily restrictive. Children knew how to look after themselves in large buildings once they had started school; five was therefore acceptable as a starting age.

So far the Committee were just tinkering in the margins. They also had four proposals to make that went closer to the heart of the matter, and a bouquet to award. Most radically, they recommended that the licensing authorities' normal practice of making children's attendance at A films conditional upon their being accompanied by a parent or guardian was totally unworkable and should be discontinued. Research had shown that within the course of one week, of the children who went to the ordinary cinema, over 60 per cent had seen at least one A film. The reason was that it was difficult to avoid A films as 80 per cent of the programmes on offer were either 'double A' or 'mixed'. New feature films, which were the main attractions, were three times more likely to be A than U. An all-U programme was hard to find, even for people prepared to travel – which most were not. Therefore, since by one means or another vast numbers of children were seeing A films despite the 'must be accompanied' rule, the Committee proposed that henceforth the A and U categories should be merely advisory, and that an entirely new category – X – should be created. No child under sixteen would be allowed into a cinema at any time when an X film was part of the programme. The X certificate would subsume the existing 'Horror' category, and add to it brutality, sex, and adult social problems such as prostitution and drug addiction. As a corollary of these censorship proposals, Wheare believed it highly desirable to bring the law as it affected children in Scotland into line with the situation in England and Wales.

There was also wounding criticism of the ONCC promise. The basic complaint came from educationists who rejected in principle the idea that virtue can be injected like that. A complementary line of attack the Committee heard was that any point the promise might in theory have was completely destroyed by the fact of its being made collectively, and by the way it was hastily gabbled without regard to its meaning. The ONCC had tried to give the promise purpose and dignity by insisting that children should stand up for it, and that all attendants should remain still; but it had become, like grace before a meal, just something that had to be got through before the fun could begin. The Committee concluded, after considering all pre-screening rituals, that the collective repetition of the promise ought to be discontinued. Club and matinee songs were, however, harmless. The ONCC must have felt very glad at having got rid if its controversial original ('We are a hundred thousand strong . . .') before the Wheare committee could hear it.

In respect of the serials, the Committee pretty much agreed with Mayer, Parnaby and Woodhouse, reinforced by the personal testimony which those three gave. None of the Committee had watched a complete serial, but they had no hesitation in describing them as 'loosely constructed and often incoherent'. More urgently, a torture scene at the end of one particular serial episode was regarded by the Committee as 'horrific'. One 'deplorable' serial that was going the rounds had turned out to be classified as an A. They recorded seeing children clearly frightened by violent action in westerns, Tarzans and gangster films. Mothers had reported that visits to the cinema sometimes resulted in children suffering nightmares or incontinence. While recognising that there is much individual variation in the causes of fright as experienced by particular children, the Committee nonetheless felt that 'the immediate effects of fright and over-excitement are so obvious and well-attested that they constitute in themselves a strong warning' against the screening of 'the kind of serial or feature film whose appeal is based on suspense or violence'. The report therefore agreed with mainstream educational and psychological opinion in recommending that exhibition of the serial 'in its present form' should be discontinued.

What they meant was that they had seen the series and serials made by CFD/CEF, and considered that the note of suspense on which these ended each week was not excessive. At the same time they provided the continuity of character which children enjoyed. In fact, overall, the Committee were unanimous in praise of everything CEF stood for, not just the serials *Dusty Bates* and *The Voyage of Peter Joe*. Field quotes with obvious relish the following passage from Wheare:

> We should like to pay high tribute to the work of the Advisory Council and the CEF for the variety and quality of the films for which they have been jointly responsible. It is a work of great originality and enterprise. Whether or not they have in every case sponsored the ideal film for children – and this they do not claim to have done – seems to us comparatively unimportant. We record with approval the existence of this machinery for the production of entertainment films for children on practical and well-considered lines, and are impressed by the imaginative grasp and pioneering spirit shown by those who direct it. Enjoyable, and often beautiful and interesting films are being increasingly made available to children through their efforts. We attach the greatest importance to the continuance and development of these projects.

Wheare's recommendation that American serials should be withdrawn was completely ignored. The proposal for the creation of an X category was implemented, but not for another five years. The praise handed out to CEF was followed by much swifter action: within three months of the report's publication, the unit was closed down.

12   *Infra-Red for Danger*

With children reared at Chippenham
The mildest plots go down,
But pictures with a zip in 'em
Are 'musts' at Camden Town.
With sawn-off shotgun rippin' 'em
The villain wins renown,
And films that make a nipper numb
From nervousness in Chippenham
Have not a hope of grippin' 'em
In callous Camden Town.

Percy Cudlipp (1954)

From the moment she took over CFD/CEF, Field was driven by a desire to get reliable information about children's responses to films. Managers' reports were not scientific enough for her. Even if they were accurate, they related to whole audiences and to overall appreciation. She wanted to know spontaneous individual as well as collective responses to particular sequences in a variety of types of film, and then to analyse the parts in relation to the whole.

Her first attempt at systematic study used sound only. During a normal Rank club show, in 1947, a microphone was positioned to record the sounds made by the audience as they watched a Disney cartoon, an issue of OCM, a travel documentary and *Bush Christmas*. The film's soundtrack was also recorded, on the same tape, so that it was possible later to synchronise the running of the film with the sounds of the audience response. This sound-only approach had the great advantage that since the microphone was relatively inconspicuous, and did not need an operator on the spot all the time, it did not inhibit children's responses.

It had obvious limitations too, and in 1948 CEF set about getting images to go with the sound. At that time, the use of infra-red plates was in its infancy, but it promised a way of capturing children's facial expressions and body language without them being self-conscious about it, because infra-red makes no noise and emits no light. Arrangements were therefore made to take infra-red pictures of an ONCC audience at Swiss Cottage, London, at various points during a film screening. The film was again *Bush Christmas*, which at that time was on its second tour of the Rank club circuits. CEF knew well that it was a highly successful film, but they wanted to be able to say why, so that they could do the trick more often. They also wanted to see whether it contained mistakes, from the point of view of child comprehension. Accordingly a variety of shots – sixteen in all – were picked out. The plan was that as each shot appeared on the screen, Field would nudge the photographer, and a group of children, always the same one, would have their response to it recorded without anyone being disturbed. However, the volatility of infra-red in trials – perfect at one moment, useless at the next – meant that at most only a 50 per cent success rate would be achieved. Accordingly, at a late stage, it was decided to abandon infra-red, and use ordinary flash photography instead. Even this was not satisfactory because the audience resented the flashes that pierced the darkness of the auditorium and broke their concentration every five minutes; and the children near the camera realised that they were the object of attention. Field (1949) describes what happened next:

> By the time the eighth light had flashed a small boy not more than nine walked solemnly down a long aisle, and addressed the picture-takers. He was confident that a reasonable request made to reasonable people would be effective. He felt he represented the fourteen hundred children present. With directness and politeness he spoke. 'Stop it', he said, and returned to his seat. So we stopped.

The eight photographs, matched up with the eight frame stills, seemed to point to the way ahead. Of the two boys nearest to the camera, one had seen the film before, on its first tour, while to the other it was completely new. As the opening title, *Bush Christmas*, appears on the screen, the second one is leaning back with his hands behind his head, looking fairly neutral. Field comments: 'He challenges the film to entertain him if it can.' When the camera pans to reveal that the horse thieves have followed the children home, the second boy has his mouth open and his tongue slightly out. Later, when the image on the screen is a long-shot of horsemen splashing through a river, the first boy is captured pointing at the screen, possibly helping his friend to understand it. Meanwhile a little girl nearby has remained in deep concentration all the while, hardly changing her expression or bodily posture for thirty-five minutes. Already, with this evidence reinforcing the impressions of various observers, the CEF were rewriting their guidelines to directors, telling them to make sure that long-shots were readily comprehensible. The running-time was also adjusted on the basis of this and other evidence; never again was a British children's film as long as *Bush Christmas*, despite its popularity and prizes. Henceforth, fifty to sixty minutes was the norm.

Field was determined to carry on, though obviously the project would have to use infra-red, despite its imperfections, not flash. For two years there was no money to continue with it, and for one of them, after CEF closed down, she was not even working on the production side of the business; rather, she was a censor. Still, she was not reticent about her plans. She spoke frequently in public about the work of CEF, and mentioned how she hoped to learn a great deal about children through the use of infra-red photography. On one occasion, in early 1950, when she was speaking to the parents of a primary school in London, one of the fathers there happened to be Maurice Ambler, a freelance photographer.

Ambler was not aware of Wheare or the impending publication of its report. His own son was at that time regularly attending the Bromley Odeon on Saturday mornings, and recalls it as 'a joyous time'. Ambler therefore had no personal cause for alarm about the films being shown to children when he had the idea of trying to achieve what Mary Field had failed to do – take a series of infra-red photographs of children's conduct at a Saturday show. He hoped to catch a variety of shots of interesting, spontaneous behaviour – kids running around, pea-shooters and catapults in action, oranges being eaten, peel being thrown, drinking, scuffles, laughter, tears – anything other than neutral absorption. Having acquired and tried out the latest infra-red photography equipment, he contacted the manager of the Tooting Granada and arranged to go there one Saturday morning. From a side-balcony, he and his assistant had a good view of a large section of the audience, so he took a series of photographs showing the children in a range of attitudes and activities, and offered them to *Picture Post*. They were interested, but not entirely convinced, and suggested that Ambler should go back and try again. He did, still not looking for anything in particular, just any subject that would make a good picture. This time the picture editor found something in them that he liked, and bought the right to publish selections from what Ambler had to offer. From the large number of photographs that Ambler submitted, he chose a few that had been taken at the end of the morning during the screening of the serial – *Jungle Girl* – and concentrated on the theme of fright. Shots of individual children showing signs of distress were isolated from their context and blown up. Children who seemed unconcerned were completely ignored – there was no story in them.

A *Picture Post* reporter, Derek Monsey, who had not been present with Ambler at the show, was then commissioned to write a commentary to go with the pictures that the magazine intended to publish. The resultant article, which

appeared in the issue of 6 May 1950, was headed *Can't We Do Better Than This*? It did not seek to describe the actual experience of being present with children for a complete Saturday morning show. Nor did it show any awareness of the imminent Wheare report. Instead, it gave some figures for national attendance, deferred to Mayer as the acknowledged expert on the subject, and then used the pictures as a way of illustrating the thesis that 'There should be *some* limit to the amount of harm parents *and* film exhibitors are prepared to do to the minds of our next generation.' The captions completed the work of interpretation.

Together, the pictures and the article did what *Picture Post* must have hoped for: they created a sensational controversy. This became a selling point of the following week's issue. Ambler himself did not know what impact his photographs had had until he noticed that posters for the following week's issue consisted of five words: STORM OVER CHILDREN'S FILM SHOWS. This 'storm' erupted in various places, including Birmingham Cathedral, where the Archbishop of Canterbury, Dr Geoffrey Fisher, mentioned the *Picture Post* story in a sermon, saying: 'This is a ghastly illustration of some of the destructive elements that beat down upon children as they grow up today.' In September the *Church of England Newspaper* reprinted one of the *Picture Post* shots, with an inaccurate and tendentious commentary: 'Photographed here is part of the audience at a special cinema show for children. On the screen a woman is being run over by a machine. Note how some children look horrified, and others hide their heads in terror while this cruelty is enacted.' Ambler received enquiries from other countries too, and was able to make several more sales. In professional and financial terms, it was the biggest thing he had done up to that time.

Huge waves of readers' letters reached *Picture Post*, from people primarily shocked by the photos and agreeing with the article. A familiar note was struck in this letter from Manchester: 'How can cinema managers possibly show such horror films to young children and get away with it? Compare the expressions of the young audience listening to, say, a Hallé concert.' This was echoed by a letter from Andover: 'Seldom have I seen more impressive

---

24, 25. (opposite): *These two illustrations show the wider view as taken by Ambler, and the extracted images which* Picture Post *preferred and printed. The* Picture Post *caption for the boy was: 'One Who Is All Alone in Terror. No-one pays any attention to him. The others have their own fears to worry about. He just puts his head down and waits for it to end.' The girl was described as: 'One Who Is Overwhelmed By Distress.' The caption added: 'She went to the matinee as usual on Saturday morning. Some of it she enjoyed. This part she didn't want to see. But even if she did want to see it, should she really be encouraged to?'*

26. *Maurice Ambler's first intimation of how effective* Picture Post's *use of his Tooting Granada infra-red studies had been*

photographs, and with your very wide circulation this will bring home the horror to so many who, like myself, had no idea that such a terrifying ordeal could be experienced by children in this country.' From Belfast came an invocation of Irish history: 'The young today learn more in cinemas than in their seminaries. The picture house has become nursery and alma mater; it equips its pupils with a complete set of false values and pernicious principles. And it teaches the young how to shoot . . . .' Kingston Hill, Surrey, contributed an analogy between cinema and religion: 'The film for children which you rightly condemn in your issue must have been devised by curiously insensitive souls. Yet the Saturday morning cinema has practically replaced the Sunday afternoon teaching.'

Among the refutations was a letter from the sixteen-year-old chairman of a Rank club in Somerset. She too was horrified, but for a different reason: 'We have now got *Jungle Girl* running as a serial. I can truly say that I have never seen any of the children in this club doing the things the children are supposed to be doing in your photographs.' A more detailed rebuttal was made by a writer from Cambridge who seemed to be the only contributor to know anything about *Jungle Girl* other than what was shown in the two frames printed by *Picture Post*: 'What is so dreadful about *Jungle Girl*? I saw several chapters of it, and, compared with many more pretentious films, it seemed good clean fun. Most of the fighting is hand-to-hand, and few of the characters are sufficiently mechanised even to possess a revolver.' This letter went on to demonstrate the total inaccuracy and lack of understanding in a caption under a *Jungle Girl* frame still. Finally, in June, the general reaction of the film trade, as represented by the CEA, was printed. Alone among all the letters, this one perceived that the article had separated moments and individuals from their context in time and space:

> Throughout a film a child's emotions are effervescent and superficial, and if the concluding moment of a serial is on a thrilling note, the reaction in a child's mind is momentary. Two minutes later he is laughing uproariously at some comic episode. From your pictures one could conclude that the outstanding feature was fear... The fact is that children exhibit an emotion more freely than adults, that it is momentary and superficial, and any effects pass as soon as the next item in which they are interested appears.

The trade newspaper *Today's Cinema* also joined in, challenging *Picture Post* to publish 'a whole series of pictures', showing the range and evanescence of children's emotions. To this the editor of *Picture Post*, Tom Hopkinson, retorted that that was unnecessary, because the article had only been about '*some* children at *some* film shows'. He did not mention that the evidence for this article about *some* children at *some* film shows had been manufactured from photographs that were about *all* children at *one* film show.

Nineteen months after the furore caused by publication of the *Picture Post* story, Mary Field managed to resume work on her own infra-red project. By that time she had finished her year with the BBFC and was set to become the first executive officer of a newly formed pan-industry organisation called the Children's Film Foundation (CFF). Her purpose in framing the project was to get confirmation or rebuttal or new enlightenment on a range of questions relating to children's response to such aspects as dialogue, beauty, boredom, the relative delights of anticipation and surprise, the effect of big close-ups and more. She initially drew up a plan to record the reactions of children in five diverse parts of England: Barnstaple, a West Country fishing village; Chippenham, a country town in Gloucester; West Ham, in London; Hull, the Yorkshire seaport; and Middlesbrough, Yorkshire, a centre for heavy industry. Each audience was to be photographed at twenty selected points during the screening of each of two separate programmes, one of ordinary commercial films, the other of CEF films. That would have involved the use of 200 infra-red plates. This project became twice as ambitious when the chance arose, and was accepted,

Opening Shot

Foreign speech

27a. *Of these shots, Field wrote: 'The poacher fires a gun before the lettering of the main titles appears. How should one catch the attention of children at the outset of a film?' Later, 'the schoolmaster addresses the class. He speaks in German. How will British children react to foreign speech?'*

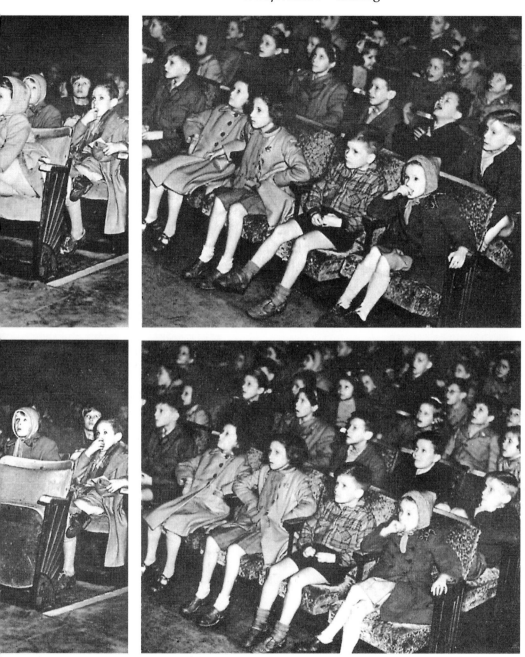

The greater willingness of the Dunfermline children to give the German dialogue a chance may have been due to the fact that they were there on a school day, with teachers around, and had not had to pay sixpence to get in

Close-up violence

Anticipation

27b. 'Is violence in close-up frightening?' was the question in Field's mind when planning the shots of children watching the hero and his friend facing Indian arrows. The shots studying anticipation were taken at the moment when Katie, the heroine, thinks she will have to smoke the peace pipe. 'Will the audience grasp the possibility and find it amusing or unpleasant? Will the sexes react differently?'

Each of the Dunfermline groups was photographed at thirty-eight points during their day in the cinema. After studying them all, Field suggested that children from mining communities were readier to wait and see how an unpromising film would develop; yet overall, she thought, the skilled artisan group was the most intelligently appreciative of all ten

Effect of music

Adult conversation

27c. 'The chief's son issues a challenge to battle. How will the audience be affected by the dramatic music at this moment?' One of the factors behind this question was that it had sometimes been reported that in matinees the dramatic use of music was frequently drowned in chatting and therefore went unnoticed. In the adult conversation, on a verandah, the points being discussed are essential to the development of the plot – 'but will the children listen?'

For thirty years after the analysis of these photographs, it was a rule with the Children's Film Foundation to keep scenes of adult dialogue to an absolute minimum, unless there was a hidden child overhearing it

of extending it by including children from the same town but with four different types of socio-economic background. This was in Dunfermline, Scotland, where the Director of Education was able to organise things so that on successive weekdays the children in front of the camera were agricultural, mining, skilled artisan and general. The whole proposal was then topped up by the inclusion of another group, bound together not by socio-economic background but by the fact that they had not attained the normal educational level for their age. The project referred to them as 'special'. In all, nearly 400 infra-red plates would now be needed, and these, plus administrative and technical support, would be expensive. Since Field no longer had Rank money to spend and CFF money was ring-fenced for production only, she applied to the Carnegie United Kingdom Trust, which too is based in Dunfermline. (In her application, she dismissed the *Picture Post* article and photographs as irrelevant: 'These efforts could not in any way be said to meet the insistent demand of the Wheare report for a scientifically directed survey of the effect of cinema on children.') Carnegie granted the necessary money.

One of the policy decisions taken in respect of the programmes was that all the children should be seeing the films for the first time. That ruled out both *Bush Christmas* and the normal commercial westerns; as a result, in both cases the film that finally filled the feature slot was not entirely routine. For the CEF programme it was *The Mysterious Poacher*, which had made its debut earlier that year, just before CEF closed down. In order to be able to feature younger actors it had been shot overseas, in Austria. The dialogue in the film was German, with an English commentary explaining it. This technique was still unusual, so reaction to it was one of the things that the infra-red studies were intended to reveal. The feature in the commercial programme – *Comanche Territory* – was in colour, which was rare for a matinee; and it had not even finished its general release, which was unprecedented. Its showing was only made possible by the fact that, as urged by Wheare, all sectors of the film industry were co-operating in the service of children.

There was one very unfortunate omission from the infra-red schedule – the serial. Since that was the part of the programme that had incurred disapproval from Wheare, a scientifically directed series of photographs that showed children's reactions to it in the context of a whole morning – unlike the isolating cut-out that *Picture Post* had employed – might have proved a welcome corrective. Field decided, however, that there was no satisfactory way of arranging that all cinemas would show the same episode of the same serial at the time that the infra-red team were there. (As it turned out, all five clubs visited were in fact showing the same serial – *Congo Bill* – but not the same episodes.) In Dunfermline the question did not arise because there the screenings were all conducted in school time, so the children had no fixed expectations. They therefore saw no serial at all in the commercial programme, but, like the clubs, saw an episode of *The Voyage of Peter Joe* as part of the CEF show in the afternoon.

After months of planning, the twenty sessions took place as scheduled between December 1951 and May 1952, but with Camden Town substituted as the London site because of total technical failure on the first two Saturday mornings at West Ham. This time, of the 390 pictures which were planned, only 5 per cent failed to come out. All of them were published exactly as they were taken; where the camera had failed to work properly, the space was left blank. For each picture information was given as to where it was taken (except for the special children); a frame still showed what was on the screen at that moment; and, in the case of the Dunfermline children, their socio-economic background was stated. Because it was a charitable body that had paid for the experiment, the material was offered for anyone in the world to interpret in their own way and, it was hoped, use in the construction of a theory of child audiences and how best to make films for them.

Field's own conclusion from the comparison between special films and commercial films was that, in general, the children had enjoyed both. What was encouraging to her, however, was that the pattern of response to the CEF films had been broadly the same in all ten groups, whereas Woody Woodpecker, *Congo Bill* and *Comanche Territory* had provoked different responses in different places. In her report on the experiment, Field noted particularly a contrast between London and Gloucestershire: 'The children of Camden Town, a notably tough area even during air raids, appear almost unmoved by what distresses Chippenham, where many of the children come into the cinema from the surrounding countryside.' Among the guidelines that she drew out for specialised film-making, some pragmatic, some philosophical, were these:

- ❑ Sudden unexpected action may cause fright or, alternatively, fail to register.
- ❑ The child's idea of beauty in a film is not the same as that of adults. Children find a travelling shot more satisfying than static composition.
- ❑ Close-ups appear to have less power to frighten in cartoons than in live action.
- ❑ There is a great drop in audience attention when the children on the screen sit down. Thus money can be saved, and interest retained, by not writing any meals into the storyline.
- ❑ Children take great pleasure in anticipation.
- ❑ Children tend to copy the actions of characters with whom they are in sympathy.
- ❑ Some apparent boredom comes from the exhaustion of concentration, rather than from rejection of the film.
- ❑ Film-viewing is a two-way affair; the pleasure of it depends very largely on what the audience itself contributes.

The work of analysing the pictures and writing the report was done in the first year of Field's tenure of the job of executive officer of the Children's Film Foundation. The twenty Carnegie strips of infra-red responses to the screen therefore became a standard reference point in discussions of films for children, and exercised a strong influence on the next thirty years of the children's matinee movement.

13 *Lollipops*

Choirs, concert-parties, football and cricket teams, visits to places of interest, community singing, fancy-dress parties and parades, talks by prominent people, visits by celebrities, road-safety campaigns, pet shows, prize competitions, and activities on behalf of old people and children in need of help, are only a few among the host of interests that have helped to make the cinema-club movement a power in the land.

(The Boys' and Girls' Cinema Clubs Annual, 1952)

We are all united in our street and all muck about together – so I should just be left behind if I didn't go.

(Child quoted in Wheare Report, 1950)

Many factors combined to make the first half of the fifties the golden age for children's Saturday cinema. After the Wheare report, the movement felt itself secure from external threat, though the attacks by no means ceased completely. In April 1951 the *Daily Mirror* ran an article headed 'Children's Saturday Morning Films are a Pest', and later that year a speaker at the annual conference of the London Schools' Film Society won loud applause from several hundred teachers by attacking the clubs as 'a pernicious racket'. However, the complaints were to a large extent the old ones being recycled, and had already been dismissed by Wheare. The cinemas therefore felt such attacks to be ignorant and outdated, and were able to fend them off with confident ease.

In this they were helped by the coincidence that 1950 saw the start of public agitation against a totally different 'menace' to children – horror comics. The full story is told by Martin Barker in his book *A Haunt of Fears*. Over five years various bodies, including a specially formed Comics Campaign Council (CCC), sought to draw public and governmental attention to what they saw as the viciousness and depravity of the American comics that had started to circulate among children. In its concern for the imminent corruption of language, culture and morality the CCC was similar to some aspects of the anti-cinema campaigns of the previous twenty years. Its rhetoric was, however, more virulent, partly because a still image is much easier to pin down or wave around than one that moves. Further, films at least had a warning system, in the form of a BBFC category, whereas there was nothing at all to stop even the youngest child reading the 'filthiest' comic. *Picture Post* joined in the argument not once but twice; articles printed in 1952 and 1954 investigated the situation and printed frames from some of the comics, with captions not unlike those used in their infra-red report (for example, The Perfect Recipe for a Nightmare). An intervention by the National Union of Teachers, which mounted an exhibition of the comics, was followed by a letter to *The Times Educational Supplement* and a lengthy ensuing correspondence. The end result was an Act which in 1955 made it illegal to print, publish or sell 'harmful' comics.

Meanwhile the film industry had set about implementing the recommendations of the Wheare report, which had urged the 'continuance and development' of the work of CEF, but JARO, massively in debt, had not been able to go on funding it alone. The various trade bodies, seeing their public reputation at stake, united in setting up a unique new organisation within less than a year of the demise of CEF. The bedrock of this new production agency, called the Children's Film Foundation, was an agreement between four trade associations representing distributors, exhibitors and producers. In the interest of making and screening films for children at matinees, they were prepared to break many of their standard rules and practices. Rank, ABC, Granada and all the smaller circuits and independents were to have equal access to the new product. This open-to-all policy was essential because the production programme was to be paid for by the British Film Production Fund, an industry body which collected a voluntary levy from all exhibitors. At the rate of one farthing per ticket costing between fourpence and a shilling, and three farthings per ticket costing over a shilling, the levy yielded around three million pounds annually, of which 5 per cent went to the CFF. The financial capacity of the CFF to stay in business was therefore linked directly to the British population's overall attendance at the cinema, so the Foundation felt reasonably secure.

As well as this new financial and operational base, the Foundation had something which CFD/CEF had yearned for – greater scope for employing young children in their films. In 1950, Ede's small committee had recommended a change in the law as soon as possible, and an immediate relaxation in the interpretation of the 1933 restrictions. Ede was sympathetic but unable immediately to frame fresh legislation, and in any case the Labour Government of which he was a member fell the following year. Still, even CEF just before its expiry had felt it safe to bend the law, giving the lead role in one of its last features, *The Dragon of Pendragon Castle*, to seven-year-old David Hannaford. Two years later Mandy Miller, aged eight, became Britain's first authentic child-star after playing a deaf girl in *Mandy*. She later made a recording of the song 'Nellie the Elephant,' and appeared in the CFF film *Adventure in the Hopfields*. But ready-made star status was not normal in a CFF film, nor was it thought to be important. What mattered was that the actors were young and could be filmed in this country. A few from the fifties, such as Michael Crawford and Francesca Annis, are still in the profession to this day, but most of them went on to do other things.

Another part of the framework of the fifties came from Wheare's proposal that there should be an X certificate. The BBFC introduced this with effect from 1951. It broadened and replaced the old H category, with the intention of keeping under-sixteens completely away from certain adult-content films. Local licensing bodies were not at first obliged to accept these certificates, but the following year the government passed a new Cinematograph Act which placed on all authorities in the UK an absolute duty of prohibiting the admission of children to X films. It did not actually come into effect till January 1956, but most authorities were enforcing it before then. The same Act contained also a provision that finally settled the Scottish Question, after more than twenty years of intermittent public concern. For the first time Scottish licensing authorities had power to place conditions on the admission of children to A films.

There were Wheare-induced changes inside the cinemas too, changes which the children must have noticed more quickly than the external ones. Rank may have found Wheare's dismissive comments on his club promise a bitter pill, but he swallowed it, accepting that its wartime relevance was over. From 1951 onwards in Rank clubs that whole ritual was abolished and forgotten. The promise was not even printed on the membership cards. The only rule now was: 'Members agree at all times to help the Club Chief'. Public affirmation of virtue was left entirely to the club song – 'We all intend to be/Good citizens when we grow up/And champions of the free'. Even the names and badges of the clubs were changed, with the words 'National', 'British' and 'Junior' being dropped. This was partly a break with the past, partly an effort to bring the two Rank circuits in line with each other. The ONCC became the Odeon Children's Cinema Club for Boys and Girls; and instead of the Gaumont British Junior Club there was now the Gaumont Children's Cinema Club for Boys and Girls. At the same time the age of admission in Rank clubs was lowered – local-authority licence permitting – in line with Wheare's finding that five was old enough. To have retained seven as a starting age would have been to give the ABC chain a two-year start in the battle for converts. Being thus uncompetitive without even (post-Wheare) getting any public credit for it, was plainly unthinkable.

The distinction between sixpennies and ninepennies, so disparaged by Parnaby and Woodhouse, had not bothered Wheare, so even the Rank clubs, which tried to be more egalitarian than the others, retained the principle of differential pricing. However, Wheare had made recommendations about levels of supervision and procedures for emergency evacuation, and these concerns too were embodied in the 1952 Cinematograph Act. No longer was it allowable for local-authority licences simply to require 'sufficient' supervision at an exhibition conducted wholly or mainly for children. Under the new Act, cinemas had to have 'not less than one attendant who has attained the age of sixteen years for every one hundred persons present' on the ground floor, and one attendant for every fifty people on higher floors (circle, balcony, gallery). Such attendants had to have been trained, and wore armbands to signify their status. Where the circle remained in service, a seat there customarily cost 9d., except in Wales, where prices were lower. Separation of sixpennies and ninepennies within the stalls, such as had happened at Bradford and Chard, may have carried on in some independent cinemas, but not within the major circuits. There was also, for all Rank cinemas, a rule that at a children's performance the front two rows in the circle must never be occupied, for safety reasons. Certain local authorities imposed this or a similar rule on all cinemas within their jurisdiction, and enforcing it was one of the tasks of the attendants on duty up there. In these circumstances, some managers concluded that opening up the upper floors for a matinee was just not worth it.

There were yet two more factors, nothing to do with Wheare, which helped shape the matinee-goers' decade. The first was the government's abolition of a regulation which, like the club promise, was a hangover from the war. In 1949 sweets and chocolate came off the ration. They could now be bought in unlimited quantities, subject to availability of stock and cash. In the early fifties there were still places that gave out free oranges as the children came in or left, but they were rapidly disappearing, and vendors of bags of peanuts in their shells were liable to be asked to move away from the cinema, as managers preferred the children to buy their snacks on the premises. An ex-ABC Minor remembers: 'Once inside the Regent, Hull, a variety of tempting edibles were on sale in the foyer – watery orange ice lollies, little tubs of ice cream with wooden spoons, toffees and boiled sweets in loud crinkly bags.' In Allerton, Derby, the lure of confectionery was so great that two sisters who had been given ninepence each and strict instructions to sit in the circle used to risk their father's anger by going in the stalls for sixpence so that they would have threepence over to spend on Butterkist Popcorn. There was a related situation at the Odeon, Llandudno, where it cost 4d. downstairs and 6d. upstairs. 'Even at those modest prices, due to the limitations of my pocket money, I never did get to enjoy the grandeur of the upper level, as this would have meant forgoing my quarter pound of liquorice allsort off-cuts.' In Edinburgh towards the end of the decade an iced drink in a triangular carton was popular – the Jubbly. 'It was orange in flavour and you could keep sucking it for about thirty minutes. By the time you had finished it the insides of your cheeks, rubbing against the orange ice, were numb.' An ex-Odeon manager confirms that though an effort was made to keep charges low in order not to open up too big a gap between those with money to spend and those without, nonetheless as the decade developed confectionery played a significant part in Saturday morning book-keeping. 'Clubs were supposed to pay their way. Without sales they would have run at a loss. We offered special confectionery – penny sticks of liquorice, ice-creams, threepenny lolly-ices, sherbet dabs – which could not be sold at normal performances.'

28. *Confectionery queues at the Troxy, Stepney, east London in 1950*
(Cinema Theatre Association)

Finally, there was a negative factor which most people were not aware of at the time. In the fifties, the clubs and matinees were free from the direct competition of television. In the first half of the decade the BBC produced popular programmes and characters such as Muffin the Mule, *Whirligig* (with Sooty and Rolf Harris) and George Cansdale's *All about Animals*. ITV, after it started in 1955, fed largely off matinee-style material, importing the Roy Rogers and

Hopalong Cassidy shows from America, before scoring a major success with the specially produced *Adventures of Robin Hood*. The BBC fought back with another bought-in series which owed its origins to B westerns – *Champion the Wonder Horse*. However, none of these went out on Saturday mornings. As far as television was concerned, Saturday mornings were a desert for children. If they wanted to see George Cansdale at that time they could – but only in a cinema, where a Cansdale film series called *Talking of Animals* was presented from the middle of the decade.

In fact, the only serious institutionalised opposition to Saturday cinema came from one of its former allies. In 1952 the BBC Light Programme broadcast the first-ever UK-wide record-request programme for children. This was *Children's Choice*, which after two years changed its name to *Children's Favourites*, with Derek McCulloch as presenter. It soon had a loyal listenership of millions, for whom McCulloch played 'The Laughing Policeman', 'The Teddy Bears' Picnic', 'The Skaters' Waltz', 'The Ugly Duckling', 'Sparky's Magic Piano', 'Champion the Wonder Horse', 'The Runaway Train', 'Robin Hood', 'Nellie the Elephant', and 'A Four-Legged Friend' (sung by Roy Rogers). Since the programme went out between 9.05 and 9.55 a.m., a child who listened to it all could not easily get to a cinema by 10.00 a.m.

The cumulative effect of all these changes was to bring a measure of uniformity to matinees in Britain. The same minimum safety standards had been imposed everywhere. The promise and the pictorial exhortations that had distinguished the Rank clubs were gone. Community-singing and talent contests were to be found in independent cinemas as well as in the circuits. And, crucially, they now all showed (or at least had the chance to show) the specially made films – features, serials and shorts – that the CFF was producing.

Initially the independents were reluctant to book CFF films, and carried on exactly as they had in the forties. In 1952 only ninety out of well over 1,000 independents were lined up to show CFF films. To combat this, the CFF worked out a system which put each cinema into one of four groups. Basically, these were Odeons, Gaumonts, ABCs, and independents (which included circuits such as Granada, Clifton, Essoldo and Caledonian). The policy was that each of these four groups should, in rotation, get first bite of the cherry. For the first year of the release of a new CFF film only the cinemas in one particular group would be able to book it. In the second year it would circulate round another group. Meanwhile the next CFF film would get its initial release in a different group from that to which the first one had gone. That way, within any district, there was never any one cinema that got all the premières; and having played once in a particular district, a film would not play there again for at least another year. When a film had been round all four circuits, it would rest for a year and then start again, on the assumption that all the children who had seen it first time round would by then have left or forgotten it.

In 1952, as an inducement, and as a sign of the good faith of the major circuits, the independents were given the first feature that CFF released – *John of the Fair*. It had its première at the Essoldo, Holloway, north London, on a Saturday morning in December of that year, with the principal actors there to take a bow. Within three years, spurred by enthusiastic reports from those who had taken the plunge – one manager of an independent in Aberystwyth even wrote to CFF in 1953 asking whether there was any means by which he could get more of their films more quickly – the number of independents regularly booking CFF product had risen to more than 700. In fact, there were so many of them that, with only sixteen release prints available, a year was no longer enough time for one film to go round that circuit; by the end of the decade the independents' right to any particular film had been extended from a year to eighteen months. (For the other three groups, one year remained ample, as the ABCs peaked at 305, the Odeons at 238 and the Gaumonts at 156.) This figure of 700+, though high, meant that there were still around 500 independents not booking CFF product. Investigation revealed that in many situations this was due to there being too many independents close to each other. Other objections were to the scarcity of the product, and to the difficulty of promoting a film that had neither a star (except, once, Mandy Miller) nor a trailer nor even a poster. And some managers must have quite simply believed that their young customers would not like the films. Even so, the mid-fifties represented the numerical high-water mark of Saturday cinema. At the end of 1955 the over-all number of matinees in Britain was 1,915; the overall weekly audience figures were over 1,000,000; and the total of cinemas showing CFF product was around 1,400.

Within this context of co-operation over film distribution the major circuits – no longer to be differentiated completely by what they showed – sought to be distinctive by the way they packaged it. Following Wheare again, the Odeon CCC now sought to have for every club an adult committee, separate from the children's committee, as the Gaumonts had always done. If possible, they tried to get the Director of Education and the Chief Constable, plus representatives of local organisations concerned with children and youth, to meet once a month. ('Through your club', managers were advised in the Rank manual, 'you can frequently obtain entry to circles which would otherwise be denied to you.') The CCCs also carried on their concern for road safety, and their training of older children as safety marshals charged with keeping the queue orderly. Beyond that, Rank managers were no longer required to promote activities which might be regarded as more properly the sphere of schools and youth clubs. Nonetheless, many still did, choirs being particularly popular. For several years from 1948 an annual carol festival, organised in association with a regional evening paper, *The Star*, attracted up to 150 choirs from London and the South of England. It ended with the eight finalist choirs competing in the Leicester Square Odeon or the Gaumont State, Kilburn.

29. *Rank with the winning choir, plus conductor and cinema manager, after the finals of the 1956 Carol Competition in the Odeon, Leicester Square*

(Cinema Theatre Association)

A less specialised club activity of these years was a development of the salvage campaigns of the thirties and forties. It involved children being asked to collect silver paper in aid of Guide Dogs for the Blind. One prime source for this was discarded cigarette packets. But there was an even more common source, not so well liked by managers. One recalls:

It was always official policy to make the clubs something more than just a film show. One year, there was a Rank campaign to raise funds for Guide Dogs. For obvious reasons we didn't ask the children for money; instead we asked them to collect metal milk bottle tops. When sufficient had been collected at a cinema they were parcelled up and sent off to a firm which melted them down for reuse. A cheque was then paid by the firm direct to the Guide Dogs Association. I believe a considerable sum was raised in this way. We held competitions to see who could collect the most bottle tops by stringing them together – big families usually won. The only trouble was that often the bottle tops hadn't been washed and so while they were in store, until we had sufficient to send away, they became very smelly.

A further socially conscious activity in CCCs was first aid. Throughout the country over a hundred CCCs attached themselves to the St John Ambulance Brigade. One contributor recalls how, as a cadet member of the Coventry Gaumont division of the Brigade, he patrolled the cinema on first-aid duty on Saturday mornings, and went to the cinema for midweek training, except on one unique occasion: 'I can clearly remember going down for the cadets on a Wednesday night in 1952, only to find that the cinema was closed, and everything was dark. It was the night that King George VI had died.'

The ensuing Coronation in 1953 stimulated the CCCs to run a Loyal Subjects competition throughout the country. Members were invited to compose messages for the new queen. Each local winner– one younger, one older – received a prize such as a table tennis bat and three balls. The two national winners had their messages inscribed in a book prepared by the Royal College of Heralds. The messages were then signed, and the books sent to the queen. One began: 'Your Majesty ~ I hope you have a happy reign. The children of the Odeon and Gaumont Clubs will be thinking of you at your Coronation and will pray for you. We will do our best to serve you well and love our country always.' An ex-Gaumont Junior from Leyton, east London, has good reason to remember also a tie-up between the club and the local celebrations. 'The cinema sponsored a fancy dress competition at our Coronation street party, and the manager awarded the prizes. Dressed as Nell Gwyn, I came first, and had my picture taken by a photographer from the local paper.'

The CCCs had no monopoly on loyalty or charity but their campaigns were larger and more orchestrated than the rest. The ABCs had a different style. They gave out commemorative red, white and blue coronation jockey caps to children at the street parties they sponsored; and members got special Minors coronation badges as well. Additionally, they rewarded loyalty to the company as well as to the monarchy. One colour picture-card for collecting or swapping, from sets of ten on such subjects as Scenes from the Films, Journeys by Water, British Birds and Famous Buildings, was given to each Minor every Saturday; and specially designed ties (for boys) and scarves (for girls) were awarded to Minors after two years of regular attendance. This was in contrast to CCC awards which, in the form of pennants, went normally to clubs rather than individuals, for collective endeavour such as, at Stourbridge, the raising of money to pay for ten children from the Infantile Paralysis Fellowship to have a seaside holiday.

The ABCs quickly latched on to the yo-yo craze of the early fifties. It figured in numerous stage presentations all over the country. A common format was for someone who was good at yo-yoing to do a demonstration, and then judge a competition. One of these experts recalls: 'As a student I went round doing yo-yo competitions at Saturday morning pictures. The manager would get kids up and I was supposed to choose a finalist and give a prize of a game. The manager usually told me which kid would win.' The climax of this phase came when Art Pickles, UK yo-yo champion, toured a large number of clubs all over the country. A memoir of a north London Ritz relates: 'I remember very clearly an appearance by Art Pickles. He performed all manner of stunts using two yo-yos, and then children were invited on the stage to learn new tricks.' For another contributor Pickles prompted a final Minor morning:

> I recall my last matinee; I was too old by far and embarrassed because Mam had insisted I took my younger brother. At twelve I was now more interested in girls than cowboys, but I went to the giant, 2,000-seater Langham on Hull's busy Hessle Road that Saturday for one big reason: the national yo-yo champion was touring the UK's cinema clubs and, as both my brother and I were in the process of mastering the yo-yo, we just had to be there. I recall a riotous, clicking forest of colliding yo-yos and miles of twisted string. It was a dangerous place to be.

Less dangerous ABC visitors in those years included England football captain Billy Wright at Wolverhampton; Julie Andrews in Nuneaton; Jimmy Logan in Dundee; Arthur Lucan (Old Mother Riley) in Walsall; and even Laurel and Hardy who, when their film-making career was over, toured the UK, performing live in variety, and visiting matinees while they were in town. Singer Ralph McTell recalls that this tour made him, as a child, aware of his own mortality:

> As kids, we assumed that all our favourites were roughly contemporary, and when a newsreel announced that Laurel and Hardy were coming to tour the UK, it really shocked me to see them as lined-faced old men. The footage was all the more frightening – sinister, even – because they were wearing their little trademark bowler hats and smiling. Ollie, as usual, had his little finger held out, as if he were holding a porcelain tea-cup. It was a horror and an awakening I'd never forget.

Did Laurel and Hardy look 'frightening' to the children who saw them in the flesh, on the stage at the Warrington Ritz and other places, with no close-up? Did the Minors recognise the sixty-three-years-old Laurel and the two-years-younger Hardy as the Beau Hunks, the Blockheads, the Saps at Sea, the Sons of the Desert whom they had seen on the screen? Were any of their routines funny, for children, when performed live? Did anyone think it sad and undignified for these two to have to come down off the screen into the real world, promoting their show and posing for the local newspaper photographer?

Whatever Laurel and Hardy may have felt about it, many celebrities were certainly not unhappy to use a matinee of 1,000 or more children as a way of pushing a product. Principal among these was Coco the Clown, referred to in ABC publicity, in and after 1953, as Minor Number One. As one of the stars of Bertram Mills' Circus, he travelled round the country, and so was able to pop up in many different ABC cinemas on Saturday mornings. Sometimes other acts went too, such as the group of midgets who accompanied him to the Regal, Hounslow. He may well have entertained the children very successfully and, with the help of a walking stick designed like a Belisha beacon and hair that could be made to stand on end at any moment, may have taught them more about road safety than any police officer could have done. Undoubtedly he also made sure that they knew the circus was in town. Probably he said to them something similar to what he wrote in the 1953 edition of the *Cinema Clubs Annual*: 'I want you all to do something for me; I want you to promise to wear your Minors' badges when you come to Bertram Mills' Circus to see me; then I shall know that you are all my friends.'

Only on very rare occasions, such as the appearance of Art Pickles at Hull, was this kind of show business tie-up the reason why children attended. Primarily it was the films (to be discussed in the next chapter) and the peer-group interaction. That is what people remember going for and enjoying. Regularity of attendance was as important for social reasons as it was for narrative continuity in the serials. An abundance of memoirs makes this very clear:

> I chose the Super, Stanford Hill, rather than the Regent, because I went there first and got locked into the continuing serials and programming there, into the culture of events and people that was different from the rare occasions when I went elsewhere. I went because I loved going to the pictures, the regularity of being with a changing combination of friends. It was second nature not to miss a week. On one fateful Saturday I decided to go to the Regent instead because I had been enthralled by an Alan Ladd movie there the night before and imagined I'd see it again. Of course, that wasn't the case, as the Regent ran its own kids' programme instead. I don't remember what they showed, only that I was on my own, couldn't join in the different songs and rituals, couldn't make any sense of the serial, and generally had a miserable time. I probably didn't even stay to see the feature.

> When my family moved to Palmers Green in 1953 I started going to the Palmadium. With friends from my new school, Saturday cinema took on an additional dimension. There were girls in the group, and

30. *The Sevenoaks Granada, August 1953. A pack of ideas for use in local advertising campaigns was sent to exhibitors showing Disney's* Peter Pan. *One of the ideas was: 'Dress a boy of about twelve years of age to resemble our illustration, getting a make-up artist to transform his face, then use him on the stage, at children's matinees, making personal appearances at stores selling Peter Pan merchandise, carrying gifts to children in hospital and other such stunting, some of which would be certain to arouse PRESS interest.' The film itself was never shown at Saturday matinees* (Allan Scott)

when the lights went down the bold could try and slide a surreptitious arm around the shoulders of their choice – though the staff often walked the aisles shining their torches to discourage the amorous. And if you were unlucky, you still had the films to watch.

My matinee-going was in Norwich, at the Regent (in the dodgy part of town). I went firstly because my big sister did; then because it was somewhere to go that parents (almost) approved of; and also because you could flirt with the boys in the dark (I was eight or nine). I loved the screaming and the orange drinks and I remember the foisty old usherettes who shushed at you with their torches.

In Edinburgh there was a kind of Saturday morning uniform. Everyone that went wore blazers, burberries, balaclavas, flying helmets and Wellingtons. No one, as I recall, took their coats off in the cinema during the films no matter how hot it got.

In Morden I went a few times in the mid-fifties, and then regularly, in a different cinema, two or three years later. In the first cinema there was something about going up on stage and singing; and in the other place there was perhaps once a Red Cross woman. But generally it was just the package of films. The significance of it was that it was about being able to go and do on your own something that was considered fairly grown up. Because Saturday morning pictures were considered respectable, parents were only too happy to let you go. When I got into a particular class at school it was very much the thing to do. It was the place where you'd meet everyone again. During the week you'd arranged who'd go with whom, who'd asked whom to sit by whom, so mostly the whole class was there – certainly all the in-crowd were. Lots of comments were thrown out, and people would be laughing at the comments rather than at the film. Also, a lot of kids went along to cause bother – that was part of the fun of it. People would start running around before the film, and chucking stuff, and ducking into different rows from where they'd been put. It was a very different feeling and atmosphere from going to a film in the evening.

The lure of the in-group was so strong that many children wanted to go, although their parents preferred them not to, either because they thought that matinees were a 'racket' or because they did not want to encourage social mixing. Such parents devised various stategies for coping with their children's demand. The simplest one was just to say 'no', and mean it. Some parents did not even have to say it; their children 'just knew' that they would never agree. Early in the decade, fear of the possibility of catching polio could be invoked. Later, Uncle Mac could be called on for help: 'Wouldn't you rather listen to *Children's Favourites*?' Another devious method was to arrange piano lessons for eleven o'clock on a Saturday morning. In some cases there were compromises: 'You can go, but only in winter'; 'You can go, but only when it rains'; 'You can go, provided that you sit in the circle'; 'You can go, provided that you do not join in any of those club activities'; 'You can go, provided that you are up to date with your homework'. Some people recall not caring much for the serial, because they never knew from one week to the next whether they would ever be allowed to go again. Many memoirs illuminate this situation of social tension, confusion and revelation:

My family was definitely middle class. We were the only people in my road to have a car – a Ford Eight. My mother wasn't keen on Saturday morning pictures, but while she was away once I was looked after by my grandmother. When my mother came back she found that my grandmother had let me go. Twice! To her credit, she realised that the toothpaste was out of the tube, so I was allowed to continue. When I first went, I didn't really know what I was going to. I had been to the cinema a couple of times before, but only to see Disney films. Having been to a Saturday matinee, I really loved it, and I didn't want not to be one of the gang. I think that's what my mother responded to – the fact that these were now my friends. To be fair to her, I must point out that Saturday mornings could get extremely unruly. One very popular thing was to take a thin glass tube. We used to have battles, blowing rice pellets through them. You took a mouthful of rice, and you could blow out twenty in rapid succession. Towards the end we were getting searched on the way in, but it was all Bash Street kids stuff – nothing seriously violent.

I come from a middle-class family in a working-class area, and was perceived to be 'a bit posh' by my mates. A lot of time was spent by me proving my credentials as one of the lads. I have a particular formative memory of my first visit to Saturday pictures, because I barely escaped ridicule when I turned up neat and tidy with scrubbed knees, Bryl-creemed hair and school blazer, to find that everyone else was wearing leather jackets (more likely plastic really) with zipped pockets. I remember being horrified and fascinated at their bad behaviour, and how the poor man who tried to control things had less power and authority than teachers, and how they (later 'we') exploited this. For months I protected my parents from the knowledge that it was a madhouse – I didn't think that they would be able to cope with the idea that I was having to endure such bad manners. I know now that they knew all along but were keen to make sure that I could operate at those social levels as well as within the middle class we aspired to.

My brother and I were the local vicar's sons and were therefore middle class. We went with a friend from junior school. My friend was definitely working class and it was he who told me about the cinema club, still called 'The Tuppenny Rush' in the fifties. My visits all took place at age ten, before I passed my 11+ and was sent off to boarding school. The manager clearly tried to make the film show a club event, and just as clearly failed. He spent a lot of time threatening us, stopping films, issuing ever more empty threats. I was fascinated by kids who were more or less completely out of control and tormented adults as a form of blood sport. My parents clearly disapproved of us going, but it got us out of their way for a while.

As the end of the decade approached, attendance started gradually to decline. In the twenty months between January 1956 and August 1957, 14 ABC cinemas, 37 Rank cinemas and 209 independents stopped running matinees, in some cases because the cinemas concerned closed down completely. The remaining 1,655 matinees were all affected to some extent. The Coventry Gaumont, for example, which had been accustomed to having all of its 2,500 seats filled (except for the first two rows of the circle) sank to 2,000, and then to 1,500. The reasons were many: improved competition from television after the arrival of ITV; increasing general affluence, which trickled down to children and enabled them to see evening films in colour rather than matinee films in black-and-white; and the emergence of 'teenager' as an available cultural identity. In Nottingham, Sheffield and parts of London, a few managers discontinued their CCCs in 1958 or 1959 and ran instead a Gaumont Teenage Show. One recalls:

> There were other Rank cinemas in the town catering for the younger children. This was something additional. As far as product was concerned, it was not all that far removed from the clubs, except that we did not show the CFF stuff – that was considered too juvenile for teenagers. We still had the *Batman* serial, and things like that. What marked us out from CCCs was that we made our stage available for up-and-coming amateur pop groups, who performed live on stage after the films. We did not impose any age limits, but in fact, most of them were twelve or over.

This change that occurred in British cultural life was symbolised for one contributor by the fact that in the mid-fifties the music that was played as the children entered the cinema and settled down included Shirley Temple singing 'On the Good Ship Lollipop', from twenty years before. Four years later, when she went for the last time, it was Millie with 'My Boy Lollipop', from the current pop chart.

14 The Stuff for Child Audiences

One of my earliest cinema memories was Hopalong Cassidy at a matinee in Carlisle in about 1956. I remember that his trousers were white (or was that the Lone Ranger?) and wondering when he went for a pee. It created my first erotic fantasy which involved an older cousin being tied to a totem pole in a state of undress while a crowd of small white boys whooped around dressed as Native Americans.

(Mike Figgis, 1996)

Basically, I hated Saturday morning pictures because it was meant for kids, and I didn't want to be associated with it. I preferred to see films that adults were seeing. However, I went to the Astoria Brixton one Saturday morning in the fifties because there was a Hopalong Cassidy film on and I'd never seen one and I found it was just a dreadful B western. I wished I hadn't gone. I remember also seeing Laurel and Hardy in *Jailbirds* at the Rex Norbury and the print was in a shocking condition, full of jumps and scratches and everything. I really thought it was insulting to show these films to children and take money off them for it.

(Allen Eyles, 1993)

Though the CFF had Rank as its chairman and Mary Field as its first executive officer, it differed from its forerunner, the CEF, in two very significant ways. First, it was the creature of the whole British film industry, independents and circuits alike, acting together voluntarily in what they saw as their common interest. Secondly, it was no longer mandated to 'do the children good'.

The considerations that brought all sectors of the industry together in this unique collaboration derived from the Wheare report and the criticisms which had prompted it. This aspect was explicitly acknowledged in the first CFF constitution, which listed among its objects: 'To demonstrate to educationists and social workers that the film industry in this country aims at producing and exhibiting films which are suitable in every way for children.' At the same time, it was interested in children's films as 'a new and special type of production' which would provide employment for British technicians and actors and, it was hoped, establish Britain as the centre of the international children's film movement. Without these long-term factors – national respectability, job creation, world prestige – to consider, the industry would not have been willing to finance production of a kind which, in the short term at least, was a guaranteed money-loser. Production of special children's films thus began as part of a public-relations campaign. The British Film Production Fund Ltd, though not a charity, granted the CFF £60,000 in the first year, £100,000 in its second, and around £125,000 per year after that till 1957 when, under a new Cinematograph Act, the levy on cinema tickets sold became compulsory, and the distribution of the money was taken over by the new British Film Fund Agency. The CFF was specifically named in the new statutes, and guaranteed a grant every year for the foreseeable future. The amount was not specified in the Act, but it remained for the rest of the decade at the level of £125,000 per year. Though it was still the cinema-goer who was financing the CFF, not the taxpayer, the fact of the Foundation being given the status of specified grant-receiver implied for the industry a welcome degree of official recognition of the worth of its work.

The leaving behind of the requirement that films for children should seek to do them good was not just a result of the industry as a whole taking over the task and not wishing to pick up Rank's personal moral crusade; it derived also from an acceptance that finger-wagging exhortation was not a successful way of influencing behaviour in a desired direction. Even while still working for Rank, Field had adopted as one of the movement's texts a passage from a Report on Moral Education written by Michael Sadler, of the Schools' Inspectorate, for the Ministry of Education. This made a distinction between moral instruction and moral education. According to the report, the former was the province of the home, the church and the school; the latter came from a range of factors, one of which was 'intimacy with good example'. This phrase gave CEF a clearer sense of purpose than it had had before; its moral concerns from then on were resolved into an attempt to put on to the screen characters whom the audience would wish to get to know well, and in whom they would see good example. Field explains: 'We interpreted this not as demanding the portrayal of "goody-goody" characters, but as requiring plots and characterization that would show ordinary children and adults behaving well, but not too well, in situations into which our audiences could project themselves.' Satisfied with the results that that approach had brought, Field took it with her to CFF. Till 1959, when she left, she carried Sadler in one hand and Carnegie in the other, one to guide her in making films 'suitable' from an adult perspective, the other to assist in meeting the first object in the CFF constitution, namely that the films it produced must be 'of a type that children will readily pay to see'.

Initially CFF concentrated on the production of features with western- and thriller-type stories, such as children were accustomed to from commercial films. The difference was that CFF versions offered child characters and a British setting. In line with this policy two early films were *The Stolen Plans* and *The Stolen Airliner*. Many other films from the early years also involved poachers, smugglers, kidnappers and crooks of various kinds. In *John of the Fair*, set in the eighteenth century, John is the rightful heir to an estate but has been cheated out of it; the *Skid Kids* help police round up bicycle thieves; the chance discovery of stolen jewels helps children who have nowhere to keep their pets in *The Dog and the Diamonds*; the British Fleet in Gibraltar is saved by two children who solve *The Clue of the Missing Ape*. As the decade developed, other types of narrative were tackled too: *Johnny on the Run* concerns an unhappy Polish boy living in Edinburgh; *The Secret Cave*, based on a Thomas Hardy story, is a musical about what happens to two villages when boys discover the source of a stream and divert it; in *Blow your own Trumpet* Michael Crawford competes for a place in the local brass band; there's perhaps a bit of Russian influence in *One Wish too Many*, about children with a magic marble; and *The Monster of Highgate Ponds* just grows and grows. In addition, the CFF imported films from other countries and adapted them either by adding a commentary or by revoicing: *Kekec*, from Yugoslavia, is a boy who frees a mountain village from a terrorising bandit; the *Smugglers at the Castle* are outwitted by French schoolboys.

After a few years the production programme was broadened to include eight-episode serials, such as *Raiders of the River*, about bank robbers being tracked down, and *The Young Jacobites*, in which Francesca Annis goes back in time and helps Bonnie Prince Charlie escape from Scotland after the battle of Culloden. On top of all these there were seventeen fifteen-minute shorts, mainly either slapstick comedy or animal misadventures, four *Pen Pictures* (for example *Letter from Ayrshire*) and sixteen editions of *Our Magazine* (no longer called *Our Club Magazine*) most of which included an item featuring children in other countries.

Although the CFF was committed to the principle that a film for children should be made to the same standards as a film for adults, there were, on the face of it, two reasons why it might be expected to cost less. First, it did not depend upon having expensive stars in the lead roles; and secondly, it was considerably shorter. These two factors were, however, to some extent offset by the requirement of more action and less dialogue than in a film for adults, and by the consequent need for a greater number of outdoor locations and camera set-ups.

Making an average of four features, one serial, two shorts and three magazines each year on a budget of £125,000 was only possible because the industry was prepared to break its own rules in respect of production, just as it was in respect of distribution. For example, a standard condition stipulates that if a production is held up by adverse weather, then the commissioning body can either cancel the whole project or pay for the extra days necessary to finish it. Either way, it can be very expensive. This affected the CFF particularly, because so much outdoor shooting was required for their films. By 1955 they were able to invoke the co-operation of the industry, and get rid of the 'bad weather claims' clause; instead, their contracts stipulated that a director must, as far as practicable, adapt to any weather that might come along, and find a way of carrying on shooting. Goodwill, in the form of reduced fees, came also from established adult actors, the BBFC, and suppliers such as laboratories and studios.

Abroad, the CFF in the fifties certainly achieved one of the objects set out in the constitution – that of gaining international recognition. In Venice especially, then the principal European forum, it became customary for CFF films to win a prize in the Children's Festival. The very first two – *John of the Fair* and *The Stolen Plans* – had to share a Silver Gondola because the judges could not decide between them. In addition to doing well at Venice, *Johnny on the Run* won an award in the USA as 'the best film of its kind', and at home was awarded an Edinburgh Diploma of Merit. The following year, *Tim Driscoll's Donkey* received a commendation in Uruguay. Equally importantly, other territories were buying and adapting CFF productions, particularly the features: most of the Commonwealth countries took some, but also Spain, South America, Poland and Czechoslovakia.

Nonetheless very few people who attended matinees in the UK at any time in the fifties seem to have any recollection of ever seeing CFF films. The basic cause of this is that even at the end of the decade, by which time the Foundation had produced or adapted thirty-three features, nine serials, twenty-three shorts and sixteen magazines, the proportion of CFF films shown over a year in any one cinema was very low. In the whole of 1959, in the ABC cinema at Torquay, the only CFF product that a Minor who attended for fifty-two weeks would have seen was three features, two shorts, the last five episodes of *Five Clues to Fortune*, and the first episode of *Mystery in the Mine*. The year before that it was three features, two shorts and three serial episodes. That amounts to less than 5 per cent of the total viewing. Nor was the situation significantly different in a Rank cinema, as all CFF product was distributed in the same way. In the Gaumont Chelsea in 1958, a child who attended for the whole year would have seen at most three CFF features, one complete CFF serial, OM *Number Five* and *A Letter from the Isle of Wight*. Again, not more than 5 per cent of Saturday morning screen time. Additionally, the Rank bookers made an effort to get specially made material from elsewhere, so in the CCCs there was a revival of *Bush Christmas*. There were also two foreign fairy tales that CFF had not thought worth buying and adapting. These were a subtitled East German film called *Little Mook*, about a fatherless Oriental hunchback boy's search for the Merchant Who Sells Happiness; and a live-action French film, *Once upon a Time*, in which all the characters are played by animals, including a monkey, a duck, a white Persian cat and some frogs riding a wall of death.

Apart from this low proportion of CFF and other specially made films, what the children saw in matinees around the country was much the same kind of thing as they had seen in the forties. Above all, they saw fifteen-episode American serials, and these were interchangeable from circuit to circuit. In September 1958 *The Adventures of Sir Galahad* was showing both in Torquay and in Chelsea, and doubtless numerous other cinemas as well. This was possible because the distributors of the serials made far more copies available than the CFF could afford to. (The CFF maximum was sixteen.) In fact, there were so many different serials available, in so many prints, and their popularity with children was judged by managers to be so high, that in Minors' matinees it was common to see episodes from two different serials each week in the first half of the fifties. For example, in Torquay on 16 October 1954 the Minors saw both episode six of *Perils of the Darkest Jungle* and episode two of *Captain Video*. It was the practice then, when a serial reached its last episode, to show also the first episode of its replacement, so that the children never went home without a cliff-hanger ending dancing in their brains. This custom was adhered to even when a cinema was already showing two serials, so on 9 April 1955 the Minors saw three: the last episode of *Buck Rogers*, the ninth episode of *Menace of the Seas* and the first episode of *Tim Tyler's Luck* – a total of one hour's screen time filled by serials. After the middle of the decade this practice was discontinued, so Minors saw only one serial episode, except when one serial came to an end, and another started. From then on the ABC programmers stuck pretty much to the same format as the Rank cinemas: cartoon, short, serial, feature.

In these boom years, cinemas often found matinees so popular that they spilled over from Saturdays to other mornings as well. The Tuesdays of half-term weeks, and the Tuesday after Easter, for example, were sometimes turned into special extra matinees. On these occasions no serial episode was shown, in deference to those members who could make it only on Saturdays, but otherwise the format of the programme would be just the same. This situation raised to over fifty the number of non-CFF features that needed to be found each year. Some of these came from the thirties – films that had been the main attraction in an evening double bill twenty years before. In this way children had the chance to become acquainted with Gert and her sister Daisy, George Formby and his ukulele, Old Mother Riley and her daughter Kitty, Shirley Temple and her curls. It was a baffling experience for some children, surely often made worse by the condition of the prints, but not all. One contributor recalls with pleasure how it made him at last familiar with films and actors he had heard his parents talking about, and thus created common ground between them. Another reflects: 'The old features were the most important to me. By the time they came on most kids had quietened down, and it's here I remember best getting lost in the primal screen fantasy. I still laugh when I think of the Crazy Gang, I can cry when I think of Shirley Temple.'

Tarzan, one of the dominant screen characters of the forties, was little seen in fifties' matinees, but his best-known incarnation – Johnny Weissmuller – was. At the end of the forties Weissmuller put on a suit and became Jungle Jim in over a dozen black-and-white B movies, and when these reached Saturday screens they were sometimes only a year or two old. At the same time Johnny Sheffield, who had played Weissmuller's screen son in some Tarzan pictures, was transformed into Bomba the Jungle Boy. Bomba's eleven adventures likewise made it to matinees fairly rapidly. Similarly swift in their passage were the westerns emerging from the final days of the back-to-back series production programme that had begun in the thirties. In this field the undoubted king was still Roy Rogers. A contributor recalls how on one occasion he abandoned his Gaumont friends and missed his serial by going to an ABC just for one week in order to catch Roy Rogers in *Down Dakota Way* in April 1954, rather than have to wait for it to come round to his Gaumont (which it did in March 1955). The previous front runner – Gene Autry – was still around too, as were Johnny Mack Brown, Hopalong Cassidy, Charles Starret, Lash LaRue and the Lone Ranger. Even Buck Jones, twenty years after his heyday, could still be seen, in the western serial *White Eagle*. And far away from the West, in downtown New York, were the Bowery Boys and the East Side Kids, two Brooklyn screen gangs of comic hoodlums who between them turned out over fifty knockabout escapades.

Finally, there was a scattering of films which sometimes had the advantage of being in colour and the disadvantage that children had in some cases already seen them, two or three years earlier, at an evening screening. Some were films that, on first release, were supports. As such they were usually not too long for the main slot in a matinee programme, and if they had a U certificate were certainly assessed for their matinee acceptability. A series of seven films centred on Francis the Talking Mule and his companion Donald O'Connor passed the test easily. A less predictable choice was the prize-winning dramatised documentary *Navajo*, which in 1955 supported *Svengali* on the Gaumont circuit, and by 1958 was the big picture in some matinees. But it was not only supports which made the crossover. Technicolor swashbucklers, such as *Anne of the Indies*, were main evening attractions early in the fifties, and five years later topped matinee bills.

In this variegated context CFF films had to fight to make their presence felt. The infrequency of their appearance meant that they provoked no comfortable anticipation. There were no posters for them, and until the end of the decade, no trailers either. Children who read film magazines and newspaper reviews noticed that CFF films were never mentioned. They had no stars whose name would enable managers to get a cheer of excitement if they were to announce: 'Next week we are going to see a ―― film'. Each of the few CFF films that a child was likely to see over the course of three or four years of attending matinees therefore had to create its audience afresh each time, an audience that might begin by wishing that it was the Bowery Boys, or Roy Rogers, or Bomba, that week. Early CFF films have fared badly in the collective memory because, as well as having no pre-life, they had no afterlife either. As one contributor comments: 'In our games we fantasised about being cowboys, pirates or Flash Gordon but there was no point in being Billy Batson except to shout "Shazam" and turn instantly into Captain Marvel. We certainly never fantasised about being other ordinary children.'

However, at the time of actually seeing a particular CFF film, many children responded positively to the ways in which it was new and different when compared to commercial product. The first CFF annual report records a range of managers' comments on the reactions of audiences (in independent cinemas) who had never seen a specially made film before, to *John of the Fair*. One wrote: 'After having overcome their disappointment that it was not a western, our children enjoyed it.' Another commented that it got 'a much better reaction than the normal type of feature'. Reflecting the expectation that most films were part of a series, a third related how 'after the show some of the older ones asked if there was to be another picture about John, and when it would be shown'. Within this overall welcome, there were reservations about a lengthy dialogue sequence, a death-bed scene, and the villain of the story, who 'made too many speeches "in his beard" so the youngsters just drowned his words in derision'.

These responses are corroborated by an experiment in determining children's natural film tastes and reactions, carried out in Edinburgh in 1955 (Barclay, 1956). The objects were similar to those of the Carnegie experiment, except that this one used human observers rather than a camera. Over twelve weeks the children were shown an assortment of films, including the last CEF feature, *The Dragon of Pendragon Castle*, and three from the CFF. When David Hannaford, who had won sympathy and laughter in *The Flying Eye* in week one, appeared also in *Dragon* in week two, the first sight of him 'brought forth overwhelming applause'. Observers noted:

> *The Flying Eye* was certainly enjoyed by all and could be called the stuff for child audiences. They appreciated the comedy of action and

obviously identified themselves with the children in the film. They loved the old professor, and the response was high when he was stalked and locked up by the spy. That the children followed the story, action and speech was borne out by remarks overheard. Several children shouted out to the old man. They were living in the story. Even a detail like leaving a door unlocked was not overlooked. They enjoyed the situations in the film where the child actors were superior to the adults.

Some children in this experiment were obviously attenders of one of the Edinburgh Saturday matinees, for *The Stolen Plans* was followed with 'close attention and excited shrieks' by all, and 'even those who had seen the film before seemed pleased to see it again and took delight in warning others of the exciting moments to come'. Even the older boys, it seemed, liked and responded to all of the child characters, including one who was very small and female. In general, said the report, referring to specially made films: 'The children are anxious for more.' This Edinburgh experiment suggested strongly that in the right conditions some CFF films could work extremely well.

There was only one criticism expressed by the observers. They sensed that in *Peter and Pat in Lapland* (actually made by CEF, not CFF), the Edinburgh audience were put off by the precise elocution of the child actors. The report says: 'Their rather "precious" English speech was received with a certain amount of ridicule and comment. Slang words such as "cissy" and "pansy" were used to describe it . . . It was obvious from questioning afterwards that more vigorous types should have been used.' This kind of reaction was by no means confined to Scotland, or to CEF films. A manager who worked at Crosby and Warrington in the fifties remembers: 'In the early days CFF films were not well received in the north of England, because the children in them were too "posh" for audiences to accept.' But it was not just a regional thing. Children in London could also be put off. A contributor who was a north London Minor recalls: 'I can still hear the groans (some of them mine) that greeted the more worthy British features (which I now realise were CFF films) with "well-spoken" kids.' This alienation did not necessarily ruin a whole film, as the Edinburgh experiment showed, but it could get things off to a bad start. In the Ebbw Vale Plaza, a memoir recalls, 'CFF films were usually booed when the first credits appeared but mostly enjoyed once the story got going'.

There were three reasons why child actors in CFF films spoke the way they did in the fifties. Primarily, it was because they nearly all came from one of the London-based stage schools, such as Italia Conti and Corona. There they were trained in received methods of acting, singing and dancing; and there was a strong orientation towards stage performance rather than film. Joe Mendoza, who wrote and directed for CFF in the fifties, recalls: 'With the stage schools, it was not exactly a matter of making the children talk "posh"; rather, their aim was to get them to speak clearly, without an accent, to project their voices, and to sound all the consonants of every word.' And indeed that was what audiences perceived. Their rejection of voices coming from the screen was a matter not only of class but of diction that sounded strained, affected, forced, 'put on'. It was not just that the children in the audience did not speak like that themselves. They sensed that no one, anywhere, actually spoke like that in real life. One of the factors making David Hannaford, from east London, such a hit even in Edinburgh was that his voice sounded idiosyncratically gruff and natural. Another exception had been Antony Newley. In the fifties, such demotic diction was rare, and did not normally come from a stage school pupil. Nonetheless, the CFF was in the main obliged to use children from stage schools because even after the general interpretation of the 1933 Act was relaxed there was still a jungle of restrictions on the employment of children. To make things worse, these restrictions varied from one part of the country to another. Permission often had to be sought not only from the local education authority where children were working, but also from those in the areas where they normally lived. Stage schools made life easier for film-makers because they were geared to meeting the requirements of the law in respect of education while at the same time having the actors available when the director needed them. To use untrained actors, as some directors might well have preferred, was very difficult within the bounds of the law.

The second reason why children in CFF films spoke as they did was that, for Field, it was part of the example they were setting. For her, there were good and bad ways of speaking, just as there were good and bad ways of behaving. Children imitated what they heard on the screen, as well as what they saw. Field's stance, recalls Mendoza, was that she would not allow children on the screen to speak in a 'deformed or casualised' way, because clarity of diction and properness of pronunciation were, for her, standards to which the audience ought to aspire. She saw herself as promoting not middle-class accents, but 'BBC English'.

There was, finally, a very practical reason why Field was happy with the way the stage school children spoke in CFF films. Having at one time received complaints from Ullapool, Scotland, that children there could not understand Glaswegian children on screen, Field believed that 'BBC English' was the only mode of speech comprehensible to children in all regions of Britain.

One of the factors that broke down such linguistic regional barriers was the expansion and development of television, given impetus by the mid-decade arrival of ITV. And that was where, at the age of sixty-four, Mary Field went. In 1959 she gave up being executive director of the CFF and went to work for the television company ATV, as director of children's programmes. There, one of her first ideas was to explore the potential of Saturday mornings as a slot for children's television.

15 *Fun and Good Fellowship*

I remember at a children's cinema club hearing shouts of 'Shame!' when a Red Indian girl who was preparing to bathe in a mountain pool did not remove her clothes.

(John Trevelyan, BBFC, 1964)

The one thing that the Maidenhead ABC did have was a Saturday morning cinema club, the peculiarly titled ABC Minors. I had no idea, at any stage of my membership, what a minor was, although as my mum drove a Morris Minor, I must have thought it was something to do with that.

(Nick Hornby, 1995)

In most areas of life, the sixties had a totally different style from the fifties, and this was reflected in children's film shows. The circuits held on to their old terminology of 'matinees' and 'clubs', but to children it was all just Saturday morning (or afternoon) pictures. The differences between one cinema and another were more to do with what confectionery they sold, whether their filing system was efficient enough to prevent you from claiming more than one birthday a year, whether you were allowed in the back row, and whether you could get away with the old trick of letting your mates in through the fire-escape doors near the toilets. The rival to a cinema was not another cinema, but television. Here the creations of Gerry Anderson – *Supercar, Fireball XL5, Stingray* and above all *Thunderbirds* – helped set the standards by which children came to judge their entertainment.

This break with the conventions, knowledge and deference of the past manifested itself in assorted ways. Nick Hornby was not the only one who was a Minor without knowing what a minor was. In East Yorkshire at the same time one contributor, then aged seven, was frightened when his parents told him that he was now old enough to go to the Minors, because he thought it meant that he was going to be sent to dig coal: 'I was afraid of the dark, so even when I found out what Minors did, the prospect of the lights going down

unnerved me. Being a Minor did not seem much more fun than being a miner
– until the first cartoon hit the screen.' A different type of incident exemplifies
a similar rupture. At the Surbiton Odeon in 1966 the only entertainment that
was on offer, apart from the actual films, was the manager going on stage
explaining about projector breakdowns, or telling the children to stop throwing things. That was routine and only mildly amusing, but soon the audience
discovered a way of getting a much better performance out of him: 'The weird-
est thing he told us off about was when, at the end of the National Anthem,
lots of kids stood up and shouted "Sieg Heil!", giving the Nazi salute. I didn't
know what it meant, but I joined in enthusiastically when I saw that it made
him go apoplectic.' And in a cinema not far away, the Tooting Granada, where
unfortunately there was no *Picture Post* photographer present this time, children
managed to achieve something that previous generations had only dreamed of.
An ex-Granadier proudly recalls the occasion:

> There is one feature that I remember – though not its name – for a
> particular reason. It was a Union and Confederate picture, which was
> all talking – the most desperately boring piece of programming you
> could imagine for ten-year-olds.The kids were thumping the seats and
> jumping up and down, and hissing and whistling, for a long time. In
> the end, we booed the film off the screen. The manager took it off and
> put something else on, and a big cheer went up. I was very impressed
> by the realisation that children could actually express their displeasure
> at what was on the screen, and get something done about it. It gave us
> a wonderful feeling of power.

Even if that bout of resistance had not got them anywhere, most of the
Tooting Granadiers would have been back there the following Saturday. Loyalty
to each other, and familiarity with the cinema and the serial, kept children
returning to the same place week after week. It just became a commitment,
regardless of what the films were, and could exercise a pull stronger than
friendship: 'We lived between an ABC and a Granada. A close friend went to
one while I went to the other. That's just the way it worked out. As a result, he
saw *Zorro*, but I didn't; and I saw *King of the Rocket Men*, but he didn't.' As
in the fifties, matinees were for most children a social rather than an audio-
visual occasion. This memoir, about an independent cinema in Abbey Hill,
Edinburgh, is typical:

> It was a pretty big cinema, and generally full on a Saturday morning.
> There were several hundreds of us. Most of the people you were at
> school with were there. Virtually the whole class would reassemble. I'd
> go there and meet everybody I'd just seen the day before. We didn't

make special arrangements to meet other people, because we knew they'd be there anyway. It was just like having a very long free period at school.

However, for every child who was part of a group like that, there was one who was not, either because they had tasted it and did not like it, or because they lived too far away, or because they did not know such institutions existed, or because of parental veto. This book is about the millions who did go, but those who wanted to yet were never allowed to have a story to tell that illustrates public perceptions. As the matinees' charitable activities faded away, without actually dying out completely, they promoted themselves as the cheapest and safest child-care service in town. The commentary to a promotional short shown to ABC evening audiences around 1963 said, over shots of a Minors' queue: 'Just look at those happy faces. They're certainly going to enjoy the fun, the films and the good fellowship while their parents get on with the shopping.' Some parents remained unimpressed. A contributor who still feels 'mildly resentful' about it recounts how she found out what she was missing:

> In the early sixties, our local Odeon cinema at Hounslow West was an exciting place to visit, even merely to walk past. I'd been taken there in afternoons or evenings to see Disney films. On one particular occasion I was with my mother waiting for a bus opposite the Odeon. I always looked at the posters on display when I could, and this time I was surprised to see a long queue of children lined up outside, waiting expectantly to be let in. What puzzled me most was the time of day. What on earth was going on this morning? And, what was more, why didn't I know about it? I was drawn as if by a magnet to the sight of other children having fun. I wanted to join in. When I asked my mother what it was, she said that it was morning cinema for children, adding quickly in response to my whining 'Why can't I go?' that it was for 'other children'. 'What sort of children?', I persisted. 'Council house children', she concluded. I did not understand such categories. Now that I knew about Saturday morning cinema, I wanted to try it. I wanted a taste of everything, occasionally to forsake ballet class in favour of the pictures. But it never happened. My mother frequently used the expression 'a little bit of suburban snobbery' as a criticism of other people's values and behaviour, but I see now that the criticism applied best to her own attitudes.

Perhaps that mother had heard on the parental grapevine about the nature of the good fellowship that prevailed in some places. Memoirs from all over the country relate that precisely because the children who did go were 'all pals together' there was a collective resistance not only to the management but also to the films. Children went there to have fun, and if a film did not offer enough of that very quickly, then they would make their own. In this context the serials were reliable, familiar and action-packed, and the cartoons were colourful and short, but the feature always had to fight for its life. Not all of them lived to tell their tale. This memoir is a composite of images and details from all over Britain:

> Saturday pictures was thought of as a good place in which to behave badly and not get caught, because you had the cover of darkness. At the very least there was always an incredible noise, either of participation in the film, or rejection of it, so that most of the time you had no sense whatever that there was a soundtrack. The situation seemed to have been designed especially as a space in which children could run riot without grown-ups interfering. The name of the game was being there with friends, and having a good time by running around, throwing things, climbing over seats, being ticked off or chased by the usherettes. We never ended up in the seat that we started in. The front row was a good place to be for a while, because then you could try to trip up the ice-cream ladies. Among the things being thrown around, blown out or dropped inside shirts were half-eaten Zoom lollies, Kia-Ora juice cartons, cornets, beakers of Coke, bits of bubble gum – girls with long hair were in particular danger from that – spit balls, peanuts, rice, dried peas, water ballons, and stink bombs. If you could not afford to go in the circle, then at the very least it was imperative not to sit in its line of fire, otherwise you'd end up with an ice-cream or a sticky boiled sweet or the remains of a packet of crisps on your head. The atmosphere was great. Those two hours belonged to us. There was always something to watch or join in, and only occasionally was it on the screen. Later, when a parent asked us what films we'd seen, we rarely knew the answer.

In the cinemas where this kind of response occurred, managers might perhaps have considered trying to modify it by not having confectionery on sale. (Indeed, in one cinema in Edinburgh, Jubblies were neither on sale nor allowed to be brought in from outside; 'but', says one memoir, 'we always wore our duffle-coats, and smuggled the offending items into the cinema inside our hoods. Later, when all the juice had been sucked out, we would chuck the ice at usherettes – great fun'.) A total ban was never really an option though, for with the basic price of admission still fixed at sixpence, till it went up to ninepence and then one shilling towards the end of the decade, the income from ancillary sales often made the difference between a profit and a loss. One ex-manager whom I talked to suggests that without the income from sales (as opposed to box office takings) the matinee movement might well have been forced to close down a decade earlier than it did. As it was, this element became so important in the matinee economy that larger cinemas opened up their regular kiosk and had their full range available all morning, rather than just the narrow selection of cheaper items that had been general in the fifties. An ex-Odeon staff member, in a fairly affluent district of London, describes the situation as she saw it in the sixties and seventies:

> When I began there were about 1,000 children each Saturday. To cope with them there were two of us in the kiosk, and two usherettes inside walking round with trays at the start and at the interval – and they did not carry hot dogs. In the kiosk we sold everything all through the morning – popcorn, ice-creams, sausages, hot dogs, chocolate, sweets, drinks, salted peanuts in packets - and we were kept busy. The children were in and out during the screening, buying hot dogs and popcorn and drinks. They loved those three things. If the film was a bit slack, or if there was an interval, they used to come dashing out. They couldn't decide what they wanted to eat first, because they had enough money for more than one thing. I was there to serve them if they had the money to spend, but I did sometimes say 'You're spending all your pocket money this morning', and they always said 'Oh no, this is not pocket money, it's just money to come to the cinema with.' This was just as true of working-class children as of the others. They all knew that if you were going to the cinema you must have popcorn, you must have a drink, and you must have a hot dog. They definitely spent more on those three things than they did on cinema admission. A hot dog alone cost at least twice as much as the price of admission. At the end there were papers, cartons and ice-cream wrappers everywhere. If you walked in there you would be crunching on popcorn, or sliding on the drink that the children had dropped. At the end the cleaners had to come back in, while most of the children were being picked up by their parents and driven home.

That cinema was exceptional in having the cleaners come back in at the end. In many others, both ABCs and Odeons, they did not need to, for they were already there. It was in the terms of their employment when they joined the company that on Saturday mornings they would start earlier than usual, clear up Friday evening's mess, doff their pinnies, look after the children during the show, walk around with confectionery trays at the start and the interval, and then clean up at the end. In the sixties, for the two-hour matinee duty they got three shillings and sixpence. This was less than usherettes would have had

31. Stocking up in the sixties. Without the income from confectionery sales, matinees might well have come to an end several years earlier than they did

(British Film Institute)

to be paid for the same job, and it avoided having to ask them to work again so soon after clocking off late the night before. Even so, in the cinemas where attendance could be several hundreds, the letter of the law in respect of the ratio of attendants to children was rarely complied with. An ex-manager's memoir comments that in the cinema where he worked the ratio of attendants to children must have been one to 150, or even at times one to 200: 'It was impossible, totally uneconomic, to meet the licensing requirements fully. I may have brought in extra members of staff sometimes, in addition to the cleaners, but still the rules would have been broken.' Another adds: 'It was an old-fashioned, tacky way of doing things.' If there had been loss of life through fire or panic in a matinee in the sixties or seventies, the subsequent inquiry would have revealed that existing safety standards were not being observed; the licensing authorities would have tightened up their enforcement procedures; and many matinees, unable to meet higher staff costs, would have had to close

down much sooner than they did. But there was no serious accident at a matinee in any of the fifty years following the Paisley disaster. Nonetheless, the
under-staffing, and the employment of cleaners to do the work of usherettes
did make a difference. It was one of the reasons why children felt not merely
free to roam around, but justified. From the children's point of view, there was
an analogy with school: 'It was like when you have a supply teacher at school,
instead of your proper teacher. Everyone knows that supply teachers are fair
game. Well, we had supply usherettes every week.'

Managers were paid rather more than the cleaner-usherettes for their work
on a Saturday morning, but for some the money made no difference. If their
heart was not in it, then an extra guinea a week did not put it there. In addition,
they were normally tired, having worked till eleven o'clock or later the night
before, and just could not get enthusiastic about birthdays, or road safety, or
competitions. Such managers felt that they had gone into the business to present entertainment on the screen, not to be an entertainment on the stage. In
larger cinemas, where there was a trainee or assistant manager, the job of
Saturday uncle or chief was frequently delegated to one of them. Thus it happened that, for example, in Hull in 1960, a seventeen-year-old trainee, who
had himself attended matinees just a few years before, found himself standing
in front of 2,500 Minors. He rose to the challenge and carried on running
matinees for twenty years. At the same time, in an ABC in Edinburgh, another
young man had a different experience:

> I was pushed into the job one Saturday morning unexpectedly, and I
> found it extremely difficult and embarrassing. I felt that what the chil-
> dren wanted was for the pictures to start as soon as possible. They
> didn't want some adult waffling on the stage. It's the kind of thing that
> you're either good at or you're not – looking after children and getting
> them enthused. There were others who were much better at it than I
> was. They could organise sing-songs, have children on the stage, clown
> about with them, but I wasn't into that at all. I found children hard to
> look after. It was quite a responsibility, being in charge of around 600.
> I would sometimes get them to make masks, of Mickey Mouse or what-
> ever, and I'd choose a winner the next week. But I was never one for
> dressing up. There was no way I would roll up my trousers for the kids'
> matinee. I didn't think I had become a manager for that.

The importance of managers' attitudes was confirmed in the middle of the
sixties when the CFF commissioned from Group Marketing Research a survey
into audience reception of CFF films and ways in which they could be improved.
Having carried out a total of 1,500 interviews, spread over thirty-two cinemas,
the survey concluded, among other things, that there was little point in isolating

films, since they were far from being the main thing that children went for. The factors that made a particular cinema's matinee 'successful' or not included the programme of films but did not stop there. Overall, said the report, 'the most important influence in maintaining the level of attendance at a particular cinema is the personality and enthusiasm of the manager'. It was not just a question of whether he was willing to roll his trousers up. It was the whole raft of attitudes that he (or she) and the staff and the organisation unconsciously conveyed. In the sixties managers whose body language made it plain that they regarded matinees as a tedious chore, and who therefore adopted an authoritarian approach, were more likely to provoke hostility than to win attention and obedience. The new style, as symbolised by the television programme *Blue Peter* (which partly took over various aspects of the matinees' charitable activity, such as collecting for Guide Dogs) was to have younger managers enthusing and coaxing rather than commanding. After receiving the results of this 1965 survey, the motto of the children's cinema movement became 'Managers Make Matinees'.

That was undoubtedly true, but so was the reverse – that matinees could make managers. One reason why the big circuits were keen to keep them going even in the face of declining attendances and sometimes anarchic behaviour was that they offered a channel of indirect communication not only to the parents, but to the wider public. Children were a good way of getting free publicity for the cinema or the circuit. Sometimes this was tied to a particular film – though almost never a matinee film. Any competition or activity or visitor that was photographed and reported in local media was guaranteed to bring approval from head office. To go further than that, and get regional or even national coverage, meant that knighthood could not be far off. In 1960 one of the big ABC publicity coups was a Minors' Conker Championship between two cinemas in Nottingham. The final – of which the winner was a girl – attracted coverage not only from the six local papers but also from four national dailies and from both television channels. The fact that all this publicity – 120 column inches – was achieved at no cost, did no harm at all to the careers of the managers concerned.

At the end of the decade a cinema in Southend ran a Hot Pants Competition among its matinee children. Photographs of a long line of little girls in hot pants on the cinema stage appeared in the local newspaper. This was part of the manager's campaign to put the cinema back on the map. It was regarded as such a success that in subsequent years there was a competition to find a Cinema Princess. This was not a Rank cinema, but the fact that this sort of competition could happen anywhere illustrates how much had changed since 1951, when the book of rules for Rank managers emphasised that in no circumstances should they run competitions such as 'Best Hair Styles' or 'Nicest Dress'.

32. *A promotional stunt for the Glasgow press, using club members at the Eglinton Toll Odeon in 1968. The 1951 rule-book for Odeon managers had stressed: 'In no circumstances are normal week-day films to be publicised through club members'*

(Scottish Film Archive)

Both the major circuits ran award schemes as incentives for their managers, and success in running matinees (particularly the amount of free publicity generated) was one of the criteria by which they were judged. This was tacit recognition of the fact that the attendance figures for matinees did not depend on the national publicity profile of a particular new release, as the evening shows largely did, but on the manager's relationship with the children, and on the cinema's local image. One contributor recalls applying for the post of manager at Canterbury Odeon in 1970: 'One of the reasons why I got it was that I convinced the area manager that I could do a good job on the Saturday club. It had been operating on an attendance figure of around fifty. I got it up to about 250–300.' That manager is now in charge of one of the company's flagship cinemas.

Such recognition of the centrality of the manager's role did not exactly mean that head office did nothing except deliver pats on the back when a manager got free publicity. In the sixties, ABC cinemas were supplied with special badges, the plan being once again to capitalise on children's love of collecting. This time, however, the items were not free. They were a way of supplementing confectionery sales. One set consisted of the label 'ABC Minors' with a letter of the alphabet underneath; it was hoped that Minors would want to collect all those they needed to spell out their name. A contributor remembers walking home in Beckenham covered in ABC badges, only to discover the danger of being so easily identifiable: 'Seeing me, some old biddy loudly commented: "There's another of those louts from the cinema." I was outraged, but too well brought up to say so.'

The selling point of another set was luminosity. In the middle was a luminous white circle, with the ABC logo and the word 'Minors' on it. Surrounding this was a narrow band which could be any one of at least eight different colours – red, light blue, dark blue, light green, dark green, yellow, pink and

33. Matinees make managers. Children in a promotional stunt for the film Flipper, *1963*   (British Film Institute)

purple. They cost threepence each, so one young boy who was inspired to attend regularly and collect the whole set had to make a hard choice for two months: 'I recall buying one badge each Saturday for several weeks. However, since my balcony seat cost 9d. out of the shilling my mother gave me, each badge I bought meant no sweets that week. At least I still have those badges.'

But there came a time when even luminosity lost its appeal, and when screen clinches seemed inspiring rather than soppy. Games might begin as an extension of a matinee visit, and then gradually take its place completely:

I can't remember making a positive decision not to go to Saturday morning pictures any more, but I can remember the incidents that led up to the parting of the ways. On one visit we'd run into a bunch of girls, three of whom were sisters distantly related to one of the lads I went with. We saw these girls every week after that, and gradually they were embroiled into our games on the wasteland just opposite the cinema. These games didn't follow the plots of the movies, just the genre. Thus after a western we would all be doing the familiar child approximation of horse-riding: a skipping type of run with the hands in front holding on to an imaginary pair of reins. The girls seemed to enjoy the films as much as we did, and entered whole-heartedly into the play afterwards. Slowly, however, the nature of the games changed, moving inexorably from western chase variations of 'it' (a tag game) to the pre-pubescent, sexually titilating 'kiss chase'. Gradually we all started to enjoy these games more than the movies, and often spent the entire morning indulging in our own brand of horseplay. Eventually we weren't going to the matinee at all. On sunny days we'd play all morning on the wasteland and on rainy days spent the time at one of the girls' houses playing the even more adventurous 'True, Dare, Kiss or Promise'. Saturday morning pictures were still important to us though – because that was where our parents thought we were.

16 *Flash Gordon Meets Thunderbirds*

I don't regularly frequent Saturday morning shows for children, but I have been an occasional visitor. I know the difficulty of supplying good and suitable programmes, and it is a pleasure to find a children's film made with affection and imagination. *Danny the Dragon* is a serial, nearly three hours divided into ten episodes. I saw four or five of them one afternoon when the whole thing was being tried out on an audience of children with a sprinkling of adults. I thought it was charming - a cheerful and ingenious mixture of broad comedy and space fiction - and the youngsters were convulsed.

(Dilys Powell, *Sunday Times*, 4 June 1967)

In the volatile social climate of the sixties, CFF had to adapt quickly, or go under. Attainment of the goal that first CEF, and then CFF, had set itself – that of ousting unsuitable commercial films from matinee screens – was nowhere in sight. Both Frank Wells, who followed Field in 1959, and Henry Geddes, who took over from Wells in 1974, had to take account not only of the relatively slight impact that CFF had so far had on children's total screen experience, but also of the fact that matinee audiences were now altered in their nature and diminishing in their numbers. In response CFF changed its outlook and methods drastically, with the result that by the end of the decade even *Flash Gordon* and *Jungle Girl* were on their way out, and the ultimate accolade – having children fantasise about characters in a CFF film – was achieved.

Over the course of the sixties the total number of cinemas running matinees in Britain fell from 994 to 742, a decline which brought with it opportunities. The smaller circuits – Star, Essoldo (later Classic), Granada and many others, some with fewer than ten cinemas – represented exactly half of the total of participating cinemas at the beginning of the decade, but something closer to three-fifths at the end. It was therefore obviously unfair to carry on lumping them all together as 'independents', and treating them as being only one quarter of the CFF market. To remedy this, the Odeons and Gaumonts were merged into one unit, and the Independents were split into two, A and B. Thus by 1962 each of the four groups (ABC, Rank, Independent A, Independent B) were roughly the same size. With the CFF having taken over its own booking arrangements, and the groups now smaller and more nearly equal to each other than they had been in the fifties, there was hope of getting product round the screens more efficiently.

But that easement on its own was not going to make a significant difference to audiences. What was needed was more films, and more enthusiastic acceptance of them. As part of a new look that CFF sought to give itself in the sixties, following Rank's departure as chairman, its production aims were revised. No longer was it looking over its shoulder at what educationists might think. The constitutional requirement was simply that the films it commissioned should 'set as high a standard as possible by appealing to children's intelligence and love of adventure'. Methods of originating films were rethought. Under Field, the CFF had always first developed a story and screenplay, injecting certain things into it, and only secondly looked for a company to film it. This had resulted in CFF product getting a reputation within the industry as being all made to the same formula. To get away from this the CFF invited established directors and writers to submit their own ideas. One result was *Go Kart Go*, which arose from the experience which producer George H. Brown had had when he encouraged his own children to construct a go-kart themselves rather than seek to buy one ready-made.

Another essential break with the past had been ducked for some years because of cost. This was the move from black and white to colour. In 1954, as a freelance film-maker Geddes had managed to shoot in colour even on a CFF budget by using Eastman Colour rather than Technicolor, and by using 16 mm. stock rather than 35 mm. (The 16 mm. was later blown up to

34. Saturday morning audience in Staffordshire at the Regent, Brownhills, early 1962. The Regent was part of the Miles Jervis Cinema Group, a small chain of between six and ten cinemas. Its matinees were the first that Brownhills had seen, which is probably why there are several parents in the audience, apparently checking it out
(The Ned Williams Collection)

35 mm., with Venice prize-winning results.) Black and white had, however, remained the norm for virtually all other productions. In 1965, as executive officer of the Foundation, he persuaded the Board that from then on all features made for the CFF must be in colour. This, and a plan to step up the rate of production of features and serials, was made possible by an increase in the size of the grant the Foundation received from the British Film Fund Agency.

As important as this change from monochrome to polychrome was an awareness that television had changed everything. In the forties and early fifties CFD/CEF and CFF had shaped their films in the belief that it could not be assumed that children were already familiar with the conventions of moving-image story-telling. For the younger ones, a matinee might well be their first-ever audio-visual experience. By the sixties this caution was plainly unnecessary. Geddes put it like this: 'Compared with the early days our audiences have grown younger, but more sophisticated. They have learned the idiom of moving pictures by watching television. Quick cuts, close-ups, and slow dissolves – but not flashbacks – are as accepted a part of the children's world as spacemen and comprehensive schools.'

This greater sophistication had an effect on the old product as well as the new, when it was found that certain films which had come to be regarded by adults as classics of the genre were now too slow for matinee audiences. A pro-gramme of re-editing was put into effect, with the result that *Bush Christmas*, once eighty minutes long, came down to sixty-two. *The Dragon of Pendragon Castle* now had to find the treasure, solve the central-heating problem, and answer the call of the deep, all within thirty-five minutes. Some films which had once been features became 'featurettes', and had to be paired up in order to fill the hour which a matinee programme typically accorded to the 'big picture'.

All these internal developments made a difference, but it was an external change that brought about the last breakthrough, and allowed Geddes to make headway in a drive to produce CFF films that were less middle class. The Children and Young Persons Act of 1963, and fresh regulations arising from it, finally swept away most of the restrictions that had been imposed thirty years earlier. Child actors still had to have chaperones, and three hours of academic tuition if they were filming in term-time, and they were not supposed to rehearse or perform for more than three-and-a half hours each day, or more than eighty days during any one year. This, however, was a much more manage-able situation than had obtained before. No longer was it virtually essential to use child actors from one of the stage schools. From new-style training grounds such as the Barbara Speake Agency, and later the Anna Scher Children's Theatre, came urban children who went to ordinary schools and were encouraged to develop their acting talents while retaining their own accents, pronunciation and diction. Jack Wild, who was later to play the Artful Dodger in *Oliver!* and get an Oscar nomination for it, was discovered by Barbara Speake, and became one of the first to bring a working-class London accent to the matinee screens when he befriended *Danny the Dragon* in 1966. Later Linda Robson, Pauline Quirk, Phil Collins, Tod Carty and others were to carry on from Wild.

Another important effect of the new regulations was that it became easier to have a large number of children in a film. *Go Kart Go* took early advantage of this new situation, and presented not just one go-karting gang but two. Later *Zoo Robbery* brought in hordes of children for the final chase-and-rescue sequence, as this had been discovered to be a surefire way to get the audience shouting vociferous encouragement. But it was in the eighteen-part series *The Magnificent Six-and-Half* that the device of having an assorted gang – two girls (one of them very young), one black boy, one boy with glasses – really paid off in terms of audience appreciation. The intention was that everyone in the audience could find someone on the screen to identify with. So popular was it that after two series of six episodes the production company took the format, and one of the actors (Brinsley Forde) to the BBC, and recreated it for television as *The Double Deckers*. (As a result, these two series are often confused in popular memory.)

Additionally, there was a fresh attempt to increase the frequency of the appearance of the CFF trademark shot (Trafalgar Square, pigeons fluttering by the fountain, the bells of St Martin-in-the-Fields ringing out), and to broaden children's cinematic experience, by acquiring and revoicing films from other countries. Many special films were being made overseas, in the Communist countries particularly, but CFF excluded anything which it perceived as being propaganda, or a fairy-tale, or based on family problems such as abandonment, or as presenting children from an adult's perspective, or as purveying classroom-style instruction. The few that got through this net came from Czechoslovakia, Bulgaria, East Germany, Japan, Hungary and Russia. One Russian film, originally called *Welcome* but retitled *No Holiday for Inochkin*, caused one of the very few brushes with the BBFC that the CFF ever had. Normally, a film shot specially for the CFF was more or less guaranteed a U because the CFF would see at script stage if there was anything that the censor was likely to object to, but when Elem Klimov made *Welcome*, he did not have the BBFC or the CFF in mind. Matt McCarthy, who was responsible for finding and adapting many of these foreign films, recalls a problem that Klimov gave him:

> Many of Klimov's later films were quite scurrilous about the Soviet regime, but this was his first one and I thought it very funny, very fast-moving, with lots of things our children could relate to. It is political, but only if you think of it in its Soviet context. It's also quite surreal in places. It's about a Young Pioneer holiday camp, and in the story Inochkin (revoiced by Keith Chegwin) is about to be expelled for being

naughty, and is terrified at the prospect of going home and facing his grandmother. So the rest of the Pioneers come to his rescue. They manage to hide him in a hole in the ground under the Leader's dais (a fairly obvious metaphor for political subversion), and all is going well until suddenly there's a Parents' Day. Not knowing that Inochkin has been expelled, Granny is coming to visit the camp, so the boys have to find some way of keeping her and all the other parents out. There's a big nettle patch outside the dormitory, and their plan is to strip off completely, roll in the nettles, and try to catch 'measles'. It's a hilarious situation. Nobody wants to go first, for obvious reasons, so they pick straws. The loser doesn't want to go, so they all get behind him and push. He goes rolling down screaming, and then suddenly jumps up and says: 'It's lovely, it's lovely.' The others then all join in. It's a very funny scene. After revoicing it I sent it to the Censor, expecting the usual semi-automatic U certificate, but it came back with a note from John Trevelyan, saying: 'There are shots of little boys' genitals, and these should be removed.' I trimmed about seventeen seconds, with on-the-spot advice from Trevelyan himself, and then resubmitted it. This time it got the U certificate that we needed – but we had to pay for the resubmission.

However, the extra Eady money, the Eastman Colour, the awareness of a changed audience, the more demotic diction, the subversive imports, the revamped versions of films from the forties – these things took a long time to seep down to the level of general experience. Even at the end of the decade, in fifty-three matinees (an extra one for Christmas Eve, which fell on a Wednesday in 1969) the Torquay ABC Minors could have seen over the course of one year only eighteen CFF features, seven CFF serials, and four CFF shorts. Total CFF screen time, at thirty-five hours out of one hundred and six, was therefore more or less exactly one-third. Out of those thirty-five hours, only nine were in colour. These proportions might have varied slightly in other cinemas, but not by much, because the booking system was geared to being scrupulously even-handed. The figures mean that, though for the CFF office it was a decade of expansion and the new look, for children in the cinemas CFF product was at most only one-third of what they saw, and by far the greater part of that third was 'old look'. The following memoirs have to be understood against that background, and in the context of the collective adventure that the act of matinee-going had become:

I loved Enid Blyton books, and so I ought to have loved the CFF films which were based on them, or in the same style, but I didn't. When I read Blyton books I could provide the voices myself, but at the Peckham

Odeon we thought the kids on the screen sounded terribly snotty-nosed and posh. We'd sneer at them, and take the piss. All the same we did get involved in their adventures – we wanted them to win, or to escape. With all their failings, they were all we had – till Jack Wild came along.

At the Tooting Granada, CFF films were very popular, especially the serials. I remember clearly *The Young Jacobites* going back in time. That made a big impression on us. We talked about what had happened, and what was going to happen. The alien historical environment, plus the time-warp thing, just caught our imagination. We had little gangs and clubs ourselves. When there was something about, say, buried treasure in a CFF film, this would lead to a lot of play-acting and messing around on the local park or common. It actually encouraged us to creep into derelict houses, and re-enact some of the scenes. There was a fair degree of identification with the children in CFF films, more than with Shirley Temple or a western. I really wanted to be King of the Rocket Men, but I knew that was a bit unrealistic, so I settled for being a CFF kid.

The Magnificent Six-and-a-Half will always be strong in my memory, because I definitely wanted to be one of them when I stepped outside the Dunstable ABC. It was a very funny series. I soon learned to recognise the opening Trafalgar Square shot because of the *Six-and-a-Half*, and I confidently expected that a CFF film would be good – either scary or funny. I can't recall the names of any other CFF films, but I know that we found them very involving and exciting. The children would scream and stamp their feet when the kids in the film were beating up the baddies.

At the ABC State, Barkingside, I usually found CFF films pretty dull. Their storylines always seemed to involve kids uncovering a plot and having to outwit adults. But there were some that I did enjoy. These featured a bunch of kids in the countryside. When I was growing up I didn't visit the countryside much. It was, in a strange way, almost as exotic as the Wild West.

In Sutton and Purley the CFF serials, which were mainly black and white, were not looked forward to much. We regarded them, particularly their endings, as rather tame and stilted, compared to the American cliff-hangers, which were much more fun. CFF features, however, were perfectly OK with us. They were not thrilling, but they were enjoyable. Some of them were even in colour, and reasonably modern. Towards the end of my matinee-going, with *The Magificent Six-and-Half*, they seemed almost up-to-date. Colour was a rarity on a Saturday morning, in any film other than cartoons, and that made us more appreciative.

What I liked best were the black-and-white serials, whether they were CFF or American. Two of the CFF films that stick in my memory are *The Young Jacobites*, which had Scottish accents rather than the usual ones, and *Five Clues to Fortune*, which fed our imaginations and games for weeks afterwards.

The two-thirds or more of screen time that did not contain CFF material is dominated, in popular memory, by the superheroes of the American cliff-hangers. This is in line with the 1965 research which concluded that children at matinees were interested in adults only when they were exceptional. The thrill of anticipation and participation when plain Billy Batson was in trouble and was obviously about to say 'SHAZAM!' and turn into Captain Marvel was common in matinees across Britain, throughout the decade. Batman too offered a quick release: because he cannot actually fly he was easier to copy than Superman or Captain Marvel. The *Batman* serial, having been made just after the Japanese bombing of Pearl Harbor, has an oriental villain named Daka, who in an earlier decade had chilled some children, and made them wary of fairgrounds. Sixties' children seem to have been equal to the challenge. Their duffle-coats serving both as hood and cape, they did not even wait till they got out of the cinema, but joined in instantly. There was a similar attraction to *King of the Rocket Men*: he could fly, but only because he had a rocket pack strapped to his back. Frances Gifford as *Jungle Girl* had a different kind of special power – sex. Each week at the end of the episode she presented an image of lightly clad innocent beauty needing to be rescued, thereby stirring romantic feelings in older boys. For at least twenty-two years after *Picture Post*'s publication of the infra-red photographs of children watching *Jungle Girl*, it remained a fixture in matinee programming.

Most serials such as these, though they dated from the forties, did not need to be refreshed in order to make them acceptable to children in the sixties. In general, their milieus were so far removed from children's daily experience that they did not show their age too much. *Flash Gordon* was not so fortunate. The sixties was not only the decade of space exploration and moon landing in real life. More importantly for children, from 1965 onwards, it was also the era of *Thunderbirds* on television. Before the war, when the Flash Gordon serials were new, some children were frightened by the buzzing and flashing that accompanied the space ships as they came in to land. Thirty years later a new generation had a different reaction: 'Most of the kids, myself included, would laugh scornfully at the unsophisticated model rockets on wires with sparklers.

We were all Thunderbirds fans then, and by comparison with the special effects in *Flash Gordon*, the Thunderbirds seemed the height of realism.' This did not immediately destroy the Flash Gordon serials, however. They continued to be enjoyed, if perhaps differently from the way they had been in earlier decades. The last two – *Trip to Mars* and *Conquers the Universe* – were shown till at least 1970.

Television affected the matinees in other ways too. It was omnipresent. Films which had spun off from television shows – often boasting colour where the TV original was in black and white – found their way on to Saturday morning screens. Examples of this are the two Dr Who films – *Dr Who and the Daleks* and *Daleks: Invasion Earth 2150 AD*. Television origination was also responsible for one of the few non-narrative films screened in the 'big picture' slot. This was *Six Five Special*, a compendium of pop performances, including Petula Clark, Dickie Valentine and Cleo Lane. There was even a *Batman* feature, derived not from the cinema serial but from the jokey, Riddler-infested television series; and a new Rin Tin Tin, based on the television revival of the old silent star.

Just as significant as television's role in sending things to the big screen was the part it played in keeping things off it. Matinees had always been at the end of the queue for renting commercial films, and when Sunday-only screenings were phased out, they might have expected to get their turn a little sooner. That never happened, however, because in the sixties television was a major buyer of films: a sale to television was worth much more than renting it to matinees.

This difficulty and others sent matinee programmers scrambling everywhere to find films to fill the slots for which no CFF film had yet been made. The principal criterion was whether a film had a U certificate. If it was a U, and was available for the price that matinees could pay, then it would have to be very unsuitable indeed before being rejected. One film that a contributor remembers as being shown, but not watched, lasted two hours. It was so long that there was no time that morning for any of the usual short items – cartoon, comedy, serial episode. What unsettled the children was that the established format had been broken. Matinees were essentially a social ritual, and depended on a large degree of pattern repetition each week. The breaks, and the changes of style, were necessary ingredients, and the manager had failed to respect that. Almost as long was *High Society*, shown to Minors early in the decade. *High Society* is in Technicolor, with major stars (Crosby, Sinatra, Grace Kelly) and an Oscar-nominated song (*True Love*). But for children it has virtually nothing. All that happens in it is that a load of unexceptional adults stand around talking and singing sophisticatedly about who is going to marry a wealthy Philadelphia socialite. It seems quite likely that on mornings or afternoons such as these the children's behaviour was not of the most orderly.

Not that children had anything against music in principle. It was all a question of style and context. Uncle Mac had given up presenting Children's Favourites when faced with volumes of requests for the same kind of music – pop – as could be heard in general programming. The music that was played before the matinee started, the songs children sang on stage in talent contests, the dances they danced – these were always pop. ABC capitalised on this by showing both Beatles films at Minors' matinees relatively soon after their first release (which had been on the Rank circuit, not the ABC). At the Selly Oak ABC, Birmingham, for example, *A Hard Day's Night* was the attraction on

35. *For sixpence, in the summer of 1965, Glasgow children could see* For the Love of Rusty *at the Odeon, Eglinton Toll. Made in 1947, in black and white, it is an American film about a father and son who are alienated from each other until the boy's Alsation dog is wounded. Together, father and son nurse him back to health. Alternatively, children could try to get extra money and go to the same cinema later that same day to see the Beatles, in colour, in* Help! *Or, though they did not know this at the time, they could wait for two years and then see* Help! *at an ABC matinee for sixpence* (Scottish Film Archive)

New Year's Eve 1966, only eighteen months after it first came out. *Help!* took a little longer to arrive: it played in ABC matinees in September 1967, having been released in July 1965. The point of this – presumably fairly expensive – programming must have been to raise the profile of the ABC matinees, to attempt to lure back some of the vanishing thousands, to become associated in young minds with the Beatles' unparalleled popularity. It certainly succeeded in some of those aims, if only in the short term. Minors in Beverley, hearing that they were to see *A Hard Day's Night* the following week, instantly invented a game called Beatles and Fans. Each child had to be either one or the other; then the Fans, screaming, chased the Beatles down the road. When the day of the screening came, there was intense anticipation and excitement. The usual preponderance of boys over girls in audiences was reduced if not reversed. Nick Hornby remembers the showing of *Help!* at Maidenhead as being the only occasion in his experience when Minors 'really were laughing and having a sing-song and shouting aloud with glee'.

A few threads run through the rest of the motley medley that filled the screen. There were muscle-men movies, such as *Hercules in the Centre of the Earth*, and *Triumph of the Ten Gladiators*. There were British comedies from the forties – Old Mother Riley and George Formby – and newer ones from Norman Wisdom. The Three Stooges, after making hundreds of two-reelers which became stock matinee fillers in the forties, graduated to features at the end of their careers and provided *The Stooges Go West*, *Snow White and the Three Stooges* and even *The Three Stooges Meet Hercules*. Among the animals on screen, along with the new Rin Tin Tin, was Trigger Junior. And there were several compilation movies – such as *The Golden Age of Comedy* and *Days of Thrills and Laughter* – which added music and commentary to a collection of clips from silent cinema.

Not quite all U films were found acceptable by the major circuits. One group of films not seen in Odeons or ABCs was the *Carry On* series. Its double-entendres and occasional displays of flesh must have been regarded as not meeting the criterion of 'clean healthy fun' that the clubs aimed to provide. An independent cinema in Portobello, Edinburgh, did show them, though, as a contributor recalls:

> My parents were lower middle class and were not at all keen on the idea of my going to Saturday afternoon pictures. I had to work hard to persuade them. They were particularly reluctant because they thought I would see *Carry On* films there. Of course I would! That was why I wanted to go. There were kids' adventures as well – animals and pirates. But the *Carry On*s were our favourites. I remember more than once having to lie to my parents about the programme, making up some film that I said had been shown, when really it had been a *Carry On*.

Faced perpetually with this problem of finding enough features to feed the hundreds of matinee mouths, the programmers sometimes opted instead for a morning filled entirely with separate short items - as many as eight in some cases. A typical programme of this kind in 1970 consisted of: episodes from two different CFF serials – *Danny the Dragon* and *Five Have a Mystery to Solve*; two Disney cartoons – *No Smoking* and *Dude Duck*; a thirty-six minute documentary about Australian wildlife – *Land of the Kangaroo*; and three miscellaneous cartoons – *Bird in a Bonnet*, *Dizzy Yardbirds* and *Three Hams on Rye*. If the standard pattern had to be departed from, then this type of replacement must have been far more acceptable and accessible to a matinee audience than a complete two-hour film was. With an eight-item programme, if there was a part you did not like, it did not matter too much because there would be another one along in a moment, whereas from an all-morning two-hour feature there was absolutely no escape.

The year 1969 was marked as the twenty-fifth anniversary of the start of special production for children (counting *Tom's Ride* as having been made in 1944), and a celebratory promotional film narrated by Rolf Harris was shown to general audiences, in cinemas that ran matinees, to try to raise public awareness of CFF's existence. The commentary introduced short clips from a selection of CFF films, promising adventure, comedy, drama, excitement, fantasy, science fiction, mystery, location-shooting in Tunisia (*Son of the Sahara*) and other films with an overseas setting (New Zealand, Kenya, Egypt, Holland, Austria). The names of adult stars who had appeared in CFF films were listed: Irene Handl, Charlie Drake, Patricia Hayes, Jimmy Edwards, Graham Stark, Bernard Cribbins, Hattie Jacques, Ronnie Barker, David Lodge, Leslie Crowther, Roy Kinnear. It ended with the exhortation: 'This world of entertainment is here every week, just for children. What about your lot? Are you gonna let them come along too? You know by now that they're certainly going to enjoy it. Think about it.'

It was understandable self-promotion, but its implication was not true. There were still plenty of matinee Saturdays that contained no CFF component at all, and many more that contained nothing but a serial episode. Eighteen years had passed since the setting-up of the industry's own solution to the problem of programming matinees in ways acceptable to everyone, and yet controllers and managers still had to scratch around and fill two-thirds of the slots with non-Foundation product. In these circumstances there arose a perception that the five-year release cycle instituted in 1951 (one year for each distribution group, one year resting) was no longer appropriate. In that year the age-range of audiences was six to thirteen, and the number of matinees being catered for was well over 1,000. By the end of the sixties children rarely attended matinees after transferring to secondary school; and the number of regular matinee screens was down to around 742. It was therefore possible to

36. *The Classics chain, part of one of the independent groups serviced by the CFF, had their own special mascot – Louee the Lion. The costume travelled round from cinema to cinema, and a member of staff put it on when appropriate. Here a club birthday party is being celebrated at the Classic, Kilburn in 1970*

(Arthur Frost)

change to a four-year cycle without creating logistical problems or having children complain that they had 'seen this one before'. The effect of this simple
change, in conjunction with the re-editing of old titles and the acquisition of
foreign films, was rapid and dramatic. In 1973, thirty-four out of fifty-two
features shown at Torquay, and all but two of the series and serial episodes,
came from the CFF. Additionally, there were six CFF shorts. Not a single week
went by without a CFF presence in the schedule. CFF product now filled at least
half of the annual screen time, and most of it, including some of the black-and-
white material, was receiving high approval ratings in managers' weekly
reports.

   With a further reduction in the release cycle planned – from four years to
three – it looked as if CFF was at last poised to take over virtually every feature
and serial slot every Saturday throughout Britain by the end of the seventies.
That is indeed what happened – but by then there were very few children
around to notice.

17 *To Be Discontinued*

As I look back on the history of the British film industry, it seems to me that we have made three unique contributions to world cinema: the documentaries of the 1920s and 30s, the Ealing comedies, and the Children's Film Foundation.

(Margaret Hinxman, *Daily Mail* film critic, 1976)

Around the turn of the decade the ABC and Rank circuits exchanged hats. In the forties and fifties Rank had by implication claimed the moral high ground, on the strength of its wartime efforts, its subsidising of CFD/CEF for six years, its charity collections and its slightly less commercial programming of Saturday mornings. But after 1969 a fourth name change resulted in the terms 'club' 'children' and 'boys and girls' being dropped completely. In most Rank cinemas there were no more badges and not much singing of 'We come along on Saturday morning . . . .' For the last twelve years of JARO's involvement in the matinee movement, young people in an Odeon or Gaumont were not attending a meeting; they were, rather, taking in a Super Saturday Show (SSS). The only relic of earlier days was the system of sending out birthday cards (newly designed in the pop art style of Alan Aldridge) inviting the recipient to bring a guest and get free entry. Even this was not maintained for long in some cinemas, as one manager recalls:

If my helpers did not turn up on a Wednesday, I had to go through the files and do the birthday cards myself. If there were quite a few, that was a problem. In itself it does not seem a very big thing – to get out a wooden box with cards in, and pick out the right ones – but the reality could be rather different. It could become a tiresome chore. You had to set aside the time, and then you'd go to the stamp tin and find it empty, and you'd have to remember to get some on your way in on the Thursday . . . .

37. *Early seventies. 'The Super Saturday Show wishes you many happy returns of the day and invites you and a friend to be guests at our next Super Show'*

J. Arthur Rank, by then Lord Rank, died in March 1972. He had not been in day-to-day control of Rank Organisation business for many years, but within the company he had been the keeper of the flame. He had been there in Morden Odeon with Arthur Askey and Uncle Mac twenty-nine years previously, and still represented the spirit of the forties. His death symbolised the final passing of the ideals he had once proclaimed to the world. He may have been unhappy to see that what was once the ONCC now had initials that reminded him of Hitler's SS. He would certainly have repudiated any manager who behaved, a year or two after his death, like the one recalled here:

I remember well an incident at my local Odeon, which occurred when an additional morning show was arranged during the school holidays. They had scheduled too many items for the event, and were in danger of colliding with the start of the first afternoon show of that week's main film. Halfway through a CFF film (which I recall was about a gang of children endeavouring to solve a crime, with one of them trying to get into the villain's house disguised as a Guy Fawkes), at a particularly exciting moment, the screen was faded out and the house lights came up. There was uproar from the crowd, with demands for 'our money back' – but to no avail. We were ushered out into the street as usual with a promise that the rest of the film would be shown at the following week's normal Saturday show. It wasn't. In fact, it never came round again while I was attending. No doubt the gang of children succeeded in bringing the crooks to justice – but I never found out exactly how.

38. By the seventies, the Minors had dropped not only the use of the word 'matinees', but also the custom of inviting a birthday Minor to bring a guest free

Meanwhile, the ABC chain's Saturday morning customers remained 'Minors' right to the end, even after EMI took over the company in 1969. Use of the term 'matinees' was, however, discontinued: some badges in the seventies referred to 'EMI ABC Minors Happy Saturday Cinema Show'. The song did not change at all though, and with the help of a bouncing ball was still being sung forty years after its first use. Behind the Minors and managers there was a new controller, Reg Helley, and a head office, which employed more staff than its Rank counterpart. In the seventies, from that office came a series of central initiatives of a kind then absent from Rank cinemas. Chief of these was the establishment of the Chiffy Awards (the telegraphic address of the CFF was 'CHIFI'). Helley conceived them as the Minors' equivalent of Oscars. The idea was that every year Minors all over Britain would vote to determine their favourite three CFF features, and one CFF serial, from those they had seen in the past twelve months. This was accompanied by a countrywide competition among Minors to design and create the awards for the makers of the winning films. The designs were required to represent the idea of children's cinema, and could be made out of almost anything. Any adult help given had to be acknowledged, and was taken into consideration in the final judging, which involved film people from both sides of the camera. For the winning director and producer, the climax was a gala showing of the film and receipt of the award. For the winning Minor, the first prize was a VIP day trip to the EMI studio at Elstree.

Additionally, Minors were once again encouraged to collect silver paper and tin foil in order to help buy Guide Dogs, even though *Blue Peter*, now well established on television, might have been thought to have taken over that type of campaign. A more up-to-date slant was put on collecting when the focus was shifted from silver paper to Green Shield trading stamps. Nearly 5,000 books were filled, making possible the donation of fourteen Chairmobiles to organisations for disabled people. Local effort was expected too: in Leeds the Minors raised hundreds of pounds for the Lord Mayor's Appeal by organising sponsored swims. But it was about public relations as well as charitable giving:

> As managers, we used to get a lot of mileage out of the Minors. There was a time when my photograph was in the local paper just about every other week, because of the charity things, the Chiffy awards, and so on. Certainly it was the Minors that put that cinema on the map, generating a load of interest – and that's what it was all about, at the end of the day, even though this goodwill could not be measured and put on the bottom line of the Minors' financial return.

For a couple of years at the start of the decade the number of Minors' matinees, perhaps coaxed along by head office policy of appointing managers partly on the basis of their willingness to open or maintain a Saturday morning organisation, actually increased slightly – from 172 to 177. During the same period the SSS total went down from 165 to 137. Hidden within such overall figures were cinemas such as the ABC Selly Oak, Birmingham, which in the mid-sixties had regularly attracted an average of 650 Minors each week, but by 1972 was down to twenty, so had to pull the plug; and the Edinburgh Odeon, which closed down and then reopened when a new manager arrived. The projectionist recalls the difference between the relaunch and what had gone before:

> It was a revamped update, with much more in the way of stage entertainment. There would be disco dancing in front of the stage for maybe half an hour, and sometimes we had kids' bands on stage. Lots of kids liked to play the guitar. As projectionists we could contribute to the fun by controlling the music and lighting, which made it more of a challenge. Such was the success of the stage activity that to the kids the films were secondary. They just wanted the bands to play.

But these two circuits combined were now in a minority. The independents, speaking through their representative organisation, the Association of Independent Cinemas, became increasingly influential as they became numerically dominant. In several cases an independent cinema that had never run matinees before started one when the local ABC or Rank closed down. Being smaller, and not having a head office to pay for, they could sometimes make a profit in situations where an ABC or Rank cinema could not. Even so, a rift was opening up between the major circuits and the independents. Before decimalisation of coinage in February 1971 the most common charge for matinee admission had been one shilling. In some cinemas the new price was 5p – the equivalent of what it had been before – but in others the chance was taken to increase it to 10p. CFF fixed on a policy of refusing to supply its product to any matinee that charged more than that amount for admission, because one of the original ideas behind the setting-up of the Foundation was that all charges must be kept as low as possible, so as not to disadvantage children from poorer families, and because of an agreement with the unions that CFF product must be non-commercial. The total price that a cinema paid to the CFF for the hire of films was less than £10, a figure which had been calculated on the basis of covering the immediate cost of print transport and eventually, in conjunction with all other cinemas, the cost of striking the print in the first place. Recouping the cost of the original production, even partially, was never envisaged. The independents had to abide by the 10p-ruling, because they, even more than the circuits with their power of block booking, had difficulty in getting non-CFF product that was short enough and had a U certificate. At the beginning of the fifties they had been suspicious of the Foundation and slow to accept its films, but twenty years later they were totally reliant on it. Even so, as more and more matinees closed down, they began to argue that 10p was a ludicrously low price, one that did not represent anything like the same proportion of a child's pocket money as 6d. had done thirty years before. In this situation ancillary sales – badges, confectionery, ice-creams, popcorn, hot dogs smothered in tomato ketchup – became more and more important. By the middle of the decade the independents' argument had made some headway and the maximum admission price that a cinema could charge, and still be eligible to receive CFF films, was raised to 15p.

Inflation had hit also the cost of producing these films. Whereas an annual grant of £125,000 had been enough in the fifties and early sixties, when the fixed price for a feature was £25,000, by the middle of the seventies the CFF was applying for, and getting, more than three times that amount. While it was true that the overall number of matinees was slowly dwindling, this reduction was at first proportionate to the number of cinemas that had closed down completely. There was therefore no sense that the CFF was conspicuously failing in its task, so the British Film Fund Agency saw no reason to cut back the grant.

One of the films that the money paid for was *The Boy who Turned Yellow*. The CFF was accustomed to seeing directors who had made a film or two for them early in their career go on to achieve national or international distinction – people like Lewis Gilbert, Don Chaffey, James Hill, John Guillermin, John Krish, Muriel Box. With *The Boy who Turned Yellow*, that situation was reversed, for it was the last film ever to result from a collaboration beween Michael Powell and Emeric Pressburger, whose previous credits included *The Red Shoes*, *Black Narcissus* and *The Life and Death of Colonel Blimp*. It came about because Powell, nominated by the British Film Producers' Association, had been serving for some years on the Foundation's Production Committee. By his own account he could not easily get work in the seventies, and knowing that Pressburger liked writing for children (he had contributed to the screenplay for the original German version of *Emil and the Detectives*), Powell proposed that the old team should get back together again and make something for the Foundation. The result was a story about a boy who loses one of his pet mice in the Tower of London, turns yellow between Chalk Farm and Hampstead while going home on the underground, and then has a dream about travelling through a television set along electronic waves back to the Tower, where he finds his mouse but almost has his head cut off by the Beefeaters. Some other members of the Production Committee, though happy with the story, were doubtful about Powell's ability to work within the constraints of a CFF budget – around £60,000 per feature at that time – because he had a record of over-spending. However, his enthusiasm and the Committee's satisfaction with the story pushed the project through, and the film was made, costing eventually just a fraction more than had been allocated. Audience restlessness during a test screening indicated strongly that there was too much talking in it, so Pressburger cut out about five minutes of dialogue, and after that it worked well, winning the top Chiffy Award for three years out of the last four (1977, 1978 and 1980).

Perhaps the film's recognition of the centrality of television in contemporary life was part of its appeal. It was certainly television that held the mass audience now. To some extent, the CFF was able to use this fact to its advantage, by providing clips from its films for use in the BBC children's television weekday quiz *Screen Test*. The clips served as trailers; and, equally importantly, the very fact of their being broadcast on television gave them, and the Foundation, and the whole matinee movement, a credibility in children's eyes which could not have been achieved through any other medium. For regular matinee-goers the experience of seeing such a clip, and either being smugly able to tell other children about the whole film, or to look forward to seeing it one Saturday, was very satisfying. In the fifties some managers had complained that the problem with CFF films was that they had no profile, no recognisability. In the seventies many hundreds of thousands of *Screen Test* viewers certainly knew the Foundation by name if nothing else.

But at the same time television was offering direct competition to matinees. For most of 1972, ITV showed *Thunderbirds* at 11.45 a.m. on a Saturday. In the autumn this changed to *Follyfoot* and *The Man from Uncle*. By December it was *Stingray* and *Merrie Melodies*. The BBC similarly put on old films, bought-in programmes and cartoons. On neither channel was there much original programming. Nonetheless, interviews with 1,500 children in 1972 revealed that 25 per cent of them usually spent Saturday morning watching television, while another 7 per cent knew about matinees and could have gone to one, but positively preferred to stay in. These proportions increased after 1974 when *Tiswas* started, because *Tiswas* was live, loud, zany, original. It recognised that the Saturday morning still-in-pyjamas audience was differently situated from the weekday home-from-school audience. Initially broadcast only by ATV, in the Midlands region, it did not immediately have a significant effect on overall matinee attendance figures; but it was the seed of much that was to come.

The same year saw another seminal event in the story of the rise and fall of matinees, when the Minors came up against the miners. As a result of the NUM strike of winter 1973, the Heath Government introduced in early 1974 severe restrictions on the non-domestic use of electrical power – the 'three-day week'. Cinemas were compelled to reduce the number of shows they put on. Naturally, the managers chose to cut out the ones they thought least likely to be profitable. In many cinemas, the children's Saturday matinees were cancelled for the duration of the restrictions. After two months there was a general election which returned the Labour Party to government. The miners' strike was settled, and normal working conditions resumed. For some matinees, however, the two-month black-out proved terminal. Managers whose heart was not in it found reasons for not restarting; one factor was that late-night Friday screenings were capable of drawing big audiences, but the thought of working late on Friday and then having to be sunny and bright early the following morning was more than some managers could bear. For their part, some children had found other things to do on Saturday mornings while their matinee was closed. In December 1973 there had been 658 regular matinees, but by December of 1974 there were only 544 – the biggest twelve-month drop the matinees ever suffered.

A few months later *Tiswas* went nationwide; and the following year the BBC pitched in with the three-hour long *Saturday Swap Shop*. Managers were soon reporting that these programmes were having a noticeable effect on matinee attendance. Through its outside broadcasts, its phone-ins, its autocue-less spontaneity and its practice of having dozens of kids in the studio, *Swap Shop* created that sense of access and participation and solidarity which had previously been one of the matinees' strong suits in their contest with television. Moreover, it offered all this free, and without the consumer having to get up at a particular time, or get dressed, or have breakfast first, or sustain concentration on one story for any length of time. It even used as one of its presenters a young actor – Keith Chegwin – who had played the lead in a recent CFF film that did well in the Chiffy Awards, won a prize in the Moscow Film Festival of 1975 and, according to its director, edged out Errol Flynn and 'caused such audience response that it shattered the glass in the exit signs' when shown by the Centre of Films for Children in Los Angeles.

This was *Robin Hood Junior*, one of the few period films ever made for CFF. Considerations of cost normally precluded the acceptance of any projects that involved recreating the past (though on the rare occasions when it had been managed, such as with *The Young Jacobites*, it had proved popular). Making *Robin Hood Junior* on a CFF budget, and with only twenty-one days of shooting, was possible only because the producer had the good fortune to find a tangled forest and a medieval castle that were not merely available; more than that, they were located within thirty miles of Piccadilly Circus. That meant, under an agreement with the trade unions, that the production budget did not have to pay for overnight accommodation for anyone. The assumption was that the place of work was near enough for cast and crew to be able to get there by 8.30 in the morning. This and other strokes of luck resulted in *Robin Hood Junior* going only £700 over budget. This memoir, from director Matt McCarthy, illustrates the economies, the goodwill, the rule-bending and the improvisation which alone made CFF films possible:

> Because of financial constraints, we were limited to casting children in London. This did not matter to the story, because it was not about the

young Robin Hood, and therefore did not have to take place near Nottingham, but I was concerned about how the children in, say, Bristol would react to these London accents. As it turned out, I need not have worried. We saved money by doing away with make-up completely, except for powdering away sweat on occasion. Also Andrew Sachs, playing a friar, needed something when he cut his nose rather badly after a donkey panicked and threw him off. But that was our limit with make-up. The art director, Maurice Fowler, had worked on *The Third Man* in the forties, and later was art director for Spielberg on *Empire of the Sun* and some of the new Superman movies. He worked on *Robin Hood Junior* for a pittance because he was a friend of mine, and because it was for the Foundation, which people in the industry still believed in. His wife came along too, and looked after hair-styles. There are a lot of children in the film, and we always had to be very careful to keep an eye on their feet. They did not like going around barefoot. You had to be very careful that they hadn't slipped a very modern pair of sneakers on.

A restriction, or at least a guideline, in the making of CFF films was that you weren't supposed to do stunts with children, or stunts that the children in the audience might want to copy. However, we actually did do quite a bit of stunt-work in *Robin*. In one scene we had Robin swing from the saddle and up into a tree. I had chosen Keith for the part because he was practically fearless and could ride like the wind, and for this stunt he was travelling at probably thirty miles an hour. A lot of people had warned me that he could break his back doing it. Keith stuck his hands up and hit that branch with a terrible crash, and I thought 'God Almighty!', but Keith was clever enough and athletic enough to swing with it, and come back and swing himself up safely into the tree, all in one shot. None of this had been rehearsed, because we just did not have time. Even if it had been only a rehearsal, I would still have filmed it, for I had learned that lesson from an earlier incident. Robin and Little John have a scene where they are escaping from the castle, and there's a horse tethered near the bottom of the stairs. They come running down the stairs and have to swing over the balcony and land plonk on the saddle, the two of them together. For that scene we did have a rehearsal, and it went like a dream. They landed together perfectly, pulled up the horse, and away it went with them on it. But after that the horse knew what was going to happen and would not co-operate. It panicked and took fright. In the end there were about seven of us hanging on to his legs, trying to hold him there so Robin and Little John could get into the saddle. All this because I had not filmed the rehearsal! Anyway it was impossible, and finally I had to film the scene in a series of two cuts, which obviously was not as dramatic as I wanted it to be.

There was a taboo on any kind of love talk in a CFF film, but I defied that too. I shot the first-ever CFF love scene. There was no kiss, but it was a love scene. It occurs when Robin and Marian meet in the forest. She recognises him because she's seen him practising archery from the battlements, but he nonetheless insists on calling her 'My Lady'. The children's village has been burned to the ground, and the nasty baron is searching for Marian, knowing that the other children must be hiding her. Robin takes them all off into the forest, and just before they settle down for the night, he and Marian have a little scene, in which she says to him, 'Why don't you call me Marian? and he replies, 'Because you're Norman, and I'm Saxon.' Then she says, 'But we're both English.' His only reply is, 'One day, my lady . . . .' Then she makes a noise of disagreement and turns her back on him and goes off to sleep. (At this point, at the Wood Green Odeon première, I heard some boys in the audience saying: 'Go on, Robin. Get in there!') Robin turns slowly over and we fade out, to the sound of romantic krummhorn music in the background.

And I had to negotiate a further breaking of CFF conventions to get that music. The standard rule for any CFF film was that you had to use original music. The idea, probably deriving from Mary Field, was that nothing but the best was good enough for children: they must not be given anything second-hand. But in practice the restrictions on budget meant that the size of the orchestra was always limited to about five or six musicians, whereas I wanted a big old-fashioned orchestral score with lots of French horns. I persuaded the Foundation to accept stock music, for which we paid a flat fee which covered the whole world, making it cheaper than if we had used an original score.

One thing it was impossible to save money on was rates of pay. They were already rock bottom. The adults got £35 a day, which was the minimum Equity rate, a special dispensation for the Foundation only. The children were paid between £5 and £7.50 a day, depending on whether they spoke or not. On top of that there was either £5 or £10 for a chaperone, each one being allowed to look after up to five children. We aimed, with CFF movies, to shoot them in the summer holidays, because then we did not have to provide a tutor, and the children could work up to eight hours a day. Most of the crew and actors, when working on a CFF film, did not press for a lot of money – they knew that there was none to press for. Even before we had finished shooting, I was planning a spin-off series of six short films based around the *Robin Hood Junior* format. Having found the right locations, I did not want to let them languish. So I made a series called *The Unbroken Arrow*, but without Keith Chegwin because by then he had moved on to other things . . . .

The success of *Robin Hood Junior* was not an isolated case. Contemporary managers' reports, and memoirs contributed to this book, all confirm a high rate of audience satisfaction among the dwindling numbers of those who could still see the point of getting up and out for Saturday morning screen entertainment, which far more often than not would consist wholly or largely of CFF product. With the reduction in the numbers present at any one matinee – in some cases only around a hundred children – collective unruly behaviour of the type that had occurred in some cinemas in the sixties had passed. It was typical of the two decades that in the sixties an audience managed to get a film they disliked taken off; while in the seventies they could not get a film they liked kept on. There was a certain amount of running up and down the aisles; and in some cinemas a circuit promotional listing sheet called *Look-In*, available to be picked up at any time, might be rolled up and become a weapon. But in general, what children went for was the ritual of social eating and viewing, and, where managers organised it, the stage entertainment. A contributor who was a Minor for only six weeks in each year recalls the mid-seventies like this:

> Living as kids in rural Wiltshire, we never had a chance to go to a cinema there. But every summer we were packed off to our grandparents in Falkirk, and they sent us to the ABC every Saturday morning. In my memory of what I saw in those years cinema and telly are all mixed up, but I remember the atmosphere of the cinema clearly enough. There seemed to be hundreds and hundreds in the Falkirk ABC, and a lot of excitement and enthusiasm, but I don't think things were being thrown around. It was lively, but not rowdy. At home in Wiltshire we watched telly on Saturday mornings – *Tiswas* or *Swap Shop* – and doing that I felt essentially alone. In Falkirk I was part of a crowd. I'd get dressed for the ABC, but not for the telly. The queuing and the anticipation were much more exciting than just walking across the room to turn on the telly. We bought lollipops or liquorice or toffees at the cinema, or we might have taken our own tablet (a very sweet kind of fudge, peculiar to Scotland). For us, the cinema was full of strangeness, specialness and fun.

A similar enthusiasm prevailed generally among children who were still attending the matinees in the last years of the seventies. They had become very much a self-selected minority. Going to a matinee was now a positive choice, not a peer-group requirement, not a case of 'nothing else to do'. Nor was the situation of children having to choose between a Saturday matinee and an evening show any longer common, according to the 1972 survey. The overall trend was that children who attended a matinee also went frequently to other shows, while children who did not go to a matinee tended not to go to a cinema at any other time either. This was in line with statistics for the whole of Britain, which by 1980 showed average cinema attendance dropping to about 2 per cent of what it had been in 1950.

It was not that matinee-goers disliked television material. Managers' reports recorded children's responses to everything that was screened, commercial product as well as that from CFF, and in 1977, in the 399 cinemas that were still running matinees, the 1963 television-derived feature film *Hey There, It's Yogi Bear* was rated a smash hit. On a five-point scale it received a rating of 3.66. Not far behind, at 3.50, was another one from the same stable – *A Man Called Flintstone*; and in between them, at 3.61, was yet a third piece of animation, this one about *Alakazam the Great*, the king of the monkeys, produced in Japan and revoiced in America. The fact that the fourth and fifth favourites from among the commercial films were also animation – a 1970 French version of *Aladdin* and a 1972 American interweaving of biopic and tale in *The World of Hans Christian Andersen* – indicates clearly the nature of the gap in CFF's package. There are very special satisfactions offered by animation – glorious gags and far-fetched feats, stories of talking animals – that cannot be accomplished in live action, yet the CFF was always forced to steer clear of attempting to produce an animated feature, because even one year's complete grant from the BFFA would not have been enough to create anything worthwhile. However, even *Yogi Bear* was not absolutely top of the overall league table. He had four CFF films ahead of him in popularity – *Copter Kids*, *Mr Horatio Knibbles*, *Raising the Roof* and *The Battle of Billy's Pond*.

Unfortunately, Yogi Bear represented only the second division among animated features. Nothing feature-length from the animation supremo Disney was ever available to be shown at matinees. Obviously, the managers showed Disney at other times when they could; and the matinee-goers turned out in droves at those other times. However, the conditions at an ordinary show, particularly because of the presence of adults, were not the same as those at a matinee, so a satisfactory comparison between audience response to a CFF and to a Disney, even an old one, could never be made. The Foundation never found out whether a sparkling new CFF film such as *The Glitterball* could have held its own against *One Hundred and One Dalmatians*, for example, or *The Sword in the Stone*.

Not that it would have made any lasting difference either way. Even a regular supply of vintage Disneys could not have halted the process of matinee decline, now running at a greater rate than the overall figure of cinema closures. More and more matinees were being found, especially by JARO and EMI, to be uneconomic. JARO tried to slip out of the unequal contest with *Swap Shop* by moving its matinees to the afternoon, but this proved to be impossible, because the major distributors would not agree to the consequent reduction in the number of times that their new releases would be shown. The independents on the whole were not so badly placed. Some of them held their matinees in the afternoon anyway, and the others had greater possibility of changing if they thought it would help. As before, they believed that an increase in admission price – this time to 25p – was justified, and would make all the difference. The CFF agreed to service cinemas that charged that amount, but still the number of matinees went down. In 1978 the loss was exactly 100 – from 399 to 299.

*39. The Glitterball *was among the last* CFF *features to be made. and one of the most successful. Produced five years before Spielberg's* ET, *it tells the story of two boys who find an alien life-form, protect it from exploitation, help it signal to its mother ship, and then sadly watch it go back home. Max is played by Ben Buckton; and Pete by Keith Jayne*   (Children's Film & Television Foundation)

In what turned out to be its dying throw, the CFF reduced its release cycle to two and a half years, in response to pressure from the independents, who in many cases were not able to get a booking of supplementary commercial stuff such as *Yogi Bear*. By thus moving the posts it was very nearly able to score the goal of self-sufficiency, and supply every matinee with a CFF feature and serial every week. In addition, by acquiring the matinee rights to large bundles of cartoons from Warner, Fox, Columbia and Rank, it was able to parcel up all these items into 125 unitary programmes, each one consisting of a cartoon, a short comedy, a serial episode, a feature and (when available) a trailer for the following week. This made booking much simpler, since it was all done by numbers, and reduced print transport costs, each cinema receiving only one container each week. But this could never be more than a temporary closing of the circle, even if 125 weeks really was a period long enough to avoid children complaining of having seen it before. The more serious problem was that the total of 125 features included everything that the CFF had ever produced or adapted, right from 1952, and some of them, especially those in black and white, were severely straining the limits of their acceptability and would have to be urgently replaced. Continuation of the programme of adding eight new hours of screen time to the CFF's catalogue every year was thus essential in order to keep the 125 units topped up – but how could the necessary grant from BFFA be justified when the product was reaching such a small constituency? In fact BFFA took the view that it could not be justified, and gave the Foundation for the year 1979–80 only half of the £666,000 which it had calculated as being the minimum necessary to maintain momentum.

Even at this late stage there were still a few matinees attracting huge numbers of children. They were invariably the ones run by managers who organised something besides the screenings. Two of these still-booming matinees were in Plymouth, where in 1979 both the Rank cinema and the ABC were each getting a weekly attendance of around 800. Together these two accounted for more than 3 per cent of the attendance over the whole of Britain, where the average per cinema was brought down to around 150 by the fact that some matinees were attended by only around sixty children. By the middle of the year the total of Rank matinees was sixty-eight; for EMI the figure was eighty-six. The overall scale of this decline is well shown by a comparison with the figures given in the Wheare report, when matinees were a power in the land. At that time there were over 1,000,000 attending in any one week, whereas in 1979 it took twenty weeks to clock up that figure.

Despite Plymouth, and despite having more cinemas operating matinees than Rank, EMI warned the CFF in 1979 that it could no longer justify the expense of running a Minors' office, and would be withdrawing from the scheme within one year unless the situation improved dramatically. Wishing to recognise the Foundation's achievements, and perhaps give it a boost at this time of trial, the British Academy of Film and Television Arts presented the CFF in March 1980 with the Michael Balcon Award for Outstanding British Contribution to Cinema. This did not bring back the missing Minors, so EMI closed down its Minors' office in the summer of that year. Individual cinema managers could carry on with shows for children if they liked, as long as they made a profit, did all the booking themselves and discontinued the use of the name 'Minors'.

One that did carry on for a while was the ABC Stourbridge which, under the name The Saturday Morning Cinema Show, screened three-hour double bills of commercial bringbacks, such as *Abba – The Movie* coupled with *Dr Who and the Daleks* and *The Golden Voyage of Sinbad* coupled with *Mysterious Island*. Sometimes there was just one film, such as Elvis Presley in *Clambake*. These shows cost 50p for children and £1 for adults, so for one year only it was much cheaper to see Elvis at an Odeon than at an ABC. The SSS continued to function through the rest of 1980 and most of 1981, to be supplied nearly every week with a CFF unitary programme, and to stick to the low admission charges with which the movement had begun. On the relatively few weeks when there was no CFF unit, then it was often Elvis instead. *GI Blues* and *Blue Hawaii* both went the rounds.

But the real money was to be made from rock on stage, not film. As part of their battle to stay in business, some larger cinemas doubled up as theatres and put on live shows on Saturday evenings. Where this happened it illustrated the lowly status that children's matinees now had within the Rank circuit. Visits from such bands as Hawkwind, Spiro Gira, Wings, Teardrop Explodes, The Clash, Nazareth, Ultravox or Status Quo meant that the SSS had to be cancelled, because the whole day was needed to set the stage show up. At Edinburgh, for example, children were on one occasion shown two episodes of a serial, told not to come again for the next two weeks, and then shown another two when they came back. The features though had to be shown on the right day or not at all. On 16 May 1981 the scheduled CFF film for the Edinburgh SSS was *Paganini Strikes Again* – but it was never shown, because of The Cure. The following week *The Salvage Gang* should have been in operation, but Sticky Little Fingers kept them out.

A few months later, Odeon followed EMI: in summer 1981 all relevant cinemas were told to wind up their matinees by the end of September. As it happened, the last features shown to Edinburgh SSS summed up some major characteristics of the past four decades of special production. From Rank's post-war black and white CEF came the boy-meets-creature fantasy of *The Dragon of Pendragon Castle*; while Mandy Miller's *Adventure in the Hopfields*, from the early years of the pan-industry CFF, had a factual background of the kind Mary Field believed to be educative. The CFF's public-warning aspect was shown, in Eastmancolour, by a sixties' dramatisation of the dangers of *70*

Deadly Pills; and its final phase, when Henry Geddes conceived of its product as 'junior features', was represented by the Chiffy-winning, ET-foreshadowing *Glitterball*. Edinburgh SSS finally went out on 3 October, not with a bang but with a *Kadoyng* (a visitor from outer space who helps children stop a new highway being built).

The departure of the two major circuits left CFF with a base of not many more than 100 independent cinemas – most of them Classics – still wishing to be serviced. This might have been a viable figure if the attendance in each had been high, but on average it was less than 100 per cinema per week, which roughly meant that, over the thirty years of CFF's life, child attendance had declined from a million every week to a million every two years. Even so, the CFF guaranteed to keep supplying programmes at least till September 1983, not knowing that long before that date was reached it would cease to exist.

Before its demise there was, however, one final overwhelming triumph. This was *Friend or Foe*, shot in August 1981 at a cost of £150,000 – nearly half the entire CFF budget for that year. Set in wartime Britain, it's about two evacuees who hear an enemy plane crash nearby. When they look for it, one of them nearly drowns but is rescued just in time by the pilot. This sets up a conflict between the boys: one wants to shelter the German, the other wants to turn him in. With characterisation more complex than that in any other CFF film, and seventy minutes in which to explore it, *Friend or Foe* caught the international mood of the moment. It swept the board, winning prizes in Berlin, Los Angeles (the Ruby Slipper), London (Evening Standard Awards), Calcutta and Laon. As a result of this prestige and publicity, it was sold to so many overseas countries that it became one of the only two CFF films (the other was *Tightrope to Terror*) ever to recoup the cost of its production.

While the prize-winning was still going on, the Foundation concluded a lengthy series of negotiations with the various unions, and turned to face a multi-media future. At the end of June 1982 the Board of the CFF met for the last time. Henceforth, with a different constitution and a fresh orientation, it was to be the Children's Film and Television Foundation Limited (CFTF). With effect from January 1984 it had a deal, brokered by Rank, under which the BBC bought the right to screen over a three-year period thirty old (but not black and white) CFF films, and nine new ones which were to be produced by the CFTF, tailored specifically for family television viewing. In return, the Foundation received an overall payment of £1,200,000. These television screenings got off to a very slow start: in the first year of the agreement only one Foundation film was aired, the one with the most famous director – Michael Powell. That went out at tea-time on the third day after Christmas 1984. In the following year three were screened – on consecutive Friday tea-times in October. Not until the last year of the agreement did the BBC begin seriously to exploit its acquisition: through April and May 1986 a series of seven Foundation titles were broadcast as Friday Film Specials; and in September there were four within one week. Even so the BBC had managed at the end of the three years to find slots for fewer than half of the titles it had bought, so paid for the right to retain them for one more year. Ten ran on consecutive Fridays in the post-Easter season of 1987; and the final Foundation flourish came over Christmas, three days before the agreement expired, when *The Glitterball*, showing for the second time within the four-year period, notched up a family audience of many millions. For a year there was a similar deal with Granada Television where Sidney Bernstein, who had given birth to the idea of special programming for children in 1928, and had called for special production long before J. Arthur Rank made it a reality, was still the head. From these agreements the Foundation got around two million pounds, while also still receiving a small grant from the BFFA. Its fame and future looked for a while reasonably secure.

This television tie-up was not, however, good for the surviving matinees. In fact, it virtually killed them. The Foundation continued to service them up to the promised date and beyond, but most managers soon found that the restricted menu made it impossible to retain their audience. Effectively, the pool of available films was shallower than it had been before, because the most attractive features had been cherry-picked by television and were for practical purposes out of circulation for a while. Later, when they returned from the big city of television, they had – in children's eyes – lost their virtue. Neither was there much compensation to be found in the new productions, since films made with television money likewise had to go to television first and were only available to cinemas after their juice had been squeezed out. Indeed, some of them never reached matinees at all because they were shot on 16 mm., which was fine for television, but no use for the cinemas. The independents found themselves looking at a downward spiral, with the same jaded units being endlessly recycled. A Classic manager with many years experience of matinees remembers when his chain, the rump of the independents, pulled out:

I have been involved with children's cinema clubs all my life. As a boy I went to the Picture House in the Old Kent Road, where in 1950 I saw *The Dragon of Pendragon Castle*. That was the first specially made film I had ever seen, and I thought it was definitely a bit different from the constant cowboy and Old Mother Riley stuff. I hoped we were going to get more like that – and we did, sometimes. As soon as I left school I was a projectionist for nine years, and got to know and like most of the CFF stuff quite well. After that I became a manager and started a club wherever I went if there was not one there already – I even ran one in the Tatler, Stockwell, which was a sex cinema the rest of the week! In the eighties, when I was at the Classic, Sittingbourne, running a Louee the Lion club, and showing all the CFF unit programmes, we were told that the only way the CFF could keep going was to change to CFTF, and that it would enable us to keep going too. However, I noticed around 1986 that the same films seemed to come round again very quickly, after only about eight or nine months – and they were mainly the black-and-white ones. Still, we kept going somehow. I remember kids telling me about the CFF films they'd seen on television the day before. Then at the end of that year, Classic's central booking department gave up their link with the Foundation. 'There's no point any more – they've sold all the best ones to television', was the explanation given to us. It was a sad day for me, after thirty-five years of believing in children's films.

The new Foundation's time in the sun was relatively brief. In 1985 the Films Act abolished the Eady levy on cinema tickets and the BFFA which had administered it. At a stroke, that source of Foundation funding, and of official recognition, was gone. When the deals with television came to an end, satisfactory terms for renewal could not be agreed, and no Foundation films have been shown on terrestrial UK television since then. With only a dozen regular matinee outlets left, the Foundation disbanded its distribution service, leasing its prints to a commercial company. Special production and special distribution of films for children had thus collapsed completely, leaving special exhibition hanging from a cliff. For children's cinema, 1987 marked the end of the post-Wheare world.

Epilogue

If anyone's looking for a holiday for the whole world to observe, why not use February 9th? Let's call it Disney Day, to celebrate the moment that our lives changed forever. For it was on February 9th this year that the Walt Disney Company merged with Capital Cities/ABC in America and, at a stroke, created the Disney Family. . . . We're all in the Mickey Mouse Club now.

(Stephen Armstrong, *The Sunday Times*, 31 March 1996)

In the nineties, the Children's Film and Television Foundation still exists, but not as an independent producer. What little income it has, derived mainly from overseas sales, is available to be considered for investment in script development when it is offered a project – for cinema or television – judged to be broadly in line with Foundation aims. The most successful film it has been associated with – Roald Dahl's *Danny the Champion of the World* – had investment also from the Disney Channel. Looking to the future, the Foundation sees itself, on the strength of its five decades of experience in the field, as becoming – perhaps through an injection of lottery money – a clearing house of scripts, a stimulator of new ideas, a disburser of production finance for junior features.

In a few places the children's clubs have never closed, despite the company's withdrawal of central support. Since the abandonment of Foundation product the Sittingbourne club has survived by showing on Saturday mornings virtually any second-release commercial features with a U or PG certificate, regardless of whether or not there is a child among the screen protagonists. Even so there are elements that invoke older club practice, among them being the tactic, pioneered more than eight decades ago by the Glasgow BBs, of giving free entry after a certain number of weeks of regular attendance. There is also a pre-screening programme of games, lucky numbers and competitions which would not have been out of place in the fifties. However, there are no badges, no sing-songs, no visiting MPs, no serials. Admission, which costs one pound, does not include the nineties' equivalent of the BBs' stick of rock – a bucket of popcorn.

That, in a special low-price line available only on Saturday mornings, costs another pound. The finishing time differs from week to week, a variation formerly avoided on the ground that it endangered children's homegoing safety. And for a while this club, in common with revivals elsewhere in the same chain, then called Cannon, had a name which in the thirties would have provoked parental uproar – The Young Guns.

In purpose-built multiplexes, where there are no direct links with the past, Kids Clubs (or Brat Packs as they may be called, or Little Rascals) have been reinvented for the nineties. Since they have several screens, some offer the children a choice between two or even three U or PG films – all recent but not brand-new commercial features – in different auditoria. Whichever one they go to, the children are also shown trailers for the newly released features which they could see, at full price, later that same day or week. The problem of competition from Saturday morning television can now be solved by offering Sunday shows as well – an option which for J. Arthur Rank would have been, literally, unthinkable. A further direct contrast with the past is that, in an age very conscious of the physical dangers that children on their own are perceived to face, most Saturday/Sunday Kids are accompanied by a parent or two, not only on the journey to the cinema but all through the screenings as well. The result is that, in atmosphere and behaviour, these shows are family outings rather than children's shows. Confectionery, a give-away enticement in the first decade of the century, is now, in the last, absolutely central to the special shows' ability to break even: the standard purchase – a bucket of popcorn and a drink – costs more than twice as much as a seat (which is normally one pound). If most children did not enter the auditorium carrying food and drink bought in the foyer, the low-price club shows would lose money and be cancelled. In any case, they do not necessarily continue all through the year: like the Edinburgh Roxy in the forties, some close down during the school vacations. The reason now is not that there are no children around; conversely, it is that there are enough high-profile new releases (especially Disney), and enough holiday-mood families, for the cinema to be able to get good morning audiences without the necessity of reducing prices.

Thus tamed in nature and low in numbers, the new weekend morning cinema clubs have caused no infra-red sensation. There have been in the nineties, as there were after the advent of sound in the twenties, allegations that children no longer speak British English – but now the culprit is television, and the alien diction is Australian rather than American. The nineties have also seen a hasty alteration to a government bill, in the interests of child protection, just as there was in 1908 after the Barnsley disaster, but this time it has not been occasioned by death and injury inflicted on children's bodies in a public auditorium. The catalyst was, rather, the alleged harm done to children's minds by watching films in their own homes. Following assumptions that the boys who killed James Bulger in 1993 had been influenced by a video of the film *Child's Play 3*, the Criminal Justice Act of 1994 incorporated a last-minute amendment strengthening the powers of the British Board of Film and Video Classification. And MPs in the nineties can still divert the House of Commons by reciting the titles of a selection of media products aimed at children, as Sir Charles Oman did in the thirties when he inveighed against the films (*The Godless Girl, Too Hot for Paris, The Man who Was Girl-Crazy*) that Birmingham children were seeing. In 1996 Peter Luff, MP for Worcester, echoed Oman when he referred in the Commons to 'Men Unzipped', 'Boys in the Buff', and 'First-Time Sex' as items he wished to prevent young girls from seeing. The difference was that these were magazine articles, not films.

Throughout the century there have been tensions, anxieties and contradictions surrounding children and their pastimes. For more than half of those years, cinema was both the main object of adult concern – expressed positively or negatively – and a primary source of children's pleasure, taken in a variety of ways. Now, as the millennium approaches, cinema is no longer in focus. Children still watch films, sometimes in a darkened auditorium and even, on occasion, without direct adult supervision. It is unlikely though that children's cinema will ever again offer the anarchy, the social adventure, the solidarity, the collective participation and the occasional physical danger that came from being All Pals Together.

Bibliography

SPECIFIC REFERENCES

Barclay, J. B. (1951), *Edinburgh Report on Junior Cinema Clubs*, Edinburgh: Scottish Educational Film Association

Barclay, J. B. (1956), *Children's Film Tastes*, Edinburgh: Scottish Educational Film Association

Barker, Martin (1984), *A Haunt of Fears*, London: Pluto Press

Bell, Oliver (1938), *An Expose of the Principles of British Organisation of Children's Recreational Films*. Paper given at the Child Welfare Commission of the League of Nations, 2 May 1938, London: BFI

Bernstein, Sidney (1937), 'Attempts Made by the Film Trade to Meet the Problems and the Difficulties Encountered', in the published record of the *British Film Institute Conference on Films for Children*, 20 and 21 November 1936

Birkenhead Vigilance Committee (1931), *Report of the Executive Committee*, Birkenhead

Birmingham Cinema Enquiry Committee (1931), *Report of Investigations April 1930–May 1931*, Birmingham: Cinema Enquiry Committee

British Board of Film Censors (1925), *Annual Report*, quoted in Robertson, James C. (1985), *The British Board of Film Censors*, London: Croom Helm

British Film Institute/National Council of Women (1946), *Children and the Cinema*, London: BFI

Camden Training College (1946), *Children's Cinema Club: An Investigation by the Students of the Camden Training College*, London: Camden Training College

Children's Entertainment Films (1950), *Annual Report*, London: Children's Entertainment Films

Crozier, T. H. (HM Inspector of Explosives) (1930), *Report to the Right Honorable the Secretary of State for Scotland on the Circumstances attending the Loss of Life at the Glen Cinema, Paisley, 31 December, 1929*, London: HMSO

Cudlipp, Percy (1955), 'Chicks at the Flicks,' from *Bouverie Ballads*, London: Eyre & Spottiswoode. The poem originally appeared as topical comment in the *News Chronicle* in 1954 in the week that Mary Field's book on the Carnegie infra-red studies was published.

Documentary News Letter (1945), vol. 5: *Tales for Children: Five Films for Odeon Children's Clubs Reviewed*

Edinburgh Cinema Enquiry Committee (1933), *An Investigation Conducted into the Influence of the Film on School Children and Adolescents in the City*, Edinburgh: Edinburgh Cinema Enquiry

Eyles, Allen (1993), 'Film Talk', in M. O'Brien and A. Eyles (eds), *Enter the Dream-House*, London: Museum of the Moving Image

Field, Mary (1945), interviewed in *The Cinema*, 2 February, p. 3

Field, Mary (1946), interviewed in *Today's Cinema*, 6 August, p. 3

Field, Mary (1949), 'Unfinished Project', *Sight and Sound*, vol. 18, no. 69, p. 8

Field, Mary (1952), *Good Company: The Story of the Children's Entertainment Film Movement in Great Britain*, 1943–1950, London: Longmans

Field, Mary (1954), *Children and Films: A Study of Boys and Girls in the Cinema*, Dunfermline: Carnegie United Kingdom Trust.

Field, Mary (1964), 'The Beginnings', *Journal of the Society of Film and Television Arts* (special issue: *Twenty-One Years of Children's Films*), winter 1964–5, no. 18, p. 2

Figgis, Mike (1996), 'Movie Memories', *Sight and Sound* (centenary-of-cinema supplement: *Movie Times*), p. 22

Ford, Richard (1939), *Children in the Cinema*, London: George Allen & Unwin

Geddes, Henry (1964), in 'The Present and the Future' *Journal of the Society of Film and Television Arts* (special issue: *Twenty-One Years of Children's Films*), p. 23

Gifford, Denis (1986), *The British Film Catalogue 1895–1985*, Newton Abbot: David & Charles

Hinxman, Margaret (1976), 'Twenty-Five Years Young', in *Young Cinema: 25 Years of the Children's Film Foundation*, London: CFF, p. 4

Hornby, Nick (1995), 'We are the ABC Minors!', in *Movie Heaven* (supplement to April issue of *Empire Magazine*), London: EMAP Metro, p. 25

Kaufman, Gerald (1985), *My Life in the Silver Screen*, London: Faber & Faber

Llewellyn, Michael Gareth (1945), 'The Kind of Film for Children', *Sight and Sound*, vol. 13, no. 54, p. 27

Locket, Marjorie (1932), 'Children at the Pictures', *Sight and Sound*, vol. 1, no. 1, p. 27

London County Council Education Committee (1932), *School Children and the Cinema*, London: LCC

Low, Rachael and Manvell, Roger (1948), *The History of British Film 1896–1906*, London: Allen & Unwin.

McBain, Janet (1985), *Pictures Past: Scottish Cinemas Remembered*, Edinburgh: Moorfoot Publishing

MacDonald, Ramsay (1935), in 'Notes of a deputation received by the Prime Minister in relation to the film industry', held by the Special Materials Unit of the BFI Library as part of their BBFC *Collection*

McTell, Ralph (1995), 'Ralph McTell remembers Laurel and Hardy', in Driver (ed.), *Funny Talk*, London: The Do-Not Press

Margerison, B. D. (1933), 'Children's Films in Yorkshire', *Sight and Sound*, vol. 2, summer issue, p. 44

Mayer, J. P. (1946), 'Films for Children, by a Special Correspondent', *The Times*, 5 January

Mayer, J. P. (1946), *The Sociology of Film*, London: Faber & Faber

Middlesbrough Head Teachers' Association (1946), *Children and the Cinema*, Middlesbrough: Head Teachers' Association

Miller, Emanuel (1947), *Report on the Bernstein Children's Film Questionnaire*, London: Granada

National Council for Public Morality (1917), *The Cinema: Its Present Position and Future Possibilities*, London: Williams & Norgate

Official Report of the House of Commons Debates (Hansard): 23 January 1930 (Forgan); 4 February 1930 (Knox); 27 January 1931 (Lovat-Fraser); 27 May 1932 (Oman); 21

March 1933 (Atholl); 27 November 1946 (Dumpleton et al. in debate on 'Children's Cinema Clubs'); 3 June 1948 (Ede)

O'Pray, Michael (1990), in I. Breakwell and P. Hammond (eds), *Seeing in the Dark*, London: Serpent's Tail

Parnaby, M. and Woodhouse, M. (1947), *Children's Cinema Clubs Report*, London: British Film Institute

Powell, Michael (1992), *Million–Dollar Movie*, London: Heinemann

Quest, W. (1953), 'Early Children's Film Shows', *The Circle*, no. 42, p. 7

Rank, J. Arthur (1945), interviewed in *Motion Picture Herald*, 6 January, p. 36

Rees, Lorimer (1984), *Somerstown*, Thames Television for Channel Four, first transmitted on 25 Nov. 1984

Sheffield Juvenile Organisations Committee (1931), *A Survey of Children's Cinema Matinees in Sheffield*, Sheffield: Sheffield Juvenile Organisations Committee

Trevelyan, John (1964), 'The Censor Looks at Children's Films' *Journal of the Society of Film and Television Arts* (special issue: *21 Years of Children's Films*), no. 18, winter 1964–5, p. 21

Wheare, K. C. (1950), *Report of the Departmental Committee on Cinema and Children*, London: HMSO

Williamson, James (1926), memoir quoted in Appendix Two of Low and Manvell, p. 114

Wood, Alan (1952), *Mr Rank: A Study of J. Arthur Rank and British Films*, London: Hodder & Stoughton

Woodhouse, M. (1949), *Children's Film Judgements*, Leeds: University of Leeds Institute of Education

GENERAL REFERENCES

Allen, Jim (1989), *Grantham Cinemas*, Grantham: Jim Allen

Barnes, John (1976), *The Beginnings of Cinema in England*, Newton Abbot: David & Charles.

Blake T. A. (1946), 'Prince Bendon', Educational Film Bulletin – Fifty Years of Scottish Cinema, no. 33, p. 31

Children's Film and Television Foundation (1985), *Catalogue and Index of Films*, London: CFTF

Children's Film Foundation: Annual Reports (1952, 1953, 1955); *Report on Work Done 1951–1960* (1960); *Twenty-Five Years of Children's Films* (1969); *Young Cinema* (1972); *Catalogue and Index of Films* (1972); *Young Cinema* (1976); *Catalogue and Index of Films* (1980) – all London, CFF

Circuits Management Association (1951), *Children's Cinema Club Guide for Managers*, London: CMA

de Cordova, Richard (1990), 'Ethnography and Exhibition: The Child Audience, the Hays Office and Saturday Matinees', *Camera Obscura*, May, p. 90

Everson, Wiliam K. (1992), *The Hollywood Western*, New York: Citadel Press

Eyles, Allen (1993), *ABC The First Name in Entertainment*, London: BFI

Eyles, Allen (1996), *Gaumont British Cinemas*, London: BFI

Gomery, Douglas (1992), *Shared Pleasures*, London: BFI

Himmelweit, H., Oppenheim, A. N. and Vince P. (1958), *Television and the Child*, London: Oxford University Press.

Home, Anna (1993), *Into the Box of Delights*, London: BBC Books

Hunnings, Neville March (1967), *Film Censors and the Law*, London: Allen & Unwin.

Jowett, G., Jarvie, I. and Fuller, K. (eds) (1996), *Children and the Movies: Media Influence and the Payne Fund Controversy*, Cambridge: Cambridge University Press

Leyda, Jay (1960), *Kino*, London: Allen & Unwin

McNab, Geoffrey (1994), *J. Arthur Rank and the British Film Industry*, London: Routledge & Kegan Paul

Manvell, Roger (1944), *Film*, London: Penguin Books

Low, Rachael (1948), *The History of British Film 1906–1914*, London: Allen & Unwin

Low, Rachael (1979), *The History of the British Film 1929–39: Documentary and Educational Films*, London: Allen & Unwin

Low, Rachael (1979), *The History of the British Film 1929–39: Films of Comment and Persuasion*, London: Allen & Unwin.

O'Brien, M. and Eyles, A. (eds) (1993), *Enter the Dream-House*, London: Museum of the Moving Image

Pearson, Geoffrey (1984), 'Falling Standards', in M. Barker (ed.) *Video Nasties*, London: Pluto Press

Richards, Jeffrey (1984), *The Age of the Dream Palace: Cinema and Society in Britain 1930–39*, London: Routledge & Kegan Paul

Richards, J. and Sheridan, D. (eds) (1987), *Mass-Observation at the Movies*, London: Routledge & Kegan Paul.

Shipman, David (1982), *The Story of Cinema*, Volume One, London: Hodder & Stoughton.

Stedman, Raymond William (1971), *The Serials*, Oklahoma: University of Oklahoma Press

Thomas, Tony (1989), *The West that Never Was*, New York: Citadel Press

Tibballs, Geoff (1991), *The Golden Age of Children's Television*, London: Titan Books

Index